Humana Festival 2015
The Complete Plays

About the Humana Foundation

The Humana Foundation was established in 1981 as the philanthropic arm of Humana Inc., one of the nation's leading health and well-being companies. Located in Louisville, KY, the Foundation seeks to improve community health and well-being through support of nonprofit partners that promote healthy behaviors, health education, and access to health services. For more information, visit www.HumanaFoundation.org.

Humana and the Humana Foundation are dedicated to Corporate Social Responsibility. Our goal is to ensure that every business decision we make reflects our commitment to improving the health and well-being of our members, our associates, the communities we serve, and our planet.

Humana Festival 2015
The Complete Plays

Edited by
Amy Wegener and Jenni Page-White

Playscripts Inc.
New York, NY

Published by Playscripts, Inc.
7 Penn Plaza, Suite 904
New York, New York, 10001
www.playscripts.com

Cover Design by Mary Kate Zihar
Text Design and Layout by Lizzie Martinez

First Edition: April 2016
10 9 8 7 6 5 4 3 2 1

LCCN: 95650734
ISSN: 1935-4452

ISBN-13: 978-1-62384-713-5

Contents

Acknowledgments

The editors wish to thank the following persons for their invaluable assistance in compiling this volume:

Jennifer Bielstein
Sophie Blumberg
Robyn Carroll
Kimberly Colburn
Kate Cuellar
Rachel Dart
Sara Durham
Kirsty Gaukel
Steve Knight
Lizzie Martinez
Meredith McDonough
Zachary Meicher-Buzzi
Hannah Rae Montgomery
Steve Moulds
Helena D. Pennington
Jessica Reese
Jeffrey S. Rodgers
Julie Roberts
Zan Sawyer-Dailey
Ariel Sibert
Les Waters
Mary Kate Zihar

Maya Choldin
Scott Edwards
Di Glazer
Susan Gurman
Kate Navin
Antje Oegel
Mark Orsini
Pig Iron Theatre Company
Mark Subias
Rachel Viola

Actors Theatre of Louisville Staff
Humana Festival 2015

ARTISTIC DIRECTOR, Les Waters
MANAGING DIRECTOR, Jennifer Bielstein

ARTISTIC

Associate Artistic Director . . . . Meredith McDonough
Associate Director . . . . .Zan Sawyer-Dailey
Arts Administration Coordinator . . . . .Zachary Meicher-Buzzi
Company Manager. . . . . Dot King
Arts Administration Intern . . . . .Rebecca Trimbur
Directing Interns . . . . .Sophie Blumberg, Rachel Dart

Literary

Director . . . . Amy Wegener
Literary Manager . . . . .Kimberly Colburn
Literary Associate. . . . . Hannah Rae Montgomery
Humana Festival Literary Assistant. . . . . .Jessica Reese
Dramaturgy/Literary Management Interns . . . . Robyn Carroll, Ariel Sibert

Education

Director . . . . Jane B. Jones
Education Manager . . . . Betsy Anne Huggins
Interim Education Associate. . . . . Sterling Franklin
Education/Teaching Artist Interns. . . . . .Casey Flyth, Ben Niewoehner
Teaching Artists . . . . Justin Dobring, Liz Fentress,
Keith McGill, Karin Partin Wells

Apprentice/Intern Company

Director . . . . Michael Legg
Assistant Director . . . . John Rooney
A/I Administration Intern. . . . . Sam Barickman
Apprentices. . . . . .Taylor Abels, Cameron Benoit, Josh Bonzie,
Ali Burch, Ure Egbuho, John Ford-Dunker,
Erika Grob, Kayla Jackmon, Lexi Lapp, José Leon,
Joe Lino, Aaron Lynn, Max Monnig, Collin Morris,
Mallory Moser, Brian Muldoon, Madalena Provo,
Blake Russell, Lorenzo Villanueva, Casey Wortmann

ADMINISTRATION

General Manager . . . . Jeffrey S. Rodgers
Human Resources Manager. . . . . .Cora Brown
Systems Manager . . . . Dottie Krebs
Executive Assistant . . . . Janelle Baker
Administrative Services Coordinator . . . . .Alan Meyer

AUDIENCE SERVICES & SALES

Ticket Sales Director . . . . .Kim McKercher
Training Manager. . . . . .Steve Clark
Season Tickets Manager. . . . . .Julie Gallegos
Box Office Manager. . . . . Kristy Kannapell
Customer Service Representatives. . . . . .Cheryl Anderson, LaShana Avery,
Matthew Brown, Marty Huelsmann,
Ben Niewoehner, Joe Sandage, Kelly Scott

Volunteer and Audience Relations

Director . . . . Allison Hammons
House Managers. . . . . .Elizabeth Cooley, Will Farrell,
Sterling Franklin, Rebecca Trimbur
Lobby Manager . . . . .Tiffany Walton
Coat Check Supervisor . . . . Tanisha Johnson
Coat Check Attendants . . . . Casey Flyth, Jory Morris

DEVELOPMENT

Director . . . . .Julie Roberts
Associate Director, Individual Giving. . . . . Kate Chandler
Associate Director, Institutional Partnerships . . . . .Danielle Manley
Grants Manager . . . . .Justin Williamson
Donor Relations Manager . . . . .Liz Magee
Annual Fund Manager. . . . . .Jacob Freund
Development Intern. . . . . .Jamie Adling

FINANCE

Director . . . . .Peggy Shake
Accounting Coordinator . . . . Jason Acree
Accounting Assistant. . . . . Jillian Innes

MARKETING & COMMUNICATIONS

Director . . . . Steve Knight
Associate Director of Communications. . . . . .Kirsty Gaukel
Communications Manager. . . . . .Sara E. Durham
Marketing Manager . . . . .Melissa Hines
Interim Festival & Events Manager. . . . . .Shane Spaulding
Graphic Designer. . . . . Mary Kate Zihar
Assistant Graphic Designer. . . . . Amie Villiger
Group Sales Manager. . . . . .Sarah Peters
Group Sales Associate . . . . Chris O'Leary
Marketing and Communications Interns . . . . .Caroline Ruark, Hannah Wehlage

OPERATIONS

Director . . . . Mike Schüssler-Williams
Operations Manager. . . . . Barry Witt
Maintenance . . . . Ricky Baldon, John Voyles
Building Services . . . . Patricia Duncan, Derrick Henderson, Joe Spencer
Receptionist . . . . .Amanda Marshbanks

PRODUCTION

Production Manager. . . . . Paul Werner
Assistant Production Manager. . . . . Michael Whatley
Production Management Intern . . . . .Megan Arbough
Production Stage Manager. . . . . Paul Mills Holmes
Resident Stage Managers . . . . .Stephen Horton, Katie Shade
Resident Assistant Stage Manager. . . . . Jessica Kay Potter
Production Assistants . . . . Hannah Barnes, Joshua Mark Gustafson, Leah Pye
Stage Management Interns . . . . Philippa Panayiotou, Julie Phillips,
Sean Ravitz, Chelsey Haslett Sorbo

Scenic

Technical Director . . . . .Justin Hagovsky
Assistant Technical Director . . . . .Braden Blauser
Scenic Charge. . . . . .Kieran Wathen
Shop Foreman . . . . .Javan Roy-Bachman
Master Carpenter . . . . Ashley Crockett Guido
Carpenters . . . . G. E. Simmons Falk, Alexia Hall,
Brandon Hickman, Eric Kneller,
Winslow Lindsay, Ian Lootens,
Collin Sage, Pierre Vendette
Deck Carpenters. . . . . Matthew Krell, Peter Regalbuto
Scenic Painter . . . . .Sabra Crockett

Costumes

Costume Director. . . . . .Kristopher Castle
Assistant Costume Director. . . . . .Beatrice Vena
Costume Coordinator . . . . .Christine Leidner
Crafts Master . . . . Shari Cochran
Wig and Makeup Supervisor . . . . .Jehann Gilman
Pamela Brown Wardrobe Supervisor . . . . Christopher Ersing
Bingham Wardrobe Supervisor . . . . .Maggie McGrann
Costume Supervisor. . . . . Jill Keys
Draper/Tailor. . . . . Jeffery Park
First Hand. . . . . Natalie Maynard
Stitcher Captain . . . . Elizabeth Hahn
Stitcher . . . . .Faith Brown
Costume Journeymen. . . . . .Molly Herman,* Adrienne Nixon*
Wig Journeyman. . . . . Marissa Kulp

Lighting

Supervisor...Jason Weber
Assistant Lighting Supervisor ....Dani Clifford
Master Electrician...John Newman
Lighting Technicians ....Jon Harden, Victoria Bain, Katie Carr
Electricians.................................... Jesse Alford, Rob Woodall,
Alexa K. Holloway, Riley Noble,
Nichole Marquez, Kathleen Dieckman

Sound

Supervisor.. Paul Doyle
Assistant Sound Supervisor................................. Jessica Collins
Sound Technicians...................................... Russell Goddard,
Zachary McKenna, Rachel Spear

Properties

Director ....Mark Walston
Properties Master.. Joe Cunningham
Assistant Properties Master...............................Heather Lindert
Carpenter Artisans........................... Karl Anderson, Noah Johnson
Soft Goods Artisan ....Jessie Combest
General Artisan ....Brad Baute
Props Journeyman .... Samantha Sayers*
Properties Intern ....Amanda Relaford

VIDEO

Media Technologist .... Philip Allgeier
Media Intern...Abigail Sweeney

USHER CAPTAINS

Dolly Adams, Shirley Adkins, Marie Allen, Katherine Austin, June Blair, Libba and Chuck Bonifer, Tanya Briley, Maleva Chamberlain, Donna Conlon, Terry Conway, Laurie Eiden, Doris Elder, Reese Fisher, Joyce French, Carol Halbleib, Avani Kabra, Sandy Kissling, Nickie Langdon, Barbara Nichols, Cathy Nooning, Teresa Nusz, Judy Pearson, Beth Phipps, Nancy Rankin, Bob Rosedale, Kirsten Swikert, Tim Unruh, David Wallace, Megg Ward

Denotes Paul Owen Fellow

Foreword

Every spring in Louisville, weeks before the Kentucky Derby, the city teems with visitors from near and far. Thousands of theatre-makers and theatre-lovers from across the nation descend on Louisville for the Humana Festival of New American Plays, which showcases the work of the most dynamic theatre artists in the field. The festival has long served as a gathering spot for our industry; over the course of five weeks, Actors Theatre audience members are as likely to hail from New York or Chicago as they are from Atlanta, Houston, Baltimore, Phoenix, Denver, San Diego, Seattle, or Miami. And of course, many hail from right here in Louisville. It's an exciting time for the city, and for the artistic teams behind each production. It's tremendously fulfilling to introduce these plays to new audiences, and to support their journeys as they find new homes in venues all across the country.

One of the many pleasures I take in curating the festival is the opportunity to present a group of plays that reflects the rich diversity of Humana Festival audiences. The plays included in the 2015 lineup represent a thrilling array of perspective, storytelling, and subject matter. And perhaps not surprisingly, each play features a vividly distinct sense of place. The characters in this collection of stories are uniquely shaped by the locations in which their lives unfold— from a recently divorced, middle-aged woman trying on a new lifestyle in the cornfields of Iowa, to a boisterous inner-city Philadelphia family coping with its matriarch's progressive dementia, to a tiny California community neighboring a ghost town, haunted by recent loss. And some characters find themselves in more outlandishly imagined spaces, visiting strange planets on an intergalactic mission. Each strikingly drawn tale transports us to a new locale, or asks us to reconsider the one we know with fresh eyes.

Considering the wide range of geographical perspectives evident in this mix, it is particularly gratifying to include two plays, commissioned by Actors Theatre for the 2015 Humana Festival, that have special resonance for Louisville audiences. *That High Lonesome Sound*, commissioned to showcase the talents of the 2014–2015 Acting Apprentice Company, explores the rich cultural legacy of bluegrass, a musical tradition deeply embedded in Kentucky and this region. And Charles Mee's *The Glory of the World* takes as its inspiration local figure Thomas Merton, a Kentucky-based Trappist monk, activist, and prolific writer whose life defies singular characterization. At the time of this writing, our Humana Festival production of Mee's play is running at BAM in New York City. It has been profoundly rewarding to enter into a direct dialogue with Louisville audiences through stories inspired by our region, and to then share those stories with a national audience hungry to encounter distinctive viewpoints.

With this publication, we are proud to expand the audience for these plays once again, and to celebrate the remarkable creativity of the dramatists who created them. This book is an important part of Actors Theatre's effort to demonstrate and champion the broad range of contemporary American playwriting, and it is a joy to see work launched by the Humana Festival head out to new stages and new audiences.

—*Les Waters*
Artistic Director
Actors Theatre of Louisville

Editors' Note

It's been said that each of us contains multitudes, our lives a patchwork of contradictory impulses and moments of transformation that defy a simple narrative. A new adventure, a new friend, or a recent loss can send a life hurtling in surprising directions, and the attempt to define any person's "true" nature only proves the irreducible complexity of every human story. While wildly different from one another in form, voice, and inspiration, the tales of the 2015 Humana Festival of New American Plays prove this principle in myriad ways, revealing the strange juxtapositions and collisions that are the stuff of our 21st-century consciousness. The plays are never chosen with themes in mind; in fact, quite the opposite, since Actors Theatre's curatorial process aims for aesthetic diversity and a breadth of cultural perspectives. But as we put this collection together, we couldn't help noting some telling echoes—whether the action unfolded at a raucous birthday party, in a ghost town, or amid weird creatures in outer space.

Several of the plays reverberate with a sense of wonder at the unexpected twists and many possible stories that a single life can encompass. In Charles Mee's *The Glory of the World*, a series of birthday toasts for legendary writer and spiritual thinker Thomas Merton, each claiming to pinpoint his essence, expansively demonstrates that we are all far too complicated to be defined by neat explanations. Meanwhile, the Midwestern housewife in Jen Silverman's *The Roommate* sheds her demure demeanor to stretch her identity in daring new directions, sparked by a burgeoning friendship with a woman who's her seeming opposite. And in *I Promised Myself to Live Faster*, Gregory S Moss and Pig Iron Theatre Company's delirious, Charles Ludlam-inspired sci-fi mash-up, a lonely everyman finds himself catapulted into a quest to save the Homosexual Race (nay, the entire universe!) with the help of a flamboyant new ally. We might be capable of so much more than what we imagine—and sometimes, it takes crashing into an alluring stranger or an intergalactic crisis to perceive those glorious (and ridiculous) dimensions.

Such revelations can come at moments of profound life transition, and the plays in this festival often depict characters grappling with unsettling change, both painful and productive. *The Roommate*'s and *Live Faster*'s protagonists find themselves at a perplexing crossroads, and so too do the middle-aged siblings in Colman Domingo's *Dot*, whose feisty mother, once a force in her inner city community, is losing herself to dementia. As they struggle to come together and to preserve the family's memories, these characters find themselves facing a transition that no one is ever ready to tackle. Loss has also recently visited the small town in Erin Courtney's *I Will Be Gone*; its denizens' awkward attempts to mourn their dead are by turns humorous and haunted by grief. As the characters wander a nearby mountain ghost town, the play deftly captures a double consciousness of past and present, of inescapable mortality and the incongruous fact that somehow, life and love keep on going.

This rich embrace of incongruity surfaces in many of the plays, particularly in the way that laughter sits alongside loss. Such is the case with both *Dot* and *I Will Be Gone*; while tonally very different, great humor accompanies sorrow in these plays (as it so often does in life). Laughter is also sought as a salve for heartache in Patricia Cotter's ten-minute play, *Rules of Comedy*, in which a chronically unfunny woman seeks lessons on the craft of joke-telling from a stand-up comedian with hang-ups of his own. Unfortunate events become the engine for comedy in the other two ten-minute plays in this volume as well: Gary Winter imagines an environmental disaster that drops a sea monster into the delightfully demented office world of *So Unnatural a Level*. And when the protagonist of Steve Yockey's *Joshua Consumed an Unfortunate Pear* achieves immortality, his less-than-thrilled mate forces him into a romantic compromise that's both hilarious and very, very bloody.

A tendency toward formal adventurousness goes hand-in-hand with the way these plays collectively wrestle with life's complexities and confusions. Whether chronicling a hero's journey with subversive glee, unleashing comedy to dark or deeply moving ends, or transforming a birthday party into (quite possibly) the most outrageous brawl ever seen onstage, these plays take bold shapes that are integral to the way they move us. Actors Theatre's ongoing interest in exploring the possibilities of form also led to the creation of *That High Lonesome Sound*, written by four commissioned playwrights—Jeff Augustin, Diana Grisanti, Cory Hinkle, and Charise Castro Smith—and performed by our 2014–2015 Acting Apprentice Company. The initial impulse was to see what might happen if artists created a play inspired by a piece or a genre of music—in this case, bluegrass, whose history is so linked with the state of Kentucky and our region. Could the team, collaborating with director Pirronne Yousefzadeh and dramaturg Hannah Rae Montgomery, make a theatrical event something like a bluegrass album? The answer was a resounding yes, resulting in a piece of theatre that's both a collection of singular voices and a cohesive meditation on a lively musical legacy.

Finally, it's worth noting that the plays of the 2015 Humana Festival paint these colorful multitudes of experience with unforgettable imagery and a good deal of wild theatricality. If you were with us in Louisville for these world premieres, you'd have witnessed an old woman turning into a banjo and a rhinoceros galumphing across the stage as men performed a synchronized water ballet, dancing through lawn sprinklers. You'd have seen ghosts—both eerie apparitions, and in the flesh—and you'd have flown with the Mrithra, a mythical space beast who can traverse galaxies. But never fear: those memorable moments (and so many more) are captured in the pages that follow, for readers' imaginations to feast upon. And we trust that the plays will be just as vivid in your mind's eye as they were for the audiences who encountered them in Louisville.

—*Amy Wegener and Jenni Page-White*

RULES OF COMEDY
by Patricia Cotter

BIOGRAPHY

Patricia Cotter is an Emmy Award-winning Groundlings Theatre alum. She's received the American Academy of Arts and Letters' Richard Rodgers Award for Musical Theater. Other honors include the Ovation Award and the Garland Award. Plays include *Rules of Comedy* (2015 Humana Festival of New American Plays; Heideman Award finalist); *The Anthropology Section* (Actors Theatre of Louisville's *Tens*, 2015); *The Break Up Notebook* (A GLAAD Award nominee); *Three*; and *Best/Worst* (Apartment A Theatre Company, Venice, CA, where she was playwright-in-residence). Cotter co-wrote the cabaret show, *Beth Malone: So Far* (Joe's Pub, New York City). Her musicals (librettist/ adaptations) include *Rocket Science: A Musical* (music by Stephen A. Weiner, lyrics by Jason Rhyne) and *The Break Up Notebook: A Musical* (based on her play, music and lyrics by Lori Scarlett). She adapted *Mulan, Jr.,* based on the Disney film *Mulan*, for Disney Theatrical. She was the co-librettist on *Justin Love*, which won the Los Angeles Drama Critics Circle Award for Best Production in 2013. She is writing a new musical with composer Lori Scarlett, *Ladykillers*, which they developed at the Rhinebeck Writers Retreat. Cotter is a member of the PlayGround Writers Pool, where she received the 2014 June Anne Baker Prize and commission which honors the top female playwright representing a gifted new comedic or political voice for the stage.

ACKNOWLEDGMENTS

Rules of Comedy premiered at the Humana Festival of New American Plays in April 2015. It was directed by John Rooney with the following cast:

CAROLINE	Emily Stout
GUY	Conrad Schott

and the following production staff:

Scenic Designer	Dane Laffrey
Costume Designer	Beatrice Vena
Lighting Designer	Mike Inwood
Sound Designer	Christian Frederickson
Stage Manager	Stephen Horton
Assistant Stage Manager	Jason Pacella
Dramaturg	Jessica Reese
Properties Master	Mark Walston

CHARACTERS

CAROLINE: Female. Early to mid-twenties—smart, odd, serious.

GUY: Male. Mid to late twenties—a stand-up comic, intense, on the verge of becoming bitter.

SETTING

Present day. Guy's studio apartment.

Conrad Schott and Emily Stout
in *Rules of Comedy*

39th Humana Festival of New American Plays
Actors Theatre of Louisville, 2015
Photo by Bill Brymer

RULES OF COMEDY

GUY's studio apartment. An oddly serious young woman, CAROLINE, stands holding a microphone. GUY, an intense stand-up comedian, watches her. CAROLINE speaks to an unseen audience. She is mid "routine." She is not a natural comedienne. At all.

CAROLINE. …Okay. Show of hands: How many of you out there thought your elementary school bus driver was really cool, until you found out that she was a fugitive from justice? Come on. I know I'm not the only one. *(To GUY.)* What do I do if they don't respond.

GUY. Yeah. They're not going to respond.

CAROLINE. Why not?

GUY. Because, basically, no one has ever thought that their elementary school bus driver was a fugitive from justice.

CAROLINE. Mine was. Money laundering.

GUY. That's…interesting…and sort of upsetting, but not funny. Why don't you focus on something a little more, I don't know, universal? Something everybody can relate to. Like say: dating.

CAROLINE. Dating. Dating. Okay. I can do that. *(Deep breath.)* How about dating? We all do it, right? Or some of us don't. I don't date much. Maybe it's because I'm an atheist. Guys don't like atheists. Because during sex, when other girls yell out stuff like: "Oh, my God, Oh, my God, Oh, my God!", atheists tend to yell out stuff like: "Oh, my no one!", "Oh, my Ayn Rand!", "Oh, my fictional representative of an antiquated belief system!" And you know that just takes too long. Am I right ladies? Can I get a witness? Holla!

GUY. Stop! I mean I like where you were going with that…I think. Talking about sex is great, 'cause, you know, you're a girl. And everybody loves it when girls talk about sex on stage. Some girls. But I don't know if you're that kind of girl.

CAROLINE. Probably I'm not.

GUY. Yeah. No. So come on, tell me a joke. Like a joke joke with a punch line.

CAROLINE. Okay, okay. *(Thinking.)* Wow. I'm blanking. This is really hard. This is surprisingly hard. Do limericks count?

GUY. Let's back up a little bit. Just put down the mic. It's not helping.

(She struggles as to where to put the microphone.)

CAROLINE. I don't want to break it. I'm assuming you value it.

GUY. Whatever. It doesn't work anyway. Listen up: there are four basic elements to comedy. Every single joke has these elements. Every joke. You may think they don't, but trust me, they do. It's just a comedy truth. Okay? .

CAROLINE. I have no reason not to believe you.

GUY. It's been true since the dawn of comedy. Since the Greeks stood on Mount Olympus or wherever the Greeks stood, and Aristotle taught Plato the art of telling the perfect fucking joke.

CAROLINE. Aristotle was a student of Plato's—so I don't think that actually happened—

GUY. —Facts don't matter in comedy.

CAROLINE. I'm a big believer in facts.

GUY. The four elements are: The set-up, the story, the twist and the punch line.

(*She stares at him.*)

You're not going to write any of this down?

CAROLINE. That seems misleadingly simple.

GUY. It's not, I had to learn this stuff the hard way. Years of bombing in front of an audience before I came up with this foolproof method. This workshop is only two hours long so you're gonna need to focus.

(CAROLINE *grabs a pen and her notebook.*)

CAROLINE. My pen is poised. Now. Now it is poised.

GUY. The set-up. The story. The twist and the punch line. So what are they?

CAROLINE. Set-up, story, punch line.

GUY. And the twist, you forgot that one.

CAROLINE. I just assumed that the twist would come under the umbrella of the "story" portion of the program.

GUY. It doesn't come under the umbrella of anything—it's its own separate element.

CAROLINE. All right. I mean I disagree, but all right. Can I ask a question?

GUY. No.

CAROLINE. Why are rabbis always walking into bars?

GUY. What?

CAROLINE. Are rabbis known for their struggle with alcohol?

GUY. I don't think so.

CAROLINE. Haven't you noticed that many, many jokes are launched by that premise? A rabbi walks into a bar or a Jew walks into a bar. It's never a Seventh Day Adventist walks into a bar.

GUY. Seventh Day Adventists don't drink.

CAROLINE. Exactly. So if they did, then indeed, walk into a bar, wouldn't that be funny? Er?

GUY. How about you forget about rabbis specifically and religion in general, for a second, because you have just accidentally stumbled upon the classic set-up. Typically you would list three people or three things that have nothing in common and then find a way to get them all in one room, say a bar, or a rowboat, or a proctologist's office. Three incongruent things all in one space. Write this down—three is a classic comedy numeral.

(*She hesitates, then deigns to write it down.*)

CAROLINE. Or maybe the world of stand-up comedy is anti-Semitic.

GUY. There are tons of Jewish comedians. I'm a half-Jewish comedian.

CAROLINE. That seems like it could be funny. A half-Jewish comedian walks into someplace...a Red Lobster, the DMV...oh, yes, a Red Lobster restaurant might be funny because it's named for a shellfish.

GUY. How did you hear about my workshop again?

CAROLINE. I saw a flyer. I even bought a book. As research.

GUY. A book.

CAROLINE. It's called: *101 Dirty Jokes*. I got it on sale. Do you want to hear one?

(*She pulls out her book.*)

GUY. Not really—

CAROLINE. (*Reads.*) A dog, a cat and a penis are sitting around a campfire... huh...let me find a better one.

GUY. Okay, Caroline don't take this the wrong way, but you don't seem particularly, you know, funny.

CAROLINE. I know. That's why I'm here.

GUY. The thing is though, I can't teach you to be funny.

CAROLINE. Yes, you can.

GUY. No. I can't. Nobody can. That's not what this class is about.

CAROLINE. That's what you advertised. You said on the flyer that I would be funny after one "hilarious session" or my money back.

(*She pulls out the flyer.*)

GUY. I said you would find out how to be funny after one, you know, hilarious session.

CAROLINE. So far I have not laughed once since I got in here. There has been no hilarity. Nothing hilarious has occurred.

GUY. Can we please just stop using the word: "hilarious"? Look, if you want your money back...

CAROLINE. No.

GUY. How about a beer? Do you want a beer. Because I think a beer might help. Or maybe a field trip—I could take you to an open mic. Who knows if you're lucky I might even get up there myself.

CAROLINE. I've seen your act.

GUY. What? You did when?

CAROLINE. Friday night. Right after I signed up for the class. I found you online—saw you had a show—so I went.

GUY. Great.

CAROLINE. Uh-huh.

(*He waits, she offers nothing.*)

GUY. So…

CAROLINE. Yup. I saw you…up on the stage. I liked your shirt.

GUY. That was a pretty tough crowd that night.

CAROLINE. They definitely weren't laughing very much.

GUY. Like I said they were a tough crowd.

CAROLINE. Three people left. They just got up and walked out in the middle of your act.

GUY. I know. I was there. What can I say—it happens.

CAROLINE. You talked a lot about your ex-girlfriend.

GUY. That's kind of the focus of my act right now.

CAROLINE. You seemed mad at her.

GUY. What? No. I'm over it. That's just what comedians do. We tell jokes to strangers, typically drunk strangers, about our lives. My job is to make a roomful of drunk people laugh their asses off at the shitty things that happen to me.

CAROLINE. I don't like drunk people. They make me nervous. My aunt is an alcoholic and a dental hygienist.

GUY. See now that's a great example of a set-up. An alcoholic dental hygienist starts to clean this guy's teeth—

CAROLINE. She's too sad to be funny. What other types of jokes are there?

GUY. There are like a million types: Lawyer jokes, Yo' Mama jokes, Dumb Blonde jokes. What did the blonde say to the doctor when she found out she was pregnant? (*Beat.*) Are you sure it's mine?

(*No response.*)

CAROLINE. That joke didn't have a twist.

GUY. I probably should have cancelled, but you know, I needed the hundred and fifty bucks. Look I understand if this isn't your thing. As a matter of fact, I'm going to give you a hundred back right now and we can call it a night.

CAROLINE. No.

GUY. Basically I just gave you a one-on-one tutorial, that seems fair to me.

CAROLINE. I don't want my money back. I want—

GUY. I'm just going to be brutally honest, Caroline. You're not funny. At all. You actually would be a nightmare to even have in the audience. You can't question, or worry about why a rabbi would walk into a bar, or why a cowboy would have a parrot on his shoulder, you just have to go with it.

CAROLINE. Maybe if you could give me an example of the perfect set-up, story, twist—parenthetical—and punch line, I'd get it.

GUY. I don't know about perfect, but if I give you a good example, you'll leave?

CAROLINE. You give me one really good example, and I am out of here.

GUY. Just so you know, this isn't one of my jokes. I do more, like, stories from my life, well, you know, you heard…whatever. But this is a classic, well-built joke, this is basically the Toyota Camry of jokes.

CAROLINE. Got it.

GUY. A couple of New Jersey hunters are out in the woods when one of them just all of a sudden collapses and falls to the ground. His friend checks him out—and the guy doesn't seem to be breathing, his eyes are rolled back in his head—it looks pretty bad. So the hunter, completely freaked out, whips out his cell and calls 911. He gets the operator and says: "Help me. I think my friend is dead! What do I do?" The operator says: "Just take it easy, sir. I can help. The first thing we need to do, is to make sure that your friend is actually dead." So the guy pulls out his rifle and shoots his friend. Then he comes back on the line, and says to the operator: "Okay, he's definitely dead. Now what?"

(CAROLINE *bursts into tears.*)

Shit. Shit. Shit.

(*She continues to cry.*)

Sorry. Sorry. I mean…are you okay?

CAROLINE. That was funny.

GUY. No it wasn't—it's pretty stupid actually, but it follows the formula. That's all. I don't even like that joke.

CAROLINE. We know the hunter is dumb because he's from New Jersey, correct?

GUY. Correct. New Jersey is kind of the go-to dumb guy state.

CAROLINE. I don't want to be a stand-up comedian.

GUY. Then why are you here?

CAROLINE. I lost my sense of humor.

GUY. I don't think that's even possible.

CAROLINE. People lose their sense of smell or their sense of taste, some people have no common sense, why isn't it possible that I lost my sense of humor? I can't access joy. In any form. That's why I'm here, in your semi-creepy living room. I knew it wouldn't work. I just thought I'd try.

GUY. Sorry this didn't produce more…hilarity.

CAROLINE. My mother died.

GUY. Oh, God.

CAROLINE. Yeah.

GUY. I'm sorry. (*Moment.*) How'd she die?

CAROLINE. I killed her.

(*Beat of weirdness.*)

GUY. What?

CAROLINE. That was a joke?

GUY. That's not funny.

CAROLINE. I know. I don't know why I said that. It just came out. She died two months ago. And I haven't laughed since. Not once. I can't even feel the potential for laughing. I don't have it anymore. I'm just…empty.

GUY. You'll, you know, get it back.

CAROLINE. I won't.

GUY. You will. People get things back.

CAROLINE. How?

GUY. I think…the only thing I know is that you just have to keep going. Like when I'm bombing, when I'm one hundred percent eating shit bombing, I know that if I just keep going, somewhere down the line, they will laugh again. It's a mathematical impossibility that they won't. And just when I think they won't? They do. So that's what you have to do—I think—just keep going.

CAROLINE. Keep going.

GUY. That's all I got. I'm just a mediocre comedian.

CAROLINE. You're not mediocre. It's just that your ex-girlfriend jokes aren't funny. You should stop telling them.

GUY. But that's half my act.

CAROLINE. It doesn't matter. They're mean. That's why people left.

GUY. She broke my heart.

CAROLINE. I know. (*Beat.*) It's hard, but maybe just start over with some new material. You can have my a dog, a cat and a penis sitting around a campfire joke if you want it.

GUY. It all seems sort of stupid, telling jokes when, you know, there's real life.

CAROLINE. No. Not stupid. I think real life is why jokes exist. Even when they don't always work. Anyway. Bye. Thank you.

(*She gathers up her stuff to leave.*)

GUY. So. What if an orphan and a half-Jewish comedian walked into a bar?

(*She waits.*)

CAROLINE. What's the punch line?

GUY. No punch line. It's an invitation. For a drink with, you know, me.

CAROLINE. An invitation and...kind of a twist.

GUY. Kind of.

CAROLINE. The twists are important.

GUY. Yes. The twists are very important.

> (CAROLINE *smiles the smallest of smiles.*
> *Blackout.*)

End of Play

I WILL BE GONE
by Erin Courtney

ABOUT *I WILL BE GONE*

This article first ran in the Limelight Guide to the 39th Humana Festival of New American Plays, *published by Actors Theatre of Louisville, and is based on conversations with the playwright before rehearsals for the Humana Festival production began.*

"Theatre provides a space for meditation, a place to think about things that we don't have an arena to process in our daily lives," says playwright Erin Courtney. In her moving, haunting, and often funny new drama, *I Will Be Gone*, Courtney transports us to a small town under the big sky of California's Sierra Nevada Mountains, whose denizens are muddling through grief and loss and dealing (somewhat awkwardly) with ample evidence of their own impermanence. "I have lost a lot of really excellent, inspiring friends over the last twenty years," explains Courtney, "and so I think about how those people are still present in my life, and at the same time, absent—I don't get to make new memories with them. And yet every moment that I've shared with them is present in my life and in many other people's lives. In writing this play, the driving thought was about that presence and absence, and how we eventually accept losing someone—as well as the theatrical question of how to make invisible things present onstage."

When the play begins, it's been barely a month since the death of seventeen-year-old Penelope's mother. Penelope has moved in with her mom's middle-aged sister, Josephine, in the mountain community where the older generation grew up. It's a town so tiny that Josephine's high school ex-boyfriend, Liam, is now the mayor. As the women try to navigate their new situation—and Penelope befriends the punk-rocker boy next door—we learn that everyone in this town is haunted by someone or something. "We behave strangely sometimes when we're dealing with loss," notes the playwright, commenting on the humor that springs from her characters' befuddlement, and from the play's many surprises. Among those odd occurrences are increasingly pronounced manifestations of the supernatural—for the dead may still be around. Amid apparitions, earthquakes, and the characters' strange attempts to mourn, the world of the play also starts to become something of a ghost story.

In fact, *I Will Be Gone*'s small town sits near a ghost town that its characters frequent, where abandoned mines and saloons once thrived in the late 19th century during California's gold rush. "I remembered going to this ghost town called Bodie in the Sierra Nevadas, and it captured my imagination," says Courtney. "In 1880, Bodie was one of the biggest towns in California, but really quickly, the whole industry faded away. It was declared an official ghost town and historic park in 1962, and no one was allowed to fix anything, but if a structure was starting to fall over, they could prop it up. The town had to be kept in a state of 'arrested decay.' When I was a kid, I loved peering into the dusty windows; everything was left the way it had been. In the schoolhouse, you'd see sharpened pencils on the desks, somebody's glasses, and children's art on the wall. It's as if everyone left in a big hurry."

So while Courtney began her play with the idea of a bereaved woman struggling with her new role as guardian to her niece, this ghost town was also threaded into the play's DNA. "I thought, I can make a town full of people going through a time of loss they're not ready to accept. Mirroring the ghost town, they're clinging to a state of arrested decay," Courtney observes. "And ghost stories and horror provide a fantastic genre to deal with the things that terrify us; they make manifest something we can't see." In addition to memories of Bodie's eerie atmosphere, Courtney mined her own background to create other dimensions of the play's theatrical world. Having grown up in Hermosa Beach, California, amid the rise of punk rock bands like the Descendents and Black Flag, she also wove moments of song into the play. "Like humor, music is a great relief," she says, "something that brings us together in a way that we don't understand."

As the inhabitants of *I Will Be Gone* grapple with moving on, both generations face big questions about what their own lives mean in the face of loss. "I think people who are middle-aged and people who are seventeen are both on the verge of change," Courtney muses. "A teenager is about to embark on a new chapter; someone in her mid-forties is moving to the second half of life, figuring out what to bring along and what to leave behind. The movement of the story is about adapting to change. And realizing that it's okay that we're so small, but very much part of a larger universe." Such revelations may be unsettling, but they can also be oddly reassuring, and Courtney believes the theatre is the ideal realm in which to explore such paradoxical and impossible thoughts. "Theatre is a place where we get to do the thing that we can't do in real life," she reflects. "In my real life, I want literal answers and I hate change. But when I go to theatre, what makes me happiest is to watch things that cannot literally happen. To watch a character who is dead and alive at the same time."

—Amy Wegener

BIOGRAPHY

Erin Courtney's play *I Will Be Gone*, directed by Kip Fagan, premiered at Actors Theatre of Louisville in the 2015 Humana Festival of New American Plays. Her play *A Map of Virtue*, produced by 13P and directed by Ken Rus Schmoll, won a special citation Obie Award in 2012. She has written two operas with Elizabeth Swados, *The Nomad* and *Kaspar Hauser*; both were commissioned and produced by The Flea Theater. Her play *Honey Drop* was developed at the Atlantic Theater, the Clubbed Thumb/Playwrights Horizons SuperLab, and New Georges. Her other plays include *Alice the Magnet*, *Demon Baby*, *Quiver and Twitch*, and *Black Cat Lost*. She is an affiliated artist with Clubbed Thumb and a member of the Obie Award-winning playwright collective 13P, as well as the co-founder of the Brooklyn Writers Space. Ms. Courtney teaches playwriting at Brooklyn College. She earned her M.F.A. in playwriting at Brooklyn College with Mac Wellman, and her B.A. from Brown University, where she studied with Paula Vogel. She has been a member of New Dramatists since 2012 and is a 2013 Guggenheim Fellow.

ACKNOWLEDGMENTS

I Will Be Gone premiered at the Humana Festival of New American Plays in March 2015. It was directed by Kip Fagan with the following cast:

THERESA	Lexi Lapp
YOUNG JOSEPHINE	Elise Coughlan
ELLIOT	Seth Clayton
PENELOPE	Amy Berryman
JOSEPHINE	Birgit Huppuch
JIM	Triney Sandoval
LIAM	Alex Moggridge
LIZ	Rachel Leslie
YOUNG JIM	Hernando Caicedo

and the following production staff:

Scenic Designer	Andrew Boyce
Costume Designer	Kathleen Geldard
Lighting Designer	Paul Toben
Sound Designer	Daniel Kluger
Original Music	Daniel Kluger and Seth Clayton
Media Designer	Philip Allgeier
Stage Manager	Kathy Preher
Dramaturg	Amy Wegener
Casting	Calleri Casting
	(James Calleri, Paul Davis, Erica Jensen)
Assistant Sound Designer	Elliot Davoren
Properties Master	Joseph Cunningham
Directing Assistant	Tara Branham
Production Assistant	Joshua Mark Gustafson
Assistant Dramaturg	Robyn Carroll

I Will Be Gone benefitted from the generous support of the John Simon Guggenheim Memorial Foundation Fellowship, a MacDowell residency, the Creativity Fund at New Dramatists, and the Clubbed Thumb Writers' Group.

CHARACTERS

The Kids:
PENELOPE, 17
ELLIOT, 17

The Adults:
JOSEPHINE, 45
LIAM, 45
LIZ, 43
JIM, 47

The Kids in the Past:
THERESA, 15 and 18
JIM, 17
JOSEPHINE, 12

PLACE

A small town in the Eastern Sierra region of California.

SETTINGS

Jo's front porch
Town Hall
The Ghost Town—Bodie

NOTE

The script printed here is the Humana Festival production draft of *I Will Be Gone*. Companies interested in producing the play should contact AO International to confirm the most current version of the script, as updates have been made by the playwright following the publication of this collection.

"It has stood for more than eighty summers. Its timber has been impregnated, four times with joy and three times with sorrow. When someone who has lived in the house dies it is repainted. The dead person paints it himself, without a brush, from the inside."
　　　　　—Tomas Tranströmer

"I hold that love, where present, cannot possibly be content with remaining always the same."
　　　　　—St. Teresa of Avila

"Drunks fear the police,
but the police are drunk too."
　　　　　—Rumi

Amy Berryman
in *I Will Be Gone*

39th Humana Festival of New American Plays
Actors Theatre of Louisville, 2015
Photo by Bill Brymer

I WILL BE GONE

PROLOGUE

On JOSEPHINE *and* THERESA's *front porch, 33 years ago.*
JOSEPHINE *is 12 and* THERESA *is 15.*
In the yard, there is a well-maintained tree house.
The moonlight through the tree house casts strange shadows on the front porch.
JOSEPHINE *and* THERESA *are in their Lanz pajamas and have side ponytails.*
It is the middle of the night and they hold candles.

THERESA. Are you scared?

JOSEPHINE. No.

THERESA. Whatever you do, do not scream.

JOSEPHINE. I am not going to scream.

> (*They stare into the flame.*
> *They turn in circles chanting.*)

THERESA and JOSEPHINE. Bloody Mary
Bloody Mary
Bloody Mary
Bloody Mary
Bloody Mary
Bloody Mary
I have your baby.

Bloody Mary
Bloody Mary
Bloody Mary
Bloody Mary
Bloody Mary
Bloody Mary
I have your baby.

> (*They stare into the black window pane.*)

Bloody Mary

> (*They blow out their candles.*
> *A face appears in the window pane.*
> *They both scream.*)

SCENE ONE

33 years later, on the same front porch.
ELLIOT and PENELOPE, both age 17, are doing their homework.
In the yard, the once perfectly maintained tree house is broken down and full of holes.
It is late afternoon and behind the house, you can see a large mountain range and
a big, open sky.

ELLIOT. Pen, did you write down the rules?
For the poem?

PENELOPE. There are six stanzas,
the second line from one stanza becomes the third line in the next stanza.
So it goes ABA then BCB then CDC.

ELLIOT. Did you write yours already?

PENELOPE. No.
I have like two stanzas.

ELLIOT. Can I read it?

PENELOPE. Uh. Sure.

ELLIOT. (*Reading the title.*) Terzanelle for Theresa.
Oh, that's for your mom. Are you sure?

    (PEN *nods yes.* ELLIOT *reads.*)

My mother built towers out of matchsticks
She found grace in numbers and equations
Finding answers like simple magic tricks

Failing body and deep frustrations
were eclipsed by mental turns and flips
She found grace in numbers and equations

    (*There is the sound of a slight rumbling.*
    The porch light flickers on and then off.
    PEN *and* ELLIOT *both notice it.*
    The rumbling stops.)

ELLIOT. But, math for me, is full of traps and trips
Our fights about the beauty of scientific proofs
were eclipsed by mental turns and flips

Wow. That's really good.
That's. really. good.

    (*Pause.*)

PENELOPE. What are you going to write your poem about?

ELLIOT. I was thinking about making it about the Moon. The Blood Moon.
See, the October Moon is called the Blood Moon, because the leaves are

starting to fall off the trees, the moon is bright, and animals are out gathering food, getting ready for winter, and if you go hunting, you have these clear nights and you can kill more animals.

(PEN's aunt, JOSEPHINE, comes out of the house.)

JOSEPHINE. Okay, gal. Time for art class! You ready to go?

(PEN really does not want to go. She shrugs her shoulders.)

Let's head down there then.

(JO and PEN walk down the road with their art supplies. ELLIOT starts to work on his Terzanelle.)

ELLIOT. Full October Moon, Blood Moon in sky

(He gives up on the Terzanelle and picks up his guitar. He has been writing a punk rock ballad. It is about PEN. He strums and sings.)

It's a Blood Moon night
and now there's light
It's my Lucky Day
Now just to say
She's my lucky day.
She's my bright moon light

(A middle-aged homeless man, JIM, walks by the porch. He has gray hair, a gray beard, a pot belly and wears an old blue hoodie, blue sweatpants and really worn sneakers.)

JIM. (Overlaps with ELLIOT's singing.) The vibrational rotation of the molecules is the energy of the particles position in space, harmonic motion of the satellite and the radio. Space behaves as if it were a Euclidean moon. More individual components than in a Saturn 5, the wire and the silicon deodorant, tremendous achievement, and that is no task that I would not hesitate to undertake if it were put before me, I know this from experience, built in 1899, built the year Lottie Johl died.

(Pause.)

Barbara did not like the flies in the house, glue strips hanging from the ceiling Superconductor cables are one of the great engineering high fields, for my part, although I have said the abandonment of the project seemed to me impossible, I merely believe the revelation to be true in the sense that it was not contrary to what was written, the alternating currents with a rotating magnetic field which is the quantization of the perfect, perfect, mono atomic gas, and the baby in the car seat and Barbara came outside to meet her and what I am saying is the whole truth, and therefore whatever is good, this is where the dog slept, right here and this where the Chevy Impala was parked on Saturdays. The paramedics came to take her to the morgue. Lay out your dead and sit with them in the parlor, in the living room.

ELLIOT. It's a lucky day
Now that she's here
Now just to say
She's my lucky day
It's a lucky day
Now that she's here
Now just to say
She's my lucky day
She's my bright moon light

> (PEN *and* JO *are walking back. They cross paths with* JIM. PEN *registers* "*homeless man."* JO *does not acknowledge* JIM *in any way.* JO *is used to seeing him walk this path.*
> JIM *is part of the landscape.*)

ELLIOT. What happened to art class?

JOSEPHINE. Cancelled.
Here's her text.

> (*Reading from her phone.*)

"Tonight. I will be gone. In my absence, draw a still life."

ELLIOT. So what are you going to draw?

JOSEPHINE. I don't know. Fruit? In a bowl?

ELLIOT. Wait. I got it! Wait!

> (ELLIOT *goes into his house which is right next door.*)

JOSEPHINE. I am so glad that class was cancelled tonight because the nude model from last week really creeped me out. He always has a little bit of something oozing out of his penis. Like pre-cum? But he's not hard, you know, so is it an infection?

> (*Pause.*
> *They are unpacking their art supplies and setting up a little area to set up a still life.*
> ELLIOT *comes back carrying something.*)

PENELOPE. What's that?

ELLIOT. Teeth. And Gums. My mom's a dentist.

PENELOPE. Huh. Okay. Yeah that could be cool. Thanks.

> (ELLIOT *hands* PEN *the teeth. There is a little bit of an emotional charge when their hands touch. They smile awkwardly with recognition of it.* ELLIOT *goes back into his house.*)

JOSEPHINE. He has a crush on you.

PENELOPE. Stop. Aunt Jo.
He does not.

JOSEPHINE. And you have a crush on him!
Just be careful. Okay.

PENELOPE. What does that mean?

(ELLIOT *comes back out to get his notebook.*)

JOSEPHINE. I'll tell you later.
Thank You Elliot.
You saved us!

(ELLIOT *goes back into his house.* JO *and* PEN *set up a still life made of teeth. They begin drawing.*)

You know who my first boyfriend was?

PENELOPE. Who?

JOSEPHINE. Liam.

PENELOPE. The mayor?

JOSEPHINE. Yeah. In High School. Oh my God, Liam and I used to torment your mom.

(*Pause.*)

PENELOPE. What would you do?

JOSEPHINE. I don't know. She just. She just loved RULES!
And she was very judgmental.
So we used to call her St. Theresa
and she would cry every time we called her St. Theresa.

(*Pause.*)

PENELOPE. Did you know that my mom carried a St. Teresa medallion?

JOSEPHINE. What? She did?

PENELOPE. I didn't know 'til after she died.

(PEN *pulls the medallion out of her pocket.*)

I found it in her wallet.

JOSEPHINE. Can I see it?

(PEN *hands it to her.* JO *reads it.*)

"Life is to live in such a way that we are not afraid to die."

PENELOPE. That's a good motto, don't you think?

JOSEPHINE. Did your mom take you to church?

PENELOPE. No.

(*Pause.*)

JOSEPHINE. Oh, hang on a minute.

(JO *walks towards the house.*)

Our parents took us to church when we were kids. But then we just stopped going and I have no idea why.

(*JO goes into the house.*
She comes back out carrying a cardboard box.
She places it down on the ground.)

I found this box of dolls.

They were your mom's.

Do you want them?

(PEN *starts pulling the dolls out of the box. One is a porcelain-type doll of*
a Dutch girl, little blonde braids and wooden clogs. One is a cloth, ancient
Egyptian doll.
PEN *looks like she is afraid to touch the dolls.*)

PENELOPE. Uh. uhm. hmm. Did my mom like these dolls?

JOSEPHINE. Actually, I don't think she did. She didn't play with them. She kept them in this glass cabinet and every now and then she would rearrange them.

PENELOPE. What should we do with them?

JOSEPHINE. Well if you don't want them, we can give 'em to the Goodwill.

(PEN *puts the dolls back in the cardboard box and closes it.*)

PENELOPE. I don't know.

(*The box of dolls begins to move.*
PEN *and* JO *scream.*
AAAAHHHH)

PENELOPE. Why is the box moving?

Why is the box moving?

JOSEPHINE. Oh God. I bet it's a rat in there. We had rats in the basement.

PENELOPE. You had rats!

JOSEPHINE. Yes. I'm sorry.

They must have come back.

Pen, would you be upset if I just take that box to the dump?

(*Box moves.*)

PENELOPE. That would be okay.

JOSEPHINE. Are you sure?

PENELOPE. Yes. Yes! Elliot!

(*The box keeps moving.* ELLIOT *comes over; he has heard the screaming.*)

ELLIOT. What's up?

JOSEPHINE. This box has a rat in it and I am gonna drive it to the dump. Will you put it in my trunk?

ELLIOT. What if it gnaws its way out and starts to live inside your car?

JOSEPHINE. Oh God.

PENELOPE. I think you better call Animal Control.

JOSEPHINE. I don't want that thing loose in my car.

(JO *goes into the house to call Animal Control.* ELLIOT *leans into* PEN *and kisses her.*

She is surprised but happy about this. It gets steamy really fast. They are both surprised.)

ELLIOT. Oh Wow. Hey, uh do you want to come over? My mom's not home right now.

PENELOPE. No.

ELLIOT. But you were all into it. We don't have to stop.

PENELOPE. It's just, uh, too much. Uhm, too overwhelming? Right now?

ELLIOT. Yeah, I get that.

(*Pause.*)

PENELOPE. I thought after my mom died that I would do all this crazy shit.

ELLIOT. Yeah. So are you?

PENELOPE. No. In fact, it's like I actually feel her around me all the time. Like she can see everything.

So I am totally behaving myself.

ELLIOT. Huh.

PENELOPE. But I do masturbate all the time.

I can't believe I just told you that!

ELLIOT. I masturbate all the time too!

PENELOPE. Oh God. I'm so embarrassed now.

(*She turns to go inside.*)

ELLIOT. Hey, we should masturbate at the same time some time. Right?

SCENE TWO

In the front office at the very small Town Hall building.

LIAM *is standing behind* LIZ *and he has his hand down the front of her pants. They are behind a large counter so only their upper bodies are visible.*

LIAM. (*Whispering in* LIZ's *ear.*) And do you see Fellini? Fellini is so horny, he's trying to fuck the sun. He's got his sunglasses on and he is fucking the center of the solar system and it's so bright and hot and he might die from the burning rays but he doesn't care because the rays of the sun are so hot and he can't stop.

(PENELOPE *walks in.* LIZ *runs off.* LIAM *stands there not really knowing what to do.*)

Um. Just a minute.

PENELOPE. I'll come back later.

LIAM. Hang on, Penelope.

PENELOPE. Uh.

>(LIAM *turns, washes his hands in a little sink, then turns back around.*)

LIAM. What can I help you with?

PENELOPE. Uh. Well. It's not a big deal.

LIAM. What's up?

PENELOPE. Oh. I was wondering if you knew about any part-time jobs? I was hoping to get something for the weekends or after school.

LIAM. Are you settling in okay? Making friends.

PENELOPE. Yeah. I think I made a friend.

LIAM. Good. Who's that?

PENELOPE. Elliot Miller.

LIAM. Hmmm. Yeah. Okay.

PENELOPE. Okay?

LIAM. No. no. He's a good kid. He's a good kid.
And what about School?
Are you catching up okay?
I know it must be hard to start up at a new school.

PENELOPE. No. It's good.
The teachers have been really helpful.
And.
You know.

LIAM. Great.

PENELOPE. So if you hear of anyone who needs a little help, anybody who is hiring? Would you let me know?

LIAM. Sure thing. Oh in fact, I know they are looking for young people to train as tour guides over at Bodie, the Ghost Town.

PENELOPE. I used to love that Ghost Town. My mom used to take me.

LIAM. I can put in a good word for you.

PENELOPE. OK, thanks. Uh, See you later.

LIAM. Bye, Pen.

>(PEN *walks out.*
>LIZ *walks back in from the back.*)

LIZ. Liam. That graffiti is disgusting. You have to pay someone to paint over it.

LIAM. Where is it?

LIZ. On the front steps. I told you about it yesterday.

LIAM. What's it say?

LIZ. It says Evelyn.

LIAM. Who is Evelyn?

LIZ. I don't know any Evelyns!

LIAM. Fine. I'll paint over it for Christ's sake.

LIZ. Or just pay Jim to do it. I don't care but it's asking for trouble leaving a tag like that on the steps of Town Hall.

LIAM. I don't think Evelyn is in a gang.

LIZ. A girl can be in a gang. You can be so provincial sometimes. I read about it in the paper. The girls in gangs are even more violent than the guys. They have to prove how tough they are and they slash people's faces.

LIAM. I read that article too but that was in the City, it wasn't way out here.

LIZ. They are coming Liam. They are coming.

LIAM. I'll have Jim paint over it.

LIZ. AND! No more finger banging when we are in Town Hall. That was freaking embarrassing.

LIAM. Oh she didn't even notice.

LIZ. She knew exactly what was going on.

LIAM. Come on, you liked it. Admit it.

LIZ. No. I did not.

LIAM. Come on Lizzie, a lot of guys I know are flipping out and cheating on their wives. I'm just trying to keep things fresh.

LIZ. I appreciate that Liam. But you could take me to Reno for a night or something.

LIAM. But it was hot.

LIZ. Fine. Fine. Yes it was. It was okay. It's just embarrassing and you are the mayor.

LIAM. Of a small town.

LIZ. Still you are an elected official

LIAM. Who is NOT cheating on his wife.

LIZ. I'm going to the grocery store. You need anything that is not on the list?

(LIZ sees JIM outside. She calls out to him.)

Jim! Jim! Can you come in here. Liam has a job for you.

(LIZ leaves as JIM enters.)

LIAM. Hey, Jim.

You want to paint something for me?

JIM. Paint something, sure. I can paint something. My mother was a painter. She was a great painter and then she had to stop.

LIAM. I didn't know your mom was a painter.

JIM. She was but John F. Kennedy was her boyfriend. And he made her stop painting. JFK was a Jesuit priest.

LIAM. Here let me get the paint supplies.

(LIAM *goes off to get the supplies.*)

JIM. The Jesuits are good people. I like the Jesuits. The soul is a crystal castle, the soul, this soul globe tries to, is, a mansion of seven, seven mansions are inside of the plaster from the 1985 renovation. Replacement beams, weatherproof windows, new boiler. Flat eggshell on the baseboard, off-white gloss on the rocky road ice cream licked seven years old from the green store, the road to the seven stop lights, leading to the enlightened moment of all unions, fabric softeners, keep a schedule, coffee and donut, a real quiet path and the miners sing "see the elephant" the pings of the radar see naked outlines of the interior castle growing in ecstasy.

LIAM. Okay, Got it. It shouldn't take too long.
It's just some spray paint.

JIM. Spray paint your sister's basement and all that, the good works are there but they are a place holder for the rollers caked in dry paint. Elizabeth Catherine gave us hell the next day. Waste of money. Waste of resource, fifth mansion is of love. And life, six, plus the extracurricular activities take us miles away from the seven sexual union with all the beloved of the flags and floorboards.

LIAM. Someone wrote Evelyn.

JIM. Evelyn Meyers. Evelyn Meyers. 1897. Accidental Death. Pickaxe to the head.

SCENE THREE

Front porch of JOSEPHINE'*s house. Much, much later that same night. Beer bottles, bits of costumes, the reflection of police lights.* PENELOPE, *drunk, is wearing a handlebar mustache and a swim cap, painted to look like a bald head with a fringe of hair around the ears.* JO *is waving at a police car as it pulls away.*

JOSEPHINE. Thanks Chris. Sorry about the noise. Won't happen again.

(*To* PEN.)

What the fuck Penelope?

PENELOPE. I didn't think that many people would come.

JOSEPHINE. There is nothing to do in this town. If you tell kids there is a party—on Halloween weekend without a guardian present—word gets out!

PENELOPE. You kind of smell like pee.

JOSEPHINE. (*Yelling!*) Don't change the subject! What made you think that this was a good idea? This is my home. You want to have a party—great—just tell me about it so I can be here. Jesus. For a smart girl, you are really stupid!

(ELLIOT *walks up wearing a homemade Man in the Moon costume.*)

You missed the whole thing.

ELLIOT. Oh. I was working on my costume.

So it got busted up I guess.

JOSEPHINE. Yes! It got busted up. I mean shit! All these girls dressed up in these teeny tiny little outfits—saloon girls, and nurses—fishnets and cleavage—I mean it looked like a brothel out here. I walk up here and Mark Reilly is dry humping the Wagner girl on my front porch. Then Ann, across the street, had already called the cops several times. And luckily it was just Chris that came over and not Philip because if it had been Philip then, well Philip is an asshole. God. And what is this? Did they burn someone in effigy? We never did shit like that. Burn people in effigy. What kind of deviant shit are you kids up to these days? I just hope there is no puke in the house and you better hope that no one was in my bed.

(PENELOPE *runs into the house.*)

JOSEPHINE. (*To* ELLIOT.) What are you supposed to be anyway?

ELLIOT. The Man in the Moon.

Well, it's from a Méliès film.

Georges Méliès?

JOSEPHINE. That's ridiculous.

(JOSEPHINE *storms into the house.* ELLIOT *punches at the effigy hanging from the tree in the front yard. He examines it. Shakes it. He sees it is a homemade broken piñata.*)

ELLIOT. (*Yelling into the house.*) It's just a piñata. I think it was an elephant?

(JOSEPHINE *returns with trash bags.*)

JOSEPHINE. Fine. It is a piñata. Fine. Okay. I am ready to calm down now. I am calm. Elliot, I know you were not at the party but I am going to have Penelope clean up and if you would like to stay and help her then you are welcome to.

(PENELOPE *returns.* PENELOPE *and* ELLIOT *are picking up bottles, and trash, and bits of costumes. They clean for awhile.* JOSEPHINE *is muttering to herself.*)

ELLIOT. A lot of people showed up huh?

PENELOPE. Yeah.

ELLIOT. (*Quietly.*) Did you have fun?

PENELOPE. (*Quietly.*) No.
I don't know anyone.
I just drank a lot of vodka.

> (*They pick up trash. PEN is nauseous.*)

Aunt Jo, why do you smell like piss?

JOSEPHINE. Oh that band I went to see tonight, was a punk band, which I was excited about because I always liked punk rock. But then tonight I remembered why I stopped going to punk rock shows. The lead singer, who thank GOD was not my friend's kid, her kid is the drummer, anyway, the lead singer whips out his dick and actually pisses on the crowd.

ELLIOT. No way.

JOSEPHINE. Yes! I mean here we are a bunch of forty-year-olds who paid money to get pissed on.

PENELOPE. What about your friend?

JOSEPHINE. Oh! She was horrified. Truly horrified. So I just got out of there.

ELLIOT. Well at least it wasn't your friend's kid that pissed on you.

JOSEPHINE. Yes. Elliot.

PENELOPE. Um. I don't feel so well. Uhm.

> (PEN *runs into the house. We can hear her barfing. There is no way she made it to the toilet.* JO *is so mad. She has that frozen mad face. She looks at* ELLIOT. ELLIOT *looks at her like, "Hey don't blame me. I'm sober."* JO *reluctantly, angrily goes inside to check on* PEN.
>
> *"Man in the Moon"* ELLIOT *keeps cleaning up the porch.*
> *It is strangely quiet as he cleans.*
> *No animal sounds.*
> *The lack of animal sounds starts to creep out* ELLIOT.
> ELLIOT *starts to feel like he is being watched.*
> *A woman's voice, as clear as if it is right over* ELLIOT's *shoulder, says:*)

WOMAN'S VOICE. What are you doing?

> (*He whips around thinking it must be* JOSEPHINE. JO *is not there. He looks over the edges of the porch. He goes over to the door of the house.*)

ELLIOT. (*Into the house.*) Jo, what did you say?

JOSEPHINE. (*From the house.*) I didn't say anything.

ELLIOT. Did Pen?

JOSEPHINE. (*In the house.*) She's passed out.

ELLIOT. You didn't say something?

JOSEPHINE. (*In the house.*) Go home, Elliot.

SCENE FOUR

*The next morning at the Ghost Town, Bodie. A very windy day, bright sun.
PEN is hung over, sweating and holding onto a clipboard. She is giving a practice
tour.*

PENELOPE. (*Reading from clipboard.*) Welcome to Bodie!
Imagine it is the year 1859. Winter is approaching.
Two prospectors Wakeman S. Body and Black Taylor have a feeling that they
are going to find gold in this region, and so they keep going even though
winter is coming and their supplies are running low.

Body and Taylor are persistent, and their persistence pays off. They find gold!
They claim the land and then they realize they have to go back to the nearest
town, which is not at all near, to replenish their supplies. They start to make
their way back and an incredible snowstorm hits. They lose each other. Taylor
makes it out of the territory but Wakeman Body gets lost. He dies, frozen in
the snow. They do not find his corpse until the snow melts in the spring. In
his honor, they name the new town after him. Although a sign painter made
a mistake and wrote BODIE instead of BODY and the town liked the new
name and so they kept it. Wakeman S. Body never got to see the boom town
that grew out of his discovery.

Just 15 years later, the town of Bodie was at its peak. It was one of the biggest,
richest, most dangerous towns in the West. As quickly as it grew, it declined.
The gold dried up, the Depression hit, and the town population dwindled.
By 1962, the State of California bought out the last of its inhabitants and
declared Bodie a National Historic Site.

> (*She gestures around at the empty, dusty street.*
> *The wind whips down the street.*)

It is a state law that these structures must be maintained only to the extent that
they will not be allowed to fall over or otherwise deteriorate in a major way.
They must be kept in a state of "arrested decay."

I think that is a pretty poetic term.
"Arrested decay."

So, as you see they have not been painted or refurbished. Support beams are
only added if the structure is going to collapse.

> (*In another part of the Ghost Town,* JO *holds a pink cupcake.*)

JOSEPHINE. It's weird that sometimes I forget how beautiful the sky is
here.

LIAM. Yeah. Me too.

JOSEPHINE. I mean look at that sky.
There is no other place on earth with a sky just like that.
Every time Theresa and I came to Bodie,
she would just admire that sky.

>(*Pause.*)

Liam, thanks for coming with me.

LIAM. Of course.

JOSEPHINE. I think this is a good spot.

>(JO *places the pink cupcake on the ground.*)

LIAM. Theresa liked cupcakes?

JOSEPHINE. Oh, yeah. But she was really strict about them.
She would only eat them on her birthday and on Valentine's Day.

LIAM. She really did have a lot of rules for herself.

>(LIAM a*nd* JO *begin their made-up Day of the Dead ritual which includes singing a favorite song of the deceased.*)

Do you have a song for her?

JOSEPHINE. Yeah.

>(*She starts talk-singing Michael Jackson's "Don't Stop 'Til You Get Enough," like a chant. As the song builds through the first several verses, LIAM joins in, at first with little backup flourishes—"ooh," "ah power," "closer now"—but then his performance grows to accompany* JO *at full voice once she reaches the refrain. They sing together.*
>*When the song ends,* JO *and* LIAM *stand in silence for a moment.*
>PEN *walks up.*)

JOSEPHINE. She loved that song.

PENELOPE. What are you guys doing?

>(*Pause.*
>*Awkward.*)

LIAM. Tomorrow's the Day of the Dead.

JOSEPHINE. So I am leaving a cupcake for Theresa.

>(PEN *looks grossed out by this idea of leaving food out for dead people.*)

PENELOPE. I don't think my mom would like that.

JOSEPHINE. Well, I think she would.

PENELOPE. Why didn't you invite me?

JOSEPHINE. You can leave her something too, if you want.

PENELOPE. I don't want to leave her something.
You should have invited me.

>(*Pause.*)

Can we go back now?
JOSEPHINE. Sure.

> (*JO, PEN and* LIAM *leave.*
> *The pink cupcake waits to be eaten by the spirits.*
> JIM *wanders on.*
> JIM *picks up the cupcake and studies it.*)

JIM. Betty Crocker Champagne cupcake, prep time 25 minutes, total time 1 hour 15 minutes
servings 24, one box Betty Crocker SuperMoist white cake mix, 1¼ cups champagne
⅓ cup vegetable oil, 3 egg whites, 5 drops red food coloring
Betty Crocker Champagne frosting: ½ cup butter softened, 4 cups powdered sugar
¼ cup champagne, 1 teaspoon vanilla, 4 drops red food coloring, Garnishes: Betty Crocker pink decorating sugar, Edible pink pearls

> (*He smiles, he remembers* THERESA *eating a cupcake at age 17 that he had made for her.*)

crumbs flying out, laughing, Barbara got her some water. Smiling like a six-year-old.

> (*Image gone, new image replaces it.*)

Before the church was built, of course, some people had to pray before the church, and they had their old Bibles from where they came from, I came, to know the magnificent rainbow skittles that Theresa stole from the store, no, I stole I put the candy in her handbag before school tuna melt lightning.

SCENE FIVE

> *Later on the same day,* JOSEPHINE, PENELOPE, ELLIOT *and* LIZ *are setting up for the Halloween Party inside the Town Hall.* ELLIOT *is wearing his big Man in the Moon head again.* PENELOPE *is not wearing a costume.* JO *is Raggedy Ann.* LIZ *is in a toga.*

PENELOPE. Stubborn.
Beautiful. You know for her age.
Quirky. Well weird. Uh Quirky.
Smart.
She loved loved word problems, math problems, riddles, oh my god, endless.
And singing.
ELLIOT. Did she have a good voice?

PENELOPE. Oh no. Terrible Voice. The worst voice but she loved to sing anyway

And loud. A proud singer.

> (*Pause.*)

What's your mom like?

ELLIOT. My mom?

PENELOPE. Yeah.

ELLIOT. She's a dentist.
So. She's like a dentist.

PENELOPE. Continue.

ELLIOT. She started to play ice hockey and she loves it.

PENELOPE. Really?

ELLIOT. Yeah, it's like her only fun thing.
Hey, how did your first day up at Bodie go?

PENELOPE. They made me do like, a practice tour, which was not so great but you know I'm just learning. What about you? What did you do today?

ELLIOT. I went to a meeting and I did my shift at Nicely's.
You should come in tomorrow.
I could give you some free French Fries.

PENELOPE. What was the meeting for?

ELLIOT. Well, it's
It's Narcotics Anonymous.
I wanted you to know.

> (*Pause.*)

My mom sent me to rehab
in Arizona
and things are going
really good.
It was Oxycontin
which is really, really, really
addictive but
things are going
better.

PENELOPE. Oh
I didn't know,
but that's great
Elliot.
that it's going well.

> (*Pause.*)

ELLIOT. I'm really glad
you moved here.
I mean,
not about the circumstances,
but just that
you are here.

> (*Awkward, but also nice.*
> LIAM *walks over with a box of decorations.* LIAM *is wearing blue sweatpants and a blue sweatshirt.*)

LIAM. Can you guys hang these in the entryway?

PENELOPE. Yup.

ELLIOT. Hey Liam, I went to the Flea over in Bridgeport and there is a guy selling vinyl now.

LIAM. Shit! That's great! Anything good?

ELLIOT. Well at first it was all like Kenny Rogers and John Denver and I was just about to give up and then I found a punk section and I got Minor Threat!

LIAM. Awesome!
Next week I'll go with you.

ELLIOT. Cool.

> (LIAM *leaves to finish his costume.*
> ELLIOT *and* PEN *begin decorating.*
> *In another part of Town Hall,* JO *and* LIZ *take a break from hanging decorations.*)

JOSEPHINE. (*Reading to* LIZ *from a piece of paper.*)
Dear Aunt Josephine,
I am sorry that I threw a party in your house. I'm sorry that I am not perfect. I was just trying to make friends. It's hard to be the new kid in town, especially when everyone knows that your mom is dead.

LIZ. Wow.

JOSEPHINE. Yeah. She played the dead mother card. First of all, that's my sister and I'm depressed too. But I'm not throwing parties in her room. Fuck.

LIZ. Well she's young.

JOSEPHINE. I know. I know. I get it. I get it.
This note still pisses me off, because it worked.
I un-grounded her.

LIZ. You actually grounded her in the first place?

JOSEPHINE. Isn't that what parents do?

LIZ. Next time, send her to her room and tell her to think about what she did and then have her think up her own punishment.

JOSEPHINE. There is no way that works.

LIZ. It works. What about Pen's dad? Are you in contact with him?

JOSEPHINE. He has another family and he's made it clear that Pen is not a part of it.

LIZ. Oh, I'm so sorry Jo.

JOSEPHINE. I did not think that I would have NO living relatives by the time I was 45.

LIZ. You have a living relative. You have Pen!

JOSEPHINE. I mean living relatives that are older than me.
I mean shit. I still feel like I am 17 years old. I don't want to be in charge of anything. I don't want to go to my job. I don't want anyone relying on me right now. Because I would like to just freak out. Like go in the desert and freak out for five years and take peyote and turn into a wolf.
But Pen is here and so I don't get to freak out.

LIZ. Listen, Pen is great. You are going to help her and she is going to go off to college and then you can freak out if you still want to.

JOSEPHINE. (*Quiet.*) I want to freak out now.

LIZ. What about the money situation? I mean what was Theresa's financial situation?

JOSEPHINE. Well, luckily, Theresa, unlike me, is…was…incredibly conservative about money and her house has gone up in value, so we can sell it and that will pay for Pen's college.

LIZ. That's really good.
Now, what about you? Are you saving for retirement?

JOSEPHINE. God No! I'm in debt!

LIZ. You gotta get out of debt and start saving. Let me help you.

JOSEPHINE. One day, I am going to hire you to help me, but please, not yet. I just don't want to think like that yet.

LIZ. But every day you wait, you are losing money. There are really simple things I can help you with.

JOSEPHINE. I want to run away into the desert and live like an animal. I DO NOT WANT TO PLAN MY RETIREMENT. GOD!

> (JO *storms off.*
> LIAM *enters. He is now wearing the same blue sweatpants and hoodie, but he has added a grey wig and a grey fake beard. He has stuffed a pillow in his stomach area so he looks like he has a big belly.*)

LIZ. I want to help her but she just keeps pushing me away.

LIAM. Just be her friend right now.

LIZ. That is what I am trying to do. Friends help friends. She needs my help but she won't take it. She is so stubborn!

LIAM. She just needs to be angry right now. And sad. Just let her.

(ELLIOT *and* PEN *return to get more spider webs.*
LIZ *registers what* LIAM *is wearing as his costume.*)

LIZ. Liam. You can't wear that.

LIAM. Come on. I look just like him. Don't I look just like him?

LIZ. Yes, you do look just like him.

LIAM. It's funny, though, right?

LIZ. He isn't a joke.

He is a person.

(JO *has returned and sees what* LIAM *is wearing. She is shocked.*)

JOSEPHINE. Liam. What are you doing?

LIAM. It's all in good fun, ladies.

PENELOPE. What's wrong with his costume?

I can't even tell what he is?

Santa? Like Santa goes jogging?

ELLIOT. Are you supposed to be that homeless guy?

JOSEPHINE. You cannot dress like Jim as your costume!

PENELOPE. Who's Jim?

LIZ. Jim is the one homeless guy in our town.

I mean he has a home, but he refuses to sleep in it.

He's mentally ill.

JOSEPHINE. Liam and I went to High School with him!

PENELOPE. Oh, that is bad. You're the mayor. You can't wear that.

LIAM. Fine! But now I don't have any costume to wear!

(LIAM *storms off like a child.*)

JOSEPHINE. It's times like this I think I should move away from here.

LIZ. Elliot. You're tall: I need you over here.

(ELLIOT *goes reluctantly over to* LIZ.
She needs help hanging a paper skeleton.)

ELLIOT. I like your toga.

LIZ. Thanks. I made it last year but then I didn't wear it so. Your moon is, wow, you must have worked a long time on that.

ELLIOT. I did.

LIZ. Hey, your mom told me that you are doing great in school this year.

ELLIOT. Well, I wouldn't say GREAT but a whole lot better than last year.

LIZ. That's good Elliot.

ELLIOT. Thanks.

> (ELLIOT *has rejoined* PEN. *She is morosely eating candy.*)

How come you aren't wearing your costume? You looked so cute as a little bald man.

PENELOPE. I couldn't find it. I think Jo threw it out.

> (LIAM *returns. Now he wears a white T-shirt with* NO SLEEP TILL BROOKLYN *written on it with Sharpie, a baseball cap worn to the side, and Mardi Gras beads around his neck. He is holding his iPhone up to his ear, like it is a boom box.*)

LIZ. So what are you now?

LIAM. I'm a Beastie Boy.

> (LIAM *plays the Beastie Boys song*—"*Girls.*"
> LIAM *and* JO *dance.*
> LIZ *watches.*
> LIAM *sings the song's final verse, and* JO *joins in too as they jump around.*
> LIZ *has finally been pulled into the dancing. All three are singing and dancing.*)

PENELOPE. They are so embarrassing.

ELLIOT. Let's get out of here. Come on.

> (ELLIOT *leads* PEN *to a different area of the Town Hall. They start making out again.*)

I want to masturbate right now.

PENELOPE. Me too.

ELLIOT. Let's do it.

PENELOPE. No everyone is here. I can't do it.

ELLIOT. Let's go into different rooms so if anyone finds us it will look less suspicious.

PENELOPE. Okay. But lean up against the wall. So I can feel that you are there.

ELLIOT. Okay.

> (*They each go into different rooms and lean up against the wall.*
> *They begin to masturbate. The adults are still dancing, now to the song,*
> "*Fight For Your Right to Party.*")

LIAM. Hey, hey, let's go into the supply closet and do it.

LIZ. What is going on with you?

LIAM. Come on babe. I wanna be young again.

LIZ. You ARE young.

LIAM. This is the youngest I will ever be from now on, come on let's go…

> (*A very slight earthquake happens. It takes everyone a moment to notice.*
> *It takes* PEN *and* ELLIOT *a moment. The earthquake increases in intensity.*)

PENELOPE. Did we do that?

(LIAM *turns off the music.*)

JOSEPHINE. Was that an earthquake?

ELLIOT. I think we did that.

LIZ. I think so.
Wait.
It's still going.

JOSEPHINE. Shit.

LIAM. Jesus!

(JO, LIAM *and* LIZ *have gathered under a door frame.*)

LIZ. This is a big one.
Where are the kids?

JOSEPHINE. Pen! Pen!
Where are you?
Are you OK?

PENELOPE. We're OK?
Are you OK?

JOSEPHINE. We are all OK!

SCENE SIX

Town Hall. Most of the Halloween decorations are gone. It is a few days later. JO and LIZ are setting up for a memorial service. They set up two large photographs of JIM. In one photograph, JIM is 40 years old and his face is weathered and he has a graying beard. In another photograph, he is a teenager, handsome, skinny, and clean-cut. There are a few Halloween decorations on the floor or sloppily hanging from door frames. As they talk, they clean up the remains of the Halloween decor.

JOSEPHINE. So how is Liam doing?

LIZ. Oh God, he hasn't slept in days.

JOSEPHINE. It's just so terrible.

LIZ. And he feels so responsible too. He likes to act like he doesn't care about anything but he cares about everything.

JOSEPHINE. It was an earthquake. He couldn't have stopped an earthquake.

LIZ. Well, he feels like he should have done more.

JOSEPHINE. There were signs everywhere.

LIZ. Those signs never stopped anyone.
He knew Jim had been sleeping up at Bodie.

Liam would have the police bring him back home from time to time
and Jim's mom would try to convince him not to sleep out there
but Jim would just wander off and go right back
and after awhile Liam just thought,
what's the harm?

JOSEPHINE. What a nightmare.

LIZ. And it's so creepy that Liam dressed up like Jim for Halloween and then
at almost that exact moment Jim dies. It's like a curse. Like he brought on a
curse or something.
I have this terrible feeling about it.

JOSEPHINE. Me too.

> (*Pause.*
> LIAM *enters carrying a cardboard box of refreshments—lemonade, cookies,
> water, etc.*)

LIAM. Liz, do you have the credit card? I couldn't find it and we gotta pay
the delivery guy.

LIZ. I got it.

> (LIZ *goes out the back to pay the delivery guy.* LIAM *puts down the box.*
> LIAM *looks at the picture of* YOUNG JIM. JO *comes over and looks at*
> YOUNG JIM *too.*
> *They hold hands for a moment.*)

LIAM. I took this picture of Jim our sophomore year. It's a good picture,
don't you think?

JOSEPHINE. So are you gonna say a few words?

LIAM. Yeah.

JOSEPHINE. That's good.

LIAM. Yeah.

> (*Then, they start unpacking the refreshments from the box.*)

JOSEPHINE. Where do you want these cookies?

> (LIAM *looks at her like "I don't care."*
> LIZ *has returned.*)

LIAM. Oh Shit.
I forgot my notes.

> (LIAM *exits.*
> LIZ *and* JO *continue with the setting up.*)

JOSEPHINE. Liz, where should we put the cookies?

> (LIZ *points to a perfect place on the countertop near the coffee.* JO *puts the
> cookies there.*
> PEN *and* ELLIOT *enter.*)

PENELOPE. Do you guys need some help?

LIZ. Oh great. Yeah, can you put out these cups and lemonade?

PENELOPE. On the way over here, I saw three different deer. Three deer!

ELLIOT. Deer are so stupid.

PENELOPE. They are not.

LIAM. Alright. Let me get this over with.

(LIAM *stands near the easel with the picture of* YOUNG JIM.)

Can I have your attention, Please. Thank You.

Thank you for coming today. Jim's family is going to have a service and a burial but I wanted to take a moment as a community to remember Jim. The first time I met James R. Machado, Jimmy back then, he was 8 and I was 6 and we were in a summer production of *Johnny Appleseed*. Actually, we met right here, the play rehearsed in this room. He played the young Johnny Appleseed and I played the turtle. Even though he was only in one scene, he played the title character and had lines. I didn't have any lines at all, my job was just to move very slowly across the stage inside of a real turtle shell. I really admired him. He was full of authority and kindness. In high school, he was a real math whiz and once I heard Mr. Parks saying to another teacher how Jim's math skill and conceptual thinking was far beyond his own and that he was going to recommend that he start studying math at the community college. Which Jim did. Then he had a great year at Berkeley. But due to the onset of his illness, he had to come back home. Although it was hard at first, for all of us, to get used to how Jim did not want to sleep at home, he did not want to bathe or brush his hair, or change his clothes. From morning 'til night, he walked. He was living his life in a way that was outside of what we were used to.

He is survived by his Uncle Walter, his sister Alma and his mother, Ida.

(*The public Eulogy has ended. It is quiet for a while.* ELLIOT *comes up to* PEN.)

ELLIOT. Hey, Pen.

PENELOPE. Hey.

ELLIOT. You okay?

PENELOPE. I think my mom knew Jim. I think I remember that my mom used to go on walks with Jim when we would visit. I forgot that. There are so many things that I am already forgetting.

(*In another part of Town Hall,* LIAM *walks up to* LIZ *and* JO.)

LIZ. Good job, Liam.

LIAM. That was hard.

LIZ. You said just the right things.

LIAM. There is really nothing to be said.

LIZ. That's not true. You're making a space for people to mourn.

LIAM. I need a drink. You guys want to go over to Nicely's?

JOSEPHINE. Sure.

LIZ. No. Everyone will be there. I'm not up for that. I've got a bottle of Jameson in the car.

> (LIZ *goes to get the bottle.*)

LIAM. I wish we had stayed together.

JOSEPHINE. What are you talking about? You and Liz are great for each other.

LIAM. No. I know. I just mean I wonder what we would be like if we had.

JOSEPHINE. Hey, we did stay together. Right? Look, we are right here together.
We would have been a terrible married couple. Terrible.

LIAM. If you say so.

> (LIZ *returns with the bottle.*)

LIZ. I have the Jameson.

JOSEPHINE. Thanks, Liz.

LIAM. You kids want some lemonade. Should we make a toast?

> (LIZ *pours the whiskey into their styrofoam cups.*
> ELLIOT *and* PEN *join them and pour lemonade into their cups.*
>
> *They lift their glasses.*
> *No one speaks.*)

LIZ. To Jim.

ALL. To Jim.

> (*They drink.*)

JOSEPHINE. I had sex with Jim once.

> (LIAM *and* LIZ *look surprised.* ELLIOT *and* PEN *look grossed out.*)

He was home for Thanksgiving during his Freshman year
and
it was after a party
and everyone was drunk
but I always had a crush on him
because he was so smart
it was so nice
actually, the kissing was out of this world, great
he was a great kisser
the sex was like okay,
sloppy, drunk you know,
but the kissing

yeah—still my favorite
kissing of all time.

LIAM. Hey!

JOSEPHINE. Oh Liam.
Don't be offended.

LIAM. I never knew you had sex with Jim.

JOSEPHINE. Well, you and I were broken up.

LIAM. We had JUST broken up!

JOSEPHINE. Well you had already had sex with Tanya Sterling.

LIAM. Everyone had sex with Tanya Sterling.

PENELOPE. Please, please stop. Tanya Sterling is my English Teacher!

JOSEPHINE. Pen, when you get older and sex becomes less new to you, then it becomes fun to talk about the times back when it was new.

PENELOPE. Just please stop. It's weird.

LIZ. Stop! I agree. It's weird.

PENELOPE. Elliot, you wanna go back home?

ELLIOT. Yeah.

JOSEPHINE. Okay, see you later, gal. Be good.

(*The kids leave, the adults drink their whiskey. A strange feeling is brewing.*)

LIZ. (*To JO.*) So were you friends with Jim in High School?

JOSEPHINE. Oh Yeah. Our Sophomore year and his Senior year, Jim and Liam and I were like together all the time!

LIZ. What? You were?

LIAM. Oh Yeah, we hung out a lot.
Jim was older than us
so he could drive
and buy beer.
So we stocked up on Rolling Rock and Pringles
and we'd cruise up to the Hot Springs.

JOSEPHINE. What was that cool car he had?

LIAM. The Impala!

JOSEPHINE. The Chevy Impala that used to be his grandma's!

LIAM. The green goose!

JOSEPHINE. Oh my God. And we used to put the top down
so I just thought we were soooo glamorous.

LIZ. But. Well. I don't understand.
Was he (*She makes air quotes with her fingers.*) "crazy" in high school?

LIAM. No.

LIZ. No. He was just a normal guy.

JOSEPHINE. Well, cooler than normal.

>   (*Pause.*)

LIZ. What happened?

JOSEPHINE. Well, he had a schizophrenic break when he was 19 and he just, you know, he just became this different person and…

LIAM. He wasn't the same person that he was.

LIZ. Because you treated him like,
like an acquaintance
and you never told me
that he was—that you were—

LIAM. What's the big deal?

>   (LIZ *is furious.*)

LIZ. He was your friend!
And you never told me!

LIAM. Why are you getting so upset?

LIZ. Liam, we are going home.

LIAM. I'm going to hang out here a little longer.

LIZ. No. You are coming home right now.

LIAM. Fine.

>   (LIZ *storms off.* LIAM *seems confused and mad.*
>   JO *goes over to the picture of* YOUNG JIM.
>   JO *kisses the picture of* JIM *gently on the lips.*)

SCENE SEVEN

>   *Summer, 30 years ago.*
>   THERESA *is in the tree house. She is 18.*
>   *She is listening to music on her Walkman.*
>   *It is probably The Smiths' "Let Me Get What I Want."*
>   JIM *climbs up the ladder to the tree house.*
>   *He is 17 years old.*
>   *She doesn't hear him at first.*
>   *He sneaks up behind her and shakes her shoulders.*
>   *She is startled and she screams.*

THERESA. You scared me, Jim!

JIM. Sorry, Saint Theresa.

THERESA. I hate it when you hang out with Jo and Liam.

JIM. They're fun!

THERESA. They're cruel.

After you hang out with them you are always mean to me.

JIM. It's just fun.

THERESA. They always see the negative in everything.

JIM. Hey we were like that too when we were their age.

THERESA. I was not a mean 15-year-old.

JIM. Oh, you were!! Remember that summer you banned Jo from the tree house? You made me build a lock for the hatch. Jo would just sit down there and cry.

THERESA. She made me cry way more than I made her cry.

JIM. When do you leave?

THERESA. Monday. You?

JIM. Friday.

THERESA. God, I can't believe it. It feels so weird, right? Are you gonna visit me?

JIM. Of course! And you're gonna come check out Berkeley too, right?

THERESA. It's like, after this, we aren't kids anymore.

JIM. Well we are sort of in between.

THERESA. You ever think about what we are going to be like when we are old? Like when we are thirty, what we will be like?

JIM. I cannot imagine it.

Except for my plan to win the Nobel Prize in Physics.

Of course.

THERESA. Of course.

JIM. Do you think you'll move back here after college?

THERESA. Oh God no. would you?

JIM. No, maybe somewhere driving distance—L.A. or San Francisco.

> (*Pause.*)

I got you a little something.

THERESA. What? No? I didn't get you anything.

JIM. Here.

> (*He hands her a little medallion. On one side is St. Teresa of Avila and on the other side is some writing.*)

THERESA. St. Teresa. Very funny.

JIM. I know. You hate that name but read what it says on the back.

THERESA. "Life is to live in such a way that we are not afraid to die."

JIM. I was going to buy it for you as a joke but when I read that, I was like, no it's not a joke.

THERESA. Thanks, Jim. This is really cool. Thank you.

(*Pause.*)

Do you want to go up to Bodie before we leave town?

JIM. Do you? I didn't think you liked it much.
You always get carsick on the road up there.

THERESA. Well, I wanted to show you something that I never showed anyone before. I never even told anyone before.

JIM. What?

THERESA. Do you believe in ghosts?

JIM. No. Do you?

THERESA. Yes! Because I saw one. Up at Bodie. The time our whole class went up there for our 8th grade graduation.

JIM. Yeah. Yeah. I remember. That was the first time I kissed a girl.

THERESA. Wait? Who did you kiss? Jill?

(*He nods yes.*)

Okay. So while you were off kissing Jill, I was having one of those existential moments of dread that I get, so I just wanted to be alone. And I walked way to the edge of that main street and I find this one building that I had never really noticed before. The side of it was slanted and the boards were like really loose. In fact, one was so loose that when I touched it, it gave way. I could move the whole thing and make an opening big enough to crawl into this house.

JIM. What? You went inside? They told us never to disrupt the structures and to never go inside! Oh my God! I am really jealous of you right now.

THERESA. Alright, so the light is getting weirder and I am feeling weirder and I am sweating and starting to feel nauseous and I get inside and I am standing in a sitting room. Two old broken chairs, totally covered in dust and dirt and over the chairs, a mirror. I sit down in the chair. And the door, that leads to the bedroom, begins to rattle, as if someone is on the other side is rattling the handle. I go "Who's there?" thinking someone from our class is playing a trick on me. The door stops rattling so I think. It's the wind, It's the wind. But I am also like, I gotta get out of here. I stand up and start to go over to the hole where I had snuck in and BAM I hear the door—the one to the bedroom—slams open. BAM BAM BAM—it's hitting the side of the wall—flapping—I'm freaked and I look over to the mirror and I am there in the mirror—and there is the reflection of another person. It's a man and he has a white beard and his mouth is open—like he is screaming—but no sound was coming out—and I just ran. I just got the hell out of there and I ran and I ran back to the school bus and I got in there and I didn't talk to anybody until I got home and I didn't tell anyone until I am telling you now.

JIM. Why didn't you tell anyone? You could have told me.

THERESA. I didn't want to get in trouble
and I didn't want anyone to laugh at me.
Also, I got my period for the first time that day,
so I was sure it was some sort of hormonal surge.

JIM. Why are you telling me now?

THERESA. Well, I sort of want to go back there. And I don't want to go
alone and I wanted to see if you would go with me?

(*JIM leans in and holds her hand.*)

JIM. Of course I'll go with you.

THERESA. And Jim. He sort of looked like you, but old and with a beard.

JIM. Well, I am never going to grow a beard!

(*Pause.*)

I'm going to miss you, Theresa.

THERESA. Yeah, yeah, I'll miss you too.

JIM. Come on say it.

THERESA. What?

JIM. I am going to miss you, Jim.

THERESA. I am going to miss you, Jim.

SCENE EIGHT

JOSEPHINE *is asleep on her front porch. It is dusk. There is the sound of the
front door of her house rattling. It wakes her up.*

JOSEPHINE. Pen?

(*She checks her watch. She goes back to napping. More front door rattling. She
gets up opens the door. No one inside. Everything fine. Suddenly she hears
BAM BAM BAM
It is the front gate swinging but there isn't any wind.
She sees* JIM's *reflection in the window pane.*
JIM *is screaming at her.*
JO *screams.*
LIAM *walks up.*)

JOSEPHINE. I just saw Jim! I saw his face in the window!

LIAM. Oh, Jo, it's just the moon.

JOSEPHINE. He was screaming. I'm really scared.

LIAM. You're alright. It's just an emotional time right now. You are just
feeling crazy right now.

JOSEPHINE. Jim looked really angry.

LIAM. He can't be angry.

He's gone.

JOSEPHINE. I think this porch is haunted.

Can you feel how cold it is?

Right here?

Like icy cold?

> (JO *is really creeped out.*)

When Theresa and I were kids, we used to come out here in the middle of the night, with candles, and we would chant BLOODY MARY, BLOODY MARY, and turn in circles. And we did it all the time and then one time, we actually saw something in the window. The SAME window. And so we never did it again.

Maybe it is just the moon.

I am so cold.

> (LIAM *takes off his coat and puts it around* JO's *shoulders.*
> JO *rubs her freezing hands together.*
> LIAM *notices that it is really, really cold right at that one spot on the porch.*
> *He shivers.*)

JOSEPHINE. Oh God.

I miss talking to her.

You know,

after Theresa moved

we didn't see each other as much,

but whenever I was really in crisis,

she was the person I would call,

and she always listened to the whole story

And she made me laugh at whatever was happening.

No matter how bad the situation was.

Who am I supposed to call now?

> (LIAM *puts his arm around* JO.
> *He wants to say, "You can always call me"*
> *but he doesn't say it.*)

LIAM. Theresa was funny because when we were in High School, she already acted like she was 40 years old and that made us crazy, but then we all turned 40, and suddenly we were like, oh, she is really fantastic!

> (JO *smiles a smile.*
> *The smile disappears.*)

Liz and I had a fight.

She kicked me out.

JOSEPHINE. What?

LIAM. She says that she is tired of being married to a child.

JOSEPHINE. I'm sorry, Liam.

LIAM. I am not a child but
she treats me like a child!
I don't want to be married to her anymore either.
Can I stay here?

JOSEPHINE. No!

LIAM. I don't want to stay in a hotel.

JOSEPHINE. I think if you want to get back with Liz,
then you definitely should not stay here.

LIAM. Honestly, I don't want to go back to Liz.

JOSEPHINE. You'll get through it.

LIAM. She is always angry,
about everything,
and I am tired of her making me feel like
shit all the time.

   (*Pause.*)

And she won't stop talking about
how I dressed like Jim for Halloween
and how could I be such a person
that would do that.

   (*Pause.*)

JOSEPHINE. I treated Jim like I never knew him.

LIAM. Well, he was like a different person.

JOSEPHINE. You and Liz are going to make up.

LIAM. Jo, please let me stay. Please.

JOSEPHINE. Do you think Jim is haunting me?

LIAM. No.
You just saw something
that wasn't there.

JOSEPHINE. Something was there.

LIAM. Can I please stay here?

   (*Pause.*)

JOSEPHINE. I don't think it is a good idea.

LIAM. Can we please try to see what is really happening here?
Jim is gone.
Theresa is gone.
We could be gone tomorrow.

JOSEPHINE. You are married.

LIAM. But

I am right here. Jo.

I am right here.

SCENE NINE

ELLIOT *and* PEN *are inside one of the houses in the Ghost Town. It is dusk and the temperature is dropping. They are sort of jumping around to stay warm.*

PENELOPE. Hey, what are you doing for Thanksgiving?

ELLIOT. My mom and I are going to my grandparents' in Reno.

PENELOPE. Oh that's cool. Do you like your grandparents?

ELLIOT. They're alright.

PENELOPE. I don't have any grandparents. If you were gonna be in town, I was going to see if you wanted to have Thanksgiving with us. Although, Aunt Jo is a terrible cook so you aren't missing anything. Liam is still sleeping on our couch, so I guess he will be there and I just hope he can cook. It's going to be a truly awful Thanksgiving.

ELLIOT. You really know how to sell an invitation.

So what did you want to show me?

PENELOPE. Oh. I wanted to ask you if you would like to have sex with me?

ELLIOT. Okay.

Yes! Here?

PENELOPE. Yes.

ELLIOT. Um. Okay.

(*They begin kissing. Slow and polite at first and very quickly it becomes very animal.*

They bump into pieces of furniture. Dust and dirt flying around like a pigpen.)

PENELOPE. Wait. Wait.

(*She gets a condom. She puts her jacket down on the ground behind the couch, like a sleeping bag, while he puts on the condom. They have sex behind the old couch. When they are finished, they stand up, get dressed and sit on the couch.*)

ELLIOT. Well that was a nice surprise!

What made you change your mind?

PENELOPE. Aunt Jo is really making me crazy.

She thinks that Jim is haunting her

and so she did all this research

on the internet about how to exorcize ghosts

and she has placed a circle of salt around the house.
There is sea salt in every corner of every room.
She is wearing this agate bracelet
and she makes me wear one
and Liam is sleeping on our couch
so when I get up to go to the bathroom
I have to walk past him
and he sleeps with his mouth open
and last night
I heard Jo and Liam having sex
and I am just so creeped out.

ELLIOT. Uh huh.

PENELOPE. I guess I just felt like
I want to be a normal teenager
that does normal things.

ELLIOT. Like have sex in a ghost town!

PENELOPE. Exactly.

ELLIOT. I totally get it.

PENELOPE. You do?

ELLIOT. Yup.

(PEN *smiles a really really big smile. This is the first time we have ever seen her smile. She keeps smiling, like she is high. Her eyes start to well up. She is still smiling so wide but now tears are streaming down her face.*)

PENELOPE. Life. Goes. On. Right?

ELLIOT. Right.

PENELOPE. One day my mom
came home with this beautiful orange handbag.
And I was like, wow,
that's a beautiful bag and she said
"I fell on the sidewalk
because these boots have
no tread and you know I need tread
because my legs don't quite
work anymore"
when she fell,
her cheek was resting on the cold sidewalk,
and she looked up into the shop window
and saw
this bright orange bag
and from lying on the ground
she thought

"I am going to buy that"
and she stood up
and she balanced herself
and walked into the shop
and bought herself a
beautiful, orange bag.

      (*Looking him in the eye.*)
I trust you.
Elliot.
I really, really, really trust you.

ELLIOT. (*Panicked.*) Oh. Uh. Oh.
You shouldn't trust me.

PENELOPE. What?

ELLIOT. You can't trust an addict.

PENELOPE. I trust YOU.

ELLIOT. I'm an addict.

PENELOPE. Please. I just need you to be here for me right now.

ELLIOT. Pen,
uhm
I can't really trust
myself
it's like every day is a
a balancing act.
And every day I am
working really really
hard not to slip…
but…ugh…
…this building is like
a corpse
decomposing
Let's get out of here.

PENELOPE. I think it's quaint.
It's like being inside a museum.

ELLIOT. It's like being inside a grave.
Let's go.

PENELOPE. Just a minute longer,
please, I don't want to go back
to Jo's house.

ELLIOT. Well, I'm going.
This place is creepy.

(ELLIOT *crawls out of the building.* PEN *stays and weeps but now it is an angrier out-of-control weeping.*)

SCENE TEN

PEN *is giving a tour of the Standard Mill.*
Noon, a few days later.

PENELOPE. The miners told stories about spirits in the mines.
They called these spirits the Tommyknockers.
The miners heard otherworldly, menacing knocks in the mines.

(PEN *begins knocking on her clipboard, ominously.*)

They would hear the knocks, and then the mines would collapse.
Some miners felt the Tommyknockers were benevolent spirits.
Dead miners sending a warning out to the living.
"Get out. Get out. Get out. Before it is too late."

But other miners felt the Tommyknockers were evil spirits.
Angry spirits that wanted to exact revenge by causing the tunnels to collapse.
They believed the Tommyknockers were there to TAKE lives not save them.

(PEN *stops knocking.*)

Once the mines all closed down, families in nearby towns began to report knocking sounds in their homes. The patient, repetitive knocking was said to foretell danger and death.

(PEN *knocks three times.*)

SCENE ELEVEN

A few days later. It is Thanksgiving. JO *is desperately sweeping the front porch.*
PEN *is returning from a walk.*

PENELOPE. Hey.

JOSEPHINE. Hello.

(PEN *is about to go into the house.*)

Wait.

PENELOPE. Yes?

JOSEPHINE. Do you believe in Jesus Christ?

PENELOPE. Hmmmm. I believe there is a God.

JOSEPHINE. But do you believe in Jesus Christ?

PENELOPE. I think he existed and he was a holy man and I think we should love our neighbors.

> (*She tries to go in the house.*)

JOSEPHINE. Wait.

We need help.

We need to surround ourselves with people who love Jesus and have him in their heart.

PENELOPE. What is going on?

JOSEPHINE. I want to exorcise the ghost.

I want to get rid of Jim.

It's getting worse, Pen.

It keeps getting worse.

Last night,

I woke up and I felt something pressing down on me

and I felt something pressing INTO me

in a sexual way

and there was no one there.

There was no one there.

> (*Very awkward silence.*)

PENELOPE. Does Liam have Jesus in his heart?

JOSEPHINE. Liam went back to Liz.

PENELOPE. What?

> (*Pause.*)

JOSEPHINE. Before I slept with Liam, I said

"Don't sleep with me if

you are going back to Liz"

and he said

"I am not going back to Liz"

and then he went back to Liz.

PENELOPE. I'm so sorry, Aunt Jo.

JOSEPHINE. This is why

This is why

I could never be with him

and he tricked me

into believing he was

different than he is.

He tricked me

and here I am.

Does Elliot believe in Jesus?

PENELOPE. I think he does.

JOSEPHINE. Elliot! Elliot!

(*She goes and knocks on his door.*)

PENELOPE. He's not home. He went to Reno with his mom.

(ELLIOT *comes out of his house.*
He is high on Oxycontin.)

JOSEPHINE. Elliot. Do you believe in Jesus?

ELLIOT. Oh Yes.

JOSEPHINE. Do you hold him in your heart?

ELLIOT. I do.

JOSEPHINE. Will you stand with us against this demon?

ELLIOT. Yes.

(JO *drags him over to her porch.*)

PENELOPE. Elliot?

ELLIOT. What?

PENELOPE. I thought you went to Reno with your mom.

(ELLIOT *doesn't answer.*)

Are you on something?

(ELLIOT *does not answer.* PEN *starts to go into the house.*)

JOSEPHINE. Pen! Wait. Let's hold hands.
After I say his name and tell him to go,
we are not allowed to mention his name for 14 days
because then he may think we miss him and want him back.
Okay. Promise me you won't say his name or talk about him.

ELLIOT. You got it.

PENELOPE. Fine. Yes.

JOSEPHINE. Yes, what?

PENELOPE. Yes, I will not say Jim's name for 14 days.

JOSEPHINE. Okay.

(*Deep breath in, with clarity and strength.*)

James R. Machado you must leave this house.
I command you to leave this house.

(*They drop hands.*)

PENELOPE. Is that it? Can I go in now?

JOSEPHINE. Yes.

(PEN *goes into the house.* ELLIOT *goes back to his house.* JO *enters her house.*)

SCENE TWELVE

> LIAM *is getting ready for a Town Hall meeting about earthquake safety and Bodie.*
> *He is looking at his presentation on his laptop.*
> *The laptop is not doing what he is asking it do.*
> *Suddenly the laptop starts playing music.*
> *It is playing the Michael Jackson song "Don't Stop 'Til You Get Enough."*
> LIAM *tries to shut down the computer, but the music doesn't stop. He unplugs*
> *the speakers. He talks to the computer. He talks to the song. Nothing works.*
> *The first two lines of the refrain keep repeating again and again, as if stuck on*
> *a loop.*

LIAM. Oh my God.

This is ridiculous.

COME ON!

Liz!

The computer is all fucked up

It's buggin out.

The PowerPoint isn't working and I can't get this music to stop!

> (LIZ *comes in. She does something to the computer. The music stops.*)

LIZ. It's fine.

> (LIAM *goes off to get something for the meeting.*
> LIZ *turns off the lights to see how the projection will look.*
> LIZ *turns the lights back on.*
> JO *is standing there.*)

JOSEPHINE. Oh. Ah.

LIZ. Hello.

JOSEPHINE. I thought I was late.

LIZ. No. The meeting starts at 7:30.

JOSEPHINE. Oh I thought 7:00.

> (*It is 7:15. They stare at each other.* JO *starts to go.* LIZ *doesn't stop her.* JO
> *returns.*)

JOSEPHINE. How are you?

LIZ. I'm fine.

JOSEPHINE. And Liam?

LIZ. Fine.

JOSEPHINE. You guys all ready for this meeting tonight?

LIZ. Yeah.

I'm surprised you came.

JOSEPHINE. Well. I care about the town.

I care about "earthquake safety."
It's important to be prepared.

> (LIAM *enters.*
>
> *This is awkward.*
>
> *This is the first time they have all been in the same room.*
>
> *JO weirdly runs up and kisses LIZ on the lips, in a really angry way.)*

LIZ. What are you doing?

JOSEPHINE. I am sorry.
I don't know what I am supposed to do.
I don't know what I am doing.

LIZ. What the fuck?

LIAM. Jesus.

> (JO *runs out.*)

LIZ. Oh my God!

LIAM. Shit.
I think she is really losing it.

LIZ. I wish she would move to another town.

LIAM. Liz!

LIZ. Well, we can't move!

LIAM. Liz. We are going to have to figure out how to live with her.
I think she needs our help.

LIZ. Liam.
I am your wife.
I need your help.

You can't help Jo.

LIAM. She's my oldest friend.
She's like my sister.

LIZ. So, you had to go and fuck your sister?!
No, Liam, No.
She is not your family.
I am your family.

> (*There is the sound of cars pulling up into the parking lot.*
>
> *Lights of the cars coming in through the Town Hall windows.*)

Oh God. They are coming. Are you ready?

> (*Both LIZ and LIAM are totally flustered.*
>
> *He checks the PowerPoint presentation.*
>
> *He is shaking.*)

LIAM. Okay so we have the safety report on each structure.
The level of sustainability/foundational support in relationship to level of

earthquake magnitude…

LIZ. We should just bulldoze the whole ghost town.

LIAM. We can't. It's a historical landmark.

LIZ. It's too dangerous!

LIAM. It's against the law.

LIZ. Maybe we could move.
Someone else can be mayor.
We can live in Culver City near my parents.
Or we could move somewhere totally new.
Can we please just get out of here
and start over?

I hate everyone right now.

LIAM. I know. Me too.

SCENE THIRTEEN

> JOSEPHINE*'s porch at night.*
> *There is screaming inside the house.*
> *The lights inside the house come on*
> JO *and* PEN *come running out.*
> *They are in their pajamas and their faces are as white as sheets.*
> *They sit on the porch.*
> *They are quiet for a while.*

PENELOPE. How did those dolls get in our beds?

JOSEPHINE. I saw Animal Control take the box of dolls.

PENELOPE. Should we call the police? I mean, someone was in your house.

JOSEPHINE. Maybe it was Jim.
Maybe Jim did it.

PENELOPE. Can a ghost do that?

JOSEPHINE. Oh my God. I mentioned his name and it hasn't been 14 days.

PENELOPE. I don't believe in ghosts. I am going in and getting the dolls out of our beds.

JOSEPHINE. Don't go back in there. I think we need a priest.

PEN. (*As she walks back into the house.*) I think we need the police.

> (JO *sits on the porch, scared.*
> PEN *returns with two dolls, the Dutch doll and the Egyptian doll.*)

JOSEPHINE. Maybe Theresa put them in our beds.

PENELOPE. No, a living person did it.

That guy at Animal Control is pretty creepy.

What's his name?

> (*She shivers.*)

JOSEPHINE. I think it is a message.

Don't you think it is a message?

I am not mourning my sister well.

I am not mourning Jim well.

PENELOPE. No one cares how we mourn.

JOSEPHINE. I think the dead care.

PENELOPE. They can't.

JOSEPHINE. The dolls are here. Why are they here?

Don't you see? It's a message.

PENELOPE. No.

JOSEPHINE. I believe it is.

PENELOPE. Alright, then what's the message?

> (JO *and* PEN *each hold a doll and look at it.*)

JOSEPHINE. I don't know. Pen!

I don't know what the message is.

> (*There is a knocking sound.*)

PENELOPE. Well I am going to call the police.

JOSEPHINE. No.

PENELOPE. You are not behaving rationally!

> (*More knocking.*)

JOSEPHINE. Wait. Are you calling the police because you are afraid of me?

PENELOPE. NO NO

We need to fill out a report because someone was in our house.

JOSEPHINE. But you think I am losing my mind.

PENELOPE. You are acting really strange but I am not calling the police on YOU.

JOSEPHINE. Well, no one was in our house!

PENELOPE. Well I do not believe ghosts put the dolls in our beds!

> (*More knocking, creaking, really loud.*)

What is that?

> (JO *is frozen, staring up at the roof of the porch.*
> *Really loud creaking, knocking sounds.*
> *SUPER SCARY DANGEROUS SOUNDS*
> *The porch collapses.*)

SCENE FOURTEEN

Town Hall. Some music equipment is set up.
LIAM and JO are sitting in two chairs.

LIAM. Thank you for agreeing to meet with me.

JOSEPHINE. Sure.

(*Pause.*)

LIAM. Hey, are you fixing up your house? I was driving by this morning and I saw you had some guys working on it.

JOSEPHINE. Oh. The front porch collapsed.

LIAM. What?

JOSEPHINE. Yeah.

LIAM. Oh Shit! Are you okay.

JOSEPHINE. Yes. Pen actually saved me.
We heard all this rumbling and I just could not move.
It was so weird
and she actually pulled me OFF the porch and then the whole thing basically collapsed.

LIAM. Oh my God. Wow.

JOSEPHINE. Yeah. I just froze. I knew it was dangerous but I literally could not move.

LIAM. Shit. It's like that time when you were learning to drive and we almost got in an accident and your instinct was to close your eyes.

JOSEPHINE. Yeah.

(*Awkward pause.*
Big sigh from LIAM.
He doesn't want to say what he knows he is going to say.
He has rehearsed it.
His plan is to start and then proceed without deviating from his script.)

LIAM. I am sorry.
Jo, I am really sorry for the way I behaved.

JOSEPHINE. You are always sorry.
You do what you want
and you want it to be fine with
everyone.
Everyone is not
fine.

LIAM. I know.
I know everyone is not fine.

That is why

(*Back to his prepared speech.*)

I wanted to tell you in person

(*Pause.*)

that Liz does not want me
to communicate with you
and I agree with her
that I should not have any communication with you
at all.

(*Pause.*)

Are you okay?

(*Pause.*)

Do you want to talk about it?

JOSEPHINE. If I see you on the street, am I supposed to pretend like I don't know you?

LIAM. Uhm. Well. I think if we see each other in some kind of public setting then we can greet each other but no conversations or texts or phone calls.

JOSEPHINE. I see.

LIAM. Are you alright?

JOSEPHINE. Does it matter?

(ELLIOT *enters.*)

LIAM. Oh, hey, Elliot can you give us a minute?

ELLIOT. Oh, yeah, sorry I got here early.
I'll come back in like twenty minutes.

JOSEPHINE. No, I'm going. I'm going.

(JO *exits.*
LIAM *starts kicking shit.*)

LIAM. Fuck fuck fuck fuck.

ELLIOT. Hey man, are you okay?
Do you want to talk about it?

LIAM. No.
I do want to.
but it's just hard.
It's just not good.
But it's hard to do the right thing.

ELLIOT. Yes, it is.

LIAM. fuck.

ELLIOT. Sometimes it just sucks

to do the right thing.

LIAM. Because how do you even know
if it is the right thing?

ELLIOT. Exactly.
Do you want to cancel practice?

> (*Pause.*)

LIAM. No. No.
Let's uh.
Let's practice.
How are you doing?

ELLIOT. Well, it's been hard.
You know.
That relapse set me way back.

LIAM. Yeah?

ELLIOT. Yeah, because the high is the greatest feeling in the whole world.
I mean there is nothing better.
It's like you are floating over the whole world
and you can see it all
and none of it hurts.

LIAM. Yeah. That sounds good.

ELLIOT. Except for the fact that the high ends
and you come back to earth way worse off.

> (*Pause.*)

LIAM. You wanna play "Small Town"?

ELLIOT. Yeah.

LIAM. I thought it would be cool if Liz sang on that one.
She and I have been practicing it.

> (LIAM *has started texting* LIZ.)

What do you think?

ELLIOT. uh.

LIAM. Oh wait. you don't want her to sing on this one?

ELLIOT. No. no. Let's try it.

> (ELLIOT *tunes his guitar.*
> LIAM *adjusts the drum kit.*)

Which name do you like better?
Wake. Man. Body.
or
Madame Moustache.
or

Wakeman Body.

LIAM. Wakeman Body.

> (*LIZ enters.*)

LIZ. Hello, gentlemen.

> (*LIZ walks over and squeezes* LIAM's *arm.*)

You okay?

> (*LIAM nods.*)

LIAM. Let's play
"Small Town."
You ready?

LIZ. Yes, sir.

LIAM. 1, 2, 3

> (*They all three sing/scream:*)

ELLIOT, LIZ, and LIAM.
Small town
we all know
everything
Small town
Yeah Yeah

Can't let go
of all we know
Can't let go
Yeah Yeah

Small town
the cops lock up the drunks
the cops are drunks too
Small town

Can't let go
of what we know
Can't let go
of what we know
Can't let go of my small town

I am the hunter
I am the hunted
I am the hunter
I am the hunted

I have no control
I have no control

I have no control

(*They kick over their musical equipment.*)

SCENE FIFTEEN

(PEN *gives a tour of the Ghost Town.* JO *is on the tour.*
There is also a 12-year-old girl on the tour.
It is the same actress that played YOUNG JO *in the Prologue.*
She is real, but she also looks like she may have emerged from 33 years ago.)

PENELOPE. Bodie was, and still is, a place of extremes.
Extreme wealth and then total abandonment.
Harsh winters and then beautiful summers.

But the air up here is ALWAYS thin, and that takes some getting used to. If you feel faint, make sure you sit down and drink some water.

The people of Bodie were extreme too.
There were the miners, who spent all day in the dark, backs bent, arms aching, but they would make more money in one day than they could make in a week or two in their old lives. Every night, they would emerge from the tunnels and spend all their money at places like the Magnolia Saloon.

But there were also families with children and dogs and more mundane jobs like running the general store or being an undertaker. The children went to school and they learned basic math and they colored in paper bunnies at Easter.

Here at the Magnolia Saloon resided one of the most famous characters of that time. Her name was Madame Moustache and she got her name, because what had begun as a slight shadow on her upper lip had grown into a full moustache. She was of French/Creole descent and she was very beautiful. She dealt cards at mining towns across the West and the men loved her because she was honest, a great flirt, and, most importantly, she always made the men clean up before sitting at her tables. Most of the men lost most of their money most nights! But they always came back.
Unfortunately, Madame Moustache's luck ran out.

For the first time in her long career, she found herself in debt and she could not get out of it. One night, she walked to the edge of town, carrying a small, glass bottle filled with morphine. They found her the next day, dead, the small empty bottle next to her and a note, written in her fine cursive,
"I'm tired of life."
I think that was a popular phrase at the time.
"I'm tired of life."

(*From far away,*
a MAN *[same actor as* OLD JIM*]*
is looking for his daughter.
The GIRL *raises her hand.*)

PENELOPE. Yes?

GIRL. My grandmother used to sing
this song to us
"When tired of life
and all of its scenes
run in the garden
and hide in the beans"

(JO *stares at the* GIRL.
She looks just like a doppelganger of JO *herself at 12.*
JO *frowns and reaches out to touch her.*
Before JO*'s hand can reach the* GIRL*'s shoulder…*)

MAN. (*Yelling from afar to the* GIRL.) Come on, gal!
We're going.

(GIRL *runs off.*
Strange feelings.)

PENELOPE. I hope you enjoyed your tour.
And remember, please leave Bodie as you found it.

(*A blast of cold air.*
JO *claps.*)

JOSEPHINE. Your tour is good!

PENELOPE. You seem surprised.

JOSEPHINE. (*Looking in the direction that the* GIRL *ran off.*) No. It's just. It's
been a long time since I went on one of these tours and the ones I used to
go on were so bad!

PENELOPE. So mine is good only by comparison?

JOSEPHINE. Just let me pay you a compliment.
Your tour is great.

PENELOPE. Thank you.

(*They sit on the remains of the Magnolia Saloon.*)

JOSEPHINE. Uh.
It's been a hard
time.

(*Pause.*)

I have not been a great
role model.

(PEN *nods.* PEN *looks down at her shoes.*)

PENELOPE. You're okay.

JOSEPHINE. No. No. I have not been okay

     (*Pause.*)

That whole business with Liam
That was totally fucked up.
I wish I had done things differently.
You know?
Your mom was such a good person.
Even after Jim lost his mind
your mom accepted him
and she loved him just the way he was.

And I know that was not easy for her
to accept him but she did it anyway.
And that takes so much strength.
And I wasn't like that,
I mean, I wasn't
strong.

PENELOPE. I think it's hard
to accept certain things.

You know, it's like,
what's the difference
between acceptance
and just giving up?

     (*Really hard to admit this:*)

I'm afraid that I will just give up.

JOSEPHINE. I do not have a fear of you giving up.
I don't.

PENELOPE. (*Scared.*) I do.

JOSEPHINE. This morning, I woke up and I had been dreaming about your mom.
and I love when I get to see her in a dream. We were up in the tree house,
and we were fighting about something really stupid and I was crying,
and then Bob Newhart (!) pops his head into the tree house
and he says
"Stop. It."
and your mom and I just started laughing
and it was like the end of a really long argument
when you just start to laugh
because

for some reason
you let go
you can finally
let go of
this thing that you were fighting
so hard
to hold on to.

"Stop. It."

PENELOPE. Okay.

JOSEPHINE. I'm just. I just.
I'm just
proud
of you
and I miss
your mom
and I miss
my sister.

PENELOPE. I miss her too.

> (PEN *and* JO *walk off.*
>
> *The Ghost Town is empty. A light change, or a straightening up of the slumping buildings.*
> *It is 30 years earlier.* THERESA *and* JIM *enter the Ghost Town. They walk into the room where* THERESA *had seen the ghost. They stare into the mirror for a while.*)

THERESA. Well, it's not like I expected that the ghost would still be inside the mirror!

> (JIM *takes the mirror off the wall. He examines the back of it. He examines the front of it. He puts it back.*)

It feels better to be here with you.
To see this room without feeling afraid.

JIM. Good! Wow, it is wild to be inside one of the houses. All those years of coming up here and we would just press our faces against the glass windows. I would just stare and I would try to memorize all the objects. Make a mental catalog and try to imagine the people who used to own the objects.

THERESA. You did that! I did that too. I thought I was the only one that did that!

JIM. I think I have the entire general store memorized.

THERESA. See, I preferred the schoolhouse and the saloon.
a small upright piano
13 brown and 7 green glass bottles

peeling wallpaper
a pool table with lions carved into the base

JIM. a sled, a saw, lanterns, canned goods,
an ornate brass cash register
an old wooden wall phone
a calendar from 1934. April.

THERESA. A Map of Wisconsin
A Drawing of a human skeleton

JIM. And there's that one house
that has a coffin in the living room

THERESA. Oh yeah!

JIM. Because people used to lay out their dead and sit with them in their own houses.
Makes it real I think.

THERESA. Yeah.

JIM. If you spend a day or two with the dead body right there.
I mean the smell of it, the decay, you cannot be in denial, then, right?

THERESA. Yup.

JIM. Do you ever think about how you want to die?

THERESA. NO. GOD. NO.

JIM. Oh come on Theresa! Liam, Jo and I spend like almost every Saturday night, listing the ways that we want to die.

THERESA. They are so weird! Why would you want to do that?

JIM. Come on, You should try it. It's fun. It's liberating!

THERESA. No.

JIM. Wait, are you afraid to?
You are.
You're afraid to name the way you want to die.
It's not an invocation, it won't happen just because you say it.

THERESA. Fine. Fine.
Old Age.
In my sleep.
Okay.
What about you?
How do you want to die?

JIM. Well I have imagined all types of scenarios
and it changes based on my mood,
but standing here
right now with you
I would say

Having sex
in outer space
as the world's oldest
astronaut.

THERESA. Oh my God!
You are such a freak.

> (JIM *and* THERESA *have a little play fight. Tickling each other, goofing around.*
>
> *Maybe a hint of sexual tension between them that comes and then goes.*)

JIM. I love it up here.
I love how quiet it is.

> (*Pause.*)

No one is gossiping.
No one is crossing the street to avoid someone they hate.
No one is embarrassed by a terrible smell.

THERESA. Yeah, but it's COLD.
Let's go home.

JIM. One more minute.

> (JIM *and* THERESA *huddle together to stay warm.*)

End of Play

DOT

by Colman Domingo

ABOUT *DOT*

This article first ran in the Limelight Guide to the 39th Humana Festival of New American Plays, *published by Actors Theatre of Louisville, and is based on conversations with the playwright before rehearsals for the Humana Festival production began.*

Home may be where the heart is, but it's also where life can get real. In *Dot*, matriarch Dotty has been an activist committed to her inner-city Philadelphia community who refused to join the middle-class flight to the suburbs. She's recently begun suffering from dementia, but it doesn't stop her from (loudly) pronouncing her views on everything from her neighbors to her daughter's hairdo. Her daughter Shelly, a lawyer and a single parent, is struggling to care for her. Shelly's brother Donnie, a New York music critic, doesn't know the extent of his mother's decline until he returns home for the holidays. Their sister Averie hasn't been much help, either—she's been too wrapped up in trying to make a name for herself to realize how much Dotty has deteriorated.

But the bomb really drops when Dotty declares she's decided that this Christmas will be her last. Playwright Colman Domingo explains: "This amps up the stakes and the urgency even more." Despite this dramatic pronouncement, Domingo was careful to craft Dotty as a fully dimensional character who's still recognizable as the same person she's always been. "I wanted to make sure this character was not someone we pity. I wanted to give her a sense of humor. I wanted her to be as human and as complex as she could be, all the way through. And to show that she's fighting against this thing that's overtaking her mind and her body, that there's courage there."

In writing *Dot*, Domingo was inspired by watching friends deal with aging parents. "I've had four friends who've had a parent with dementia or Alzheimer's. I was watching one friend and the way that she dealt with her mother. It was a bit of dark comedy that was going on—I think between the both of them," he says. He was struck by the way that the crisis at hand did not dim their ability to find the humor and laughter in the situation, even with "this huge elephant in the room about memory and change," as Domingo puts it. He saw how important it became for them to explore family stories. "They had to grab those memories and get them to my friend's son, her only child," the playwright explains. "Because that was going to inform legacy. There was this need to try and preserve these stories."

Dot's fighting spirit is evident in her children as well. All of the siblings have their own dreams about what they'd like their lives to be. "They all define success in very unusual ways," Domingo comments. This generation—which includes the three siblings, Donnie's partner Adam, and family friend Jackie—all have age 35 in their rear-view mirrors. They're grappling with what it means to approach middle age and reevaluate their lives. "Everyone is asking these questions," Domingo reflects. "Is Shelly a successful attorney? Does she feel successful in her life? With her choices?" Domingo says he always writes families that include an artist character: "So I chose Donnie to be the writer of the family." Donnie finds financial success elusive, but bristles at Shelly's suggestion that he pursue more lucrative paths. Meanwhile, Averie has been working at odd jobs and pursuing her fifteen minutes of fame after a brief brush with reality television. "It's part of our society now, the idea that you can get rich doing anything," laughs Domingo. "Just by saying something crazy in the street. What is celebrity? That's a small theme in the play as well."

In creating this dark comedy fueled by the chaos of family dynamics, Domingo's own family provided significant material for his writing. "Averie is based on a characterization of my sister," Domingo elaborates. "I didn't even change her name, because Averie was a character in my solo show, *A Boy and His Soul*. I made a big, bold rendition of her—sort of a version of her personality when she was younger." A recent trip home included a family dinner party that he hinted might offer even more humorous fodder for *Dot*.

As the play unfolds over a few days leading up to Christmas, the characters must figure out how to manage the situation together in order to move forward. "I'm not trying to give anyone answers," Domingo clarifies. "I'm just trying to say that maybe as a family they can figure this out together. It'll be hard, but they're all taking steps."

Also a well-known actor, Domingo considers himself to be an emerging playwright exploring his voice. "*Dot* is my dining room drama experiment," he says. "It's my attempt to keep people in realistic time and not mess with time too much. Usually I would go to the surreal. The only thing surreal in this play is memory, and memory loss." The true-to-life portrayal of these characters and their dilemmas, treated with Domingo's light, comical touch, is irresistibly charming. Grounded in family, *Dot* touches the heart of home, with laughter and compassion.

—Kimberly Colburn

BIOGRAPHY

Colman Domingo is the author of the produced works *Wild with Happy* (Dramatists Play Service), *A Boy and His Soul* (Oberon Books), and *Up Jumped Springtime*. The artistic work of Mr. Domingo has been honored with Olivier, Tony, Drama Desk, and Drama League nominations. His work has won the Obie, Lucille Lortel, GLAAD, Connecticut Critics Circle, Bay Area Theatre Critics Circle, and Internet Theater Bloggers Awards. He has received fellowships and/or residencies from The Sundance Institute Theatre Lab, People's Light and Theatre Company, and the Banff Playwrights Colony. Mr. Domingo is under commission from American Conservatory Theater, People's Light and Theatre Company, and Inner Voices. His plays have been produced at The Public Theater, the Vineyard Theatre, TheatreWorks, Baltimore Center Stage, the Tricycle Theatre (London), Brisbane Powerhouse/World Theatre Festival (Australia), Theatre Rhinoceros, Lincoln Center Theater Directors Lab/American Living Room Festival/HERE, Thick Description Theatre Collective, and American Conservatory Theater. *Dot* was developed in part during a residency with New York Theatre Workshop. *Dot* received its world premiere at the Humana Festival at Actors Theatre of Louisville and subsequently was produced Off-Broadway at the Vineyard Theatre, directed by Susan Stroman.

ACKNOWLEDGMENTS

Dot premiered at the Humana Festival of New American Plays in March 2015. It was directed by Meredith McDonough with the following cast:

DOTTY .... Marjorie Johnson
SHELLY .... Sharon Washington
JACKIE... Megan Byrne
DONNIE .... Kevin R. Free
ADAM.. Sean Dugan
FIDEL.. Vichet Chum
AVERIE... Adrienne C. Moore

and the following production staff:

Scenic Designer .... Dane Laffrey
Costume Designer..................................... Connie Furr Soloman
Lighting Designer.. Mark Barton
Sound Designer .... Christian Frederickson
Stage Manager.. Stephen Horton
Assistant Stage Manager.. Jason Pacella
Dramaturg .... Kimberly Colburn
Casting.. Kelly Gillespie
Properties Master .... Mark Walston
Directing Assistant.. Rachel Dart
Assistant Dramaturg.. Ariel Sibert

Dot received support from the New York Theatre Workshop Annual Usual Suspects Summer Residency at Dartmouth College.

CHARACTERS

DOTTY: African American. 65 years old.

SHELLY: African American. 45 years old.

JACKIE: Caucasian. 40 years old.

DONNIE: African American. 40 years old.

ADAM: Caucasian/Latin/Arab. 40 years old. A gay boy's gay boy.

AVERIE: African American. 35 years old.

FIDEL: Kazakh. Mid to late 20's.

NOTES

// Denotes overlaps. Silences are to be used as a silent opportunity. They are as important as rests in music. These characters speak before they think. The people that I know in West Philly have the DRYEST delivery. Especially about difficult subjects or even saying I love you. Try not putting ANYTHING on a line first and read it for its rhythms and then go deeper. No one in this play is deliberately mean or callous. The stakes are just too high and there is no need to mince words. And these people are lightning quick with shifts of tone or intention. Brace yourselves. Welcome to *Dot*.

This play is for Stacey Thomas, Lisa Thompson, Anika Noni Rose, Chuck Schultz and the amazing women that live on in their memory. This is for families that are coping and finding their way. And everything I do, I do in honor of my parents, Edith and Clarence Bowles.

Marjorie Johnson and Kevin R. Free
in *Dot*

39th Humana Festival of New American Plays
Actors Theatre of Louisville, 2015
Photo by Bill Brymer

DOT

THE NORTHERN LIGHTS

"Twisted" by Lambert, Hendricks and Ross plays as we open on three women in a beautiful upscale kitchen. Very Martha Stewart meets Claire Huxtable. DOTTY is a 65-year-old African American woman. SHELLY is her 45-year-old daughter. JACKIE is a 40-year-old Caucasian. DOTTY is looking at a pill container with segments for each day of the week. SHELLY is by the stove cooking. JACKIE sits at the table with DOTTY. Everyone is a bit on edge.

DOTTY. Today is Tuesday?

SHELLY. Yes, today is Tuesday.

DOTTY. Christmas is in two days.

SHELLY. I know Mom, I know.

DOTTY. You getting the tree today?

SHELLY. Yes, I told you ten times, I'm getting the tree today. Jackie you sure you don't want a drink?

JACKIE. It's almost ten o'clock in the morning.

SHELLY. Are you sure?

JACKIE. Yes.

SHELLY. I'm having one.

JACKIE. No, no thank you.

SHELLY. A.A. or something?

JACKIE. No, It's just—

DOTTY. I could swear I took 'em this morning when Fidel came by!

SHELLY. Fidel came by yesterday morning!

JACKIE. Mrs. Shealy, Shelly, I can come back later.

DOTTY. (*To* SHELLY.) You sure?

SHELLY. Yes, he comes on Monday and Wednesday.

JACKIE. Fidel?

SHELLY. Yes, Fidel.

JACKIE. Who's Fidel?

SHELLY. This boy that—Give me a few minutes and we can have a proper visit. In the other room.

(She lays a piece of paper and a pen on the table.)

JACKIE. I just came to borrow some linen from your mom.

SHELLY. Mom, I need you to sign that! You didn't sign it.

DOTTY. Don't I need a lawyer to be present or something?

SHELLY. I am a lawyer, remember?

DOTTY. Eight years of school! And you failed the Pennsylvania bar three times, I remember.

SHELLY. Sign it. She's your witness.

JACKIE. Who?

DOTTY. Three times.

SHELLY. You.

JACKIE. For what?

SHELLY. Don't worry about it, it's all legal—Mom please sign!

DOTTY. Oh, okay I will. On the dotted line, on the dotted line.

(*She picks up the pen and then she gets distracted.*)

Good ole Jackie! How you doing?

JACKIE. I'm fine, Mrs. Shealy.

DOTTY. Ain't seen you in a while.

JACKIE. It's been awhile.

DOTTY. You still living in New York?

JACKIE. Yes, Mrs. Shealy.

DOTTY. You can call me Dotty now, honey, you a grown woman.

JACKIE. Yes, Mrs. Shealy, I am still living in New York. Maybe this is a bad time?

SHELLY. It's all the same.

DOTTY. Where?

JACKIE. Where what?

DOTTY. Where do you live in New York?

JACKIE. Oh! Um, Harlem.

DOTTY. Is it still dirty?

JACKIE. When is the last time you been there?

DOTTY. '83.

SHELLY. Mom, do you want eggs?

DOTTY. What time is it?

SHELLY. Ten o'clock. Mom you need to eat. Do you want eggs?

DOTTY. Yes I want eggs. I can make my own eggs.

(*She gets up to make her eggs.*)

SHELLY. Mom, I thought we agreed that I will make breakfast and you make dinner.

DOTTY. Is that what we agreed on?

SHELLY. Yes, that's what we agreed on.

JACKIE. I can just come back—

SHELLY. (*Sotto voce.*) Just give me a minute—

DOTTY. Just don't put cheese in it. Richard always puts cheese in my eggs.

SHELLY. Richard? Mom? Dad? SHIT!

DOTTY. Language—

SHELLY. Never mind.

DOTTY. I told you I wanted to stop all those unnecessary expletives in my house.

SHELLY. Look who's talking. Ms. Cuss everybody out in the police station!!!

DOTTY. No I didn't!

SHELLY. Yes you did!

DOTTY. No I didn't!

SHELLY. (*To* JACKIE.) Yes, she did.

DOTTY. We should be a good example to little Jason. He is very impressionable at his young age.

JACKIE. I *really* can come back later. I just needed to borrow a few things, Mrs. Shealy. I can come back later, I can come back later!

DOTTY. What do you need Jackie?

JACKIE. Well I just wanted to borrow a few things. Linen, lightbulbs, things like that.

DOTTY. That's not a problem.

JACKIE. Thank you.

DOTTY. I almost forgot what you looked like!

JACKIE. I changed my hair.

DOTTY. So did this one.

JACKIE. Blonde!

SHELLY. Something different.

DOTTY. You used to be down here all the time for a meal and our little talks.

SHELLY. Talks?

JACKIE. Yeah.

SHELLY. What talks?

DOTTY. None of yo business talks.

JACKIE. Nothing really.

DOTTY. Did you find my tape recorder Shelly?

SHELLY. (*Looking in the cabinet.*) Shit—

DOTTY. Language—

SHELLY. Mom did you move things around in these cabinets since yesterday?

DOTTY. What? No!

SHELLY. Yes you did!

DOTTY. No, I didn't.

SHELLY. Yes, she did.

JACKIE. (*Changing the subject.*) Um…Harlem has changed a lot probably since the last time you were there. It is pretty clean now. There is even talk of a Whole Foods going up in my neighborhood!

DOTTY. Our neighborhood has just gone down. Hmph, Democrats.

(DOTTY *gets up from the table and goes into the fridge and brings out some mushrooms.*)

SHELLY. Mom, what are you talking about? You're a Democrat!

DOTTY. I know, I know, but when I was coming up it was all turned around. (*To* SHELLY.) I got it.

SHELLY. Mom—

DOTTY. I got it. I want mushrooms in mine.

SHELLY. Fine.

(SHELLY *makes herself another drink and uses the cocktail shaker.* DOTTY *cooks her eggs.*)

DOTTY. The Republicans were the ones that ended slavery and looked after front stoops. I don't remember when it happened, but it looked like the only people that looked after one another were the Democrats. Jimmy Carter and them.

SHELLY. I know Mom, you campaigned for every primary since // 1960!

DOTTY. // 1960! People took care of the front steps and put out potted plants that would line the stoop. When we first moved in here in 1953, we were some of the first few blacks in this neighborhood! //

SHELLY. (*To* JACKIE *sotto voce, sarcastically.*) // How are you today, Jackie? Me…I'm fine. (*Beat.*) My son is staying over with a classmate of his. (*Beat.*) I needed to get him out of my hair so I can sort out a bunch of mess so that we could actually think of having a holiday. (*Beat.*) When she goes in on something these days she goes all the way in. Or completely OUT! //

JACKIE. // I don't understand. What do you mean by OUT? What's going on?

DOTTY. (*Leaving the eggs cooking on the stove.*) // Mayor Joseph Clark. One of them good white men. Even had a TV show, called "Tell it to the Mayor"! So the people could "Tell it to the Mayor" on TV. I "told it to the Mayor" a couple of times. Asked questions about sanitation and summer kids' programs. I was the block captain and I was responsible for the summer lunch program. You know as working class people we depended on breakfast and lunch being served in school. Remember Shelly I had you going in at seven a.m. to get that breakfast? Cock a doodle doo!

SHELLY. Yes. Powdered eggs.

DOTTY. Probably like how mine are right now. Ain't nothing but powdered eggs down below Marlo.

SHELLY. Mom that's Jackie.

DOTTY. That's what I said, Jackie.

SHELLY. No, you didn't.

DOTTY. What was I talking about?

JACKIE. Uh, well, "Tell it to the Mayor"?

DOTTY. Why?

SHELLY. (*Notices the eggs left cooking on the stove and runs over to retrieve them.*) I have no idea! // Mom—shit—

DOTTY. // I loved that show. I was on there plenty of times. "Tell it to the Mayor." Honey, I would wear my finest June Cleaver dress and pearls. //

SHELLY. // How many times are you going to tell this story? Oh, one more time? Okay.

DOTTY. // Well not real pearls, costume jewelry. The Mayor wasn't ready for me, with my keen insight on how to solve the problems of the inner city. I threw out ruminations on how to get women involved in all forms of neighborhood associations because as we three know…

DOTTY, SHELLY, and JACKIE. Women are the ones who really get things done.

JACKIE. At least we try. I'm trying.

DOTTY. Chile, I was a feminist before there was a word for it. Without women, there is no life. We are the titty of the world!

SHELLY. // OK, that's enough!

JACKIE. // Is that coffee in that cup, Mrs. Shealy?

DOTTY. All I'm saying is, I'm from people who struggled to get a little piece of something. Now that that little something is so easy to get, no one cares about stoops and potted plants. Sheila down the street drives a—what is that Shelly?

(SHELLY *puts the eggs down in front of* DOTTY.)

SHELLY. A Range Rover.

DOTTY. And keeps her porch filled with garbage cans and NIGGAS!

JACKIE. Oh, wow—

DOTTY. You know what they are—

SHELLY. MOM, eat your eggs.

DOTTY. She don't like it when I talk about these Niggas!

SHELLY. MOM, would you eat your eggs!!!

DOTTY. I'm eating them, I'm eating them! Did you burn 'em?

(DOTTY *begins to eat the eggs.*)

SHELLY. No, YOU burned them!

(*To* JACKIE.)

So what do you need?

DOTTY. They are Niggas! That is what Niggas do! Ride around in Range Rovers and don't take care of their front stoops!

SHELLY. Eat Mom! I don't have time for this! I have to go back to the hairdresser and then pick up the tree if you want a real tree.

DOTTY. I was wondering what was going on with your hair. You look like a mean pineapple.

SHELLY. Don't mess with me. I will go to the basement and pull out Daddy's hot pink artificial tree like I want to.

DOTTY. No, no, no, no, no, no, no, I want a Spruce!

SHELLY. Then let's get the jokes in check!

DOTTY. This year a Blue Spruce! I got to have a Blue Spruce. Like my daddy used to get! Used to cut it down with his own two hands. Like Paul Bunyan! Jackie, chile, I ain't had a real tree in years!

JACKIE. Neither have I, Mrs. Shealy.

SHELLY. Then let's leave the hair alone.

DOTTY. I'll leave it alone, I'll leave it alone. It's just brassy, is all I'm sayin'.

SHELLY. I know, I know, I know. It's too brassy.

JACKIE. You always wore your hair long with a perm. Why did you cut it so short?

SHELLY. When I am stressed out, I tell Andre to give me something different.

DOTTY. Why are all hairdressers named Andre?

SHELLY. If you ask me one more question I'm gonna light myself on fire.

DOTTY. (*Laughs.*) It's brassy. She looks like a mean pineapple.

SHELLY. You said that! Wasn't funny a minute ago. EAT! They must have made this Watermelon Vodka just for me.

DOTTY. Why you drinkin' so early in the day?

SHELLY. I am grown! I can drink when the rooster crows if I feel like it.

DOTTY. What a mouth! I don't know where you got a mouth like that.

SHELLY. Apple doesn't fall far from the tree.

DOTTY. And what you talking 'bout roosters crowing? This is the city. Ain't no roosters—

SHELLY. (*Referring to a cocktail.*) MOM! You sure you don't want one?

JACKIE. No, Shelly, I'm fine. I *really* should—

DOTTY. Jackie, do you talk to your mother this way?

JACKIE. No.

SHELLY. Well, that would be a miracle! Being as though Ms. Marlo has been dead for years.

DOTTY. That's not what I meant. Four, Five?

JACKIE. Ten.

DOTTY. Ten!!!

JACKIE. Time flies.

(DOTTY *is completely perplexed.*)

Are you okay Mrs. Shealy?

DOTTY. I'm fine honey, I'm fine. (*Sotto voce.*) Shelly can you get Jackie some sheets and things from the linen closet?

JACKIE. And can I borrow some sweats?

SHELLY. Oh I see, you are on the run.

JACKIE. I'm not on the run.

SHELLY. Oh really?

JACKIE. I'm not!

SHELLY. You are either running out of here or out of New York.

JACKIE. That is not fair—

SHELLY. Talk to her while I get you some linen. (*To* DOTTY.) Remember Ms. Marlo died?

(SHELLY *goes upstairs to retrieve the linen and sweats.*)

DOTTY. Yes I remember! I remember. We sent all of those white roses.

JACKIE. Yes you did. Donnie picked them out.

DOTTY. Picked what out?

JACKIE. The roses. He knew that she loved those.

DOTTY. Yeah, he knew. Donnie knows.

JACKIE. She loved white roses.

DOTTY. (*To herself.*) Her passing was long...drawn out...and the life rung out of her, all the way to the finish line. People die. Everybody has to go.

(*Silence.*)

You got a cigarette?

JACKIE. A cigarette?

DOTTY. She hid mine.

(DOTTY *gets up and searches the drawers.*)

JACKIE. I never knew you smoked.

DOTTY. There's a lot of things that you don't know about me. You got any weed?

JACKIE. Weed?

DOTTY. Yeah, weed.

JACKIE. Um…no. Mrs. Shealy. When did you start smoking weed?

DOTTY. Weed?

JACKIE. Yes, weed.

DOTTY. Where you been?

JACKIE. New York. Don't change the subject Mrs. Shealy. Since when do you smoke weed?

DOTTY. Everybody's doing it. Tiny, Boo, Dawn.

JACKIE. Who is Tiny, Boo and Dawn?

DOTTY. Where you been? Why haven't I seen you in so long.

JACKIE. No, Mrs. Shealy don't change the subject.

DOTTY. You changing the subject.

JACKIE. No, you are.

DOTTY. Am I?

JACKIE. Yes.

DOTTY. Where you been?

JACKIE. Um. Well, I-I-I just needed to get a little distance.

DOTTY. From us?

JACKIE. Well, not from you, but, yes from the family. If I was ever going to expect to get a family of my own, I had to get a little distance, you know? Now back to Tiny, Boo and Dawn—

DOTTY. Just because Donnie is gay // doesn't mean that you are not a part of this family.

JACKIE. // I don't think me hanging around here was very healthy for me—

(SHELLY *returns with the linen and sweats.*)

SHELLY. Sheets, blanket and the only sweats I could find were some of Donnie's old sweats from his track and field days.

JACKIE. Okay, thank you. Thank you.

SHELLY. Not a problem.

(DOTTY *stares into space.*)

DOTTY. What time is it?

SHELLY. Mom? It's ten o'clock. Eat please. And take your medication.

(DOTTY *eats the eggs and she looks at the pill container. She looks at* JACKIE.)

JACKIE. What's going on. You asked that a few times now Mrs. Shealy. Shelly what's going on?

SHELLY. Ask her.

DOTTY. Ask me what?

JACKIE. Are you alright Mrs. Shealy?

DOTTY. I just need salt.

(*She gets up to go search the cabinet.*)

SHELLY. Mom, you can't have salt!

DOTTY. It needs something. You can't expect me to give up everything? I need salt.

SHELLY. Go ahead then. Have salt! Kill yourself!

DOTTY. I just need salt! Doctors don't know everything.

(DOTTY *searches the cabinets.*)

SHELLY. She apparently NEEDS salt.

JACKIE. Shelly, I should go. I don't know what is going on and it's probably not my business so I will let you guys work out whatever you need to work out. I have to pick up a few things.

SHELLY. Just give me a minute. How long you staying?

JACKIE. I'm not really sure.

SHELLY. What do you have to pick up?

JACKIE. I came down here in the spur of the moment.

SHELLY. I knew it! Spill the tea.

(DOTTY *returns from the cabinets with Oreo cookies.*)

DOTTY. Good ole Jackie! How you doing? You still living in New York?

JACKIE. Um… Yes! Mrs. Shealy. I am still living in New York.

SHELLY. Mom, you left the cabinets open again.

DOTTY. Where?

JACKIE. I told you, Harlem.

DOTTY. Is it still dirty?

SHELLY. Mom, you asked her that.

DOTTY. Asked her what?

SHELLY. Is New York still dirty.

DOTTY. I did?

SHELLY. Yes, you did. Why you got Oreos? Where's the salt?

DOTTY. The salt?

SHELLY. The salt.

DOTTY. The salt?

SHELLY. Mom, you wanted salt and you got Oreos.

JACKIE. It's okay Shelly.

SHELLY. (*Emotionally cracks.*) NO, IT'S NOT OKAY! THESE ARE OREOS AND SHE WANTED SALT!!!

> (*Dead silence.*)

JACKIE. (*Soberly.*) What the fuck is going on???

> (*Silence.*
> *Silence.*
> *Silence.*)

Mrs. Shealy? (*Beat.*) Shelly?

SHELLY. You gonna tell her?

DOTTY. Tell her what?

JACKIE. Tell me what?

SHELLY. About… Don't make me do this. It's something that your doctor said that YOU should share.

JACKIE. What? Oh my God. Doctor? What is it?

DOTTY. I'm fine, I'm fine, my daughter is being overly dramatic.

SHELLY. Mom?

DOTTY. I got some memory problems.

SHELLY. Mom?

DOTTY. Just forgetful. Getting old.

SHELLY. MOM?

DOTTY. I get confused sometimes.

SHELLY. Mom tell her.

JACKIE. Tell me what? What? What is it?

DOTTY. What day is this?

JACKIE. Tuesday.

DOTTY. Tuesday.

SHELLY. See?

DOTTY. See what?

JACKIE. What?

DOTTY. Two days 'til Christmas. Tuesday. I got to find my tape recorder. I gotta tape some things for little Jason. What time is—

SHELLY. Mom, please, ten, ten, TEN!!!!

DOTTY. Can I use the bathroom officer?

SHELLY. You don't have to ask me to use the bathroom.

DOTTY. My daughter is like a Marine. She got it from her father.

SHELLY. Mom. Granddad was in the Marines. Just go.

DOTTY. (*She salutes.*) YES SIR!

> (DOTTY *exits into the bathroom.*
> *Silence.*)

JACKIE. Shelly what's going on—

SHELLY. Ssh. Just give me a…minute.

> (*Silence.*
> *Silence.*
> *Silence.*)

JACKIE. Shelly—

SHELLY. Ssh.

> (*Silence.*
> SHELLY *pours three jiggers of Vodka into her glass. She downs the drink. She holds her index finger up in the air.*
> *A full thirty seconds go by!*)

SHELLY. Woo. Okay. I'm good. (*Beat.*) It's Dementia. Alzheimer's.

JACKIE. Oh my God!!!

SHELLY. Shhhh. Yeah. Alzheimer's. It's a bitch.

JACKIE. Oh my God, Oh my God. Oh my God!!!

SHELLY. Yeah.

JACKIE. How long has this been going on?

SHELLY. She was diagnosed, what, about a year ago?

JACKIE. A year ago???

SHELLY. A year ago!

JACKIE. Oh Shelly!

SHELLY. And she has been on the decline.

JACKIE. I am so sorry.

SHELLY. We think that she was hiding it from us for a while. Probably hiding it from herself.

JACKIE. I am so sorry.

SHELLY. It's alright. You didn't do it.

JACKIE. Oh my God. Alzheimer's?

SHELLY. It has a horrible sound to it, right? Alzheimer's.

JACKIE. Yes, awful.

SHELLY. Named after some German doctor.

JACKIE. I've never been in love with the German language.

SHELLY. Harsh.

JACKIE. Like the chewing sound of a beast.

SHELLY. Well the beast that lives in this house is called Alzheimer's. I got a call at my office sometime last fall. It was in September. September 5th to be exact. Jason had just started third grade. And I was just catching my breath from having him home terrorizing me all summer. I got the call that she got pulled over for driving 95 miles an hour—

JACKIE. —95 miles an hour?

SHELLY. Yup. On Kelly Drive.

JACKIE. Around all those curves and bends?

SHELLY. Right where Teddy Pendergrass crashed his car with that transsexual. When the cop asked why she was driving so fast, she said that "the wind felt good on her"—

JACKIE. Oh, Shelly.

SHELLY. The cop asked where she was going and she didn't know.

JACKIE. Oh my God.

SHELLY. She had no idea where she was going. They found my number as one of the last numbers dialed in her phone and called me—

JACKIE. Thank God for cell phone recall—

SHELLY. I came and picked her up from the police station down on Girard Avenue.

JACKIE. The one down by Westmoreland School for Girls?

SHELLY. For bad ass girls. Now you know, I don't go down on Girard Avenue.

JACKIE. Remember Nic Nic's cousin Dawn?

SHELLY. Yeah.

JACKIE. That is the school that she got transferred to in the seventh grade after she punched me in the face and pulled my hair. The police station is right across the street. It took years for that patch of hair to grow in.

SHELLY. Oh yeah, that's right. Anyway, it was such a scene as I was trying to verify that she was my mother and then she freaked out and cussed EVERYBODY out and they had the paramedics take her to the hospital and deal with all THAT and then they kept her for a few days and did all of these tests and then the questions about her health and sanity and well, they told me that it was Alzheimer's.

JACKIE. Shelly, I'm so sorry.

SHELLY. It's just been getting worse and taking its toll. It's getting really…

(*Silence.*)

I just can't let her be in this house alone. I am afraid of what she will get into or forget to do.

JACKIE. You can't leave her alone?

SHELLY. Hell NO! Not unless I put her to bed. Give her a mild sleeping aid and I'm good.

JACKIE. Perhaps you should look into other alternatives.

SHELLY. I'm doing what I can. I take one too. It's all good.

JACKIE. Okay.

SHELLY. For the past few weeks, I've had to take her with me to work. On Friday, she drove me so crazy trying to organize my files at my office. Said she was trying to help. I come in from a staff meeting and she is pointing to a crazy looking file, telling me to take a hard look at it.

JACKIE. What was it?

SHELLY. Something she made with newspaper articles and a whole lot of random chaos.

JACKIE. Well that's what is going on. Right? In her head at times. I read an article in the *Times* about that. It's Chaos.

SHELLY. Chaos. One minute she is so lucid, remembering names of Mayors of 1953 and the next, she doesn't remember what she asked one minute ago. So, it has been me and her locked in my office on the days when Fidel // is not here to be with her.

JACKIE. // Who is Fidel?

SHELLY. This boy that I hired off of Craigslist. He is not a certified nurse but he has a lot of experience taking care of the elderly. He is from Kazakhstan.

JACKIE. Kazakhstan? What is that?

SHELLY. Former Soviet Union. He doesn't speak much which is a great quality in a caregiver. There is enough noise around here. He and my mother seem to have a little bond going. Looking like they are plotting at times. Communicating in their own crazy way. One with Alzheimer's and the other one with nods and stares. He comes in, cleans, cooks, does laundry, makes sure that the house is not burned down two to three times a week and I pay him fifty dollars a day.

JACKIE. That's good. Can he be here full-time?

SHELLY. With Jason's private school, my mortgage, car note, and all my own personal expenses that is the best that I can do until I get my hands on my brother and sister. It is long overdue for them to take over some responsibility and take up some slack. She's going to need full-time care, like, YESTERDAY.

JACKIE. Funny thing is that she looks fine.

SHELLY. And I look like a mean pineapple.

JACKIE. You just need to soften it. Is there anything I can—

SHELLY. I look like a dyke, don't I?

JACKIE. No, you don't look like a dyke. Shelly—

SHELLY. My son said I looked like his teacher's partner, Ms. Woods.

JACKIE. His teacher is a lesbian?

SHELLY. It's a Quaker school. Ms. Woods is a big old knuckle dragging bull dagger.

JACKIE. Really?

SHELLY. Now you know I ain't got no problem with lesbians. I was one for a few months in college.

JACKIE. Weren't we all?

SHELLY. But Ms. Woods is a man! When I asked Jason, how did my haircut look and he said like Ms. Woods, my knees buckled, my eyes rolled to the back of my head and I almost passed out, right there in the kitchen with *SpongeBob* playing in the background.

JACKIE. It actually looks more like SpongeBob's cut.

SHELLY. (*Sotto voce.*) Whatchu doin' here?

JACKIE. (*Sotto voce.*) For a visit. I just decided to come home for a while.

SHELLY. Girl, no one comes to this neighborhood for a visit. A funeral maybe, but not a visit.

JACKIE. Why can't I just visit? I haven't been here in what?

SHELLY. Let's see…two years ago. Since you popped over here and ran into Donnie and Adam cuddled up on the couch?

JACKIE. Really?

SHELLY. Mmm-hmm.

JACKIE. Don't people just drop in to say hello to the old neighborhood?

SHELLY. NO.

JACKIE. Sometimes!

SHELLY. No they don't.

JACKIE. Yes, they do!

SHELLY. Get to it!

JACKIE. I'm pregnant!

SHELLY. Shut up!

JACKIE. Eight weeks.

SHELLY. Shut up!

JACKIE. By a man that ain't mine.

SHELLY. SHUT. UP.

JACKIE. He's got a wife and kids—

SHELLY. And a chick that is knocked up!

JACKIE. I know. Shhh, be quiet. I feel terrible. I don't know how I got in this situation. I feel awful.

SHELLY. You should... Huzzy.

JACKIE. (*Blurts out with high velocity.*) I QUIT!!! QUIT!!! I think I quit my JOB and NEW YORK, as I did leave right in the middle of a wedding that we were catering at the Waldorf Astoria. Watching these two people who looked so in love and so happy. They looked right out of those magazines like *Brides!* I HATED them. I wanted to EXPLODE! I was a Molotov cocktail ready to be thrown into the fray of bliss! They suddenly shoved my life in my face. The YEARS of living in the BIG CITY with BIG DREAMS and thinking I was Carrie Bradshaw or Samantha or some shit. Dating what available men there were in New York and FAILING miserably and hoping HOPING and believing that my prince charming would come, like every little girl, but then the YEARS tick tock and then you look up and you're FORTY and the only men trying to holler at you are married or fucked up or a creep, because a bunch of BITCHES already got dibs on the good men that you let slip through your fingers because you hated the way they chewed their food or something else insignificant and just that morning you went to the doctor and found out that you were eight weeks pregnant a couple of days after the white stick turned blue and you look over in the middle of the wedding and see the smug married asshole whose side piece you have been for a year and a half, and turn back to the happy bride in Vera Wang and her Don Draper-looking husband and you just decide to giddyyap and leave in the middle of "I do's" and hightail it through the Lincoln Tunnel as if you have a scarlet letter tattooed on your forehead. I just had to come home. That is all I could think about. To get my head together and re-evaluate my so-called LIFE. I got a MESS of a life. A MESS OF A LIFE! Just gimme a sip of that Watermelon Vodka.

SHELLY. A sip.

(*She downs a few sips.*)

JACKIE. New York can just be TOO MUCH. You know what I mean? The pace of it all. And I got caught up in the pace. Caught up with Gilberto. That's his name.

SHELLY. Of course it is.

JACKIE. Gilberto San Jose. He owns the event company that I manage. You know me, I am always so busy and he was just...THERE. It's good to be home. Home.

SHELLY. You're a smart girl. You will figure it out. MOM WHAT CHU DOING IN THERE?

JACKIE. Life was so easy before we became adults! If your brother just kept his promise, I wouldn't be in this mess.

SHELLY. No, you'd be in ANOTHER mess! He's as gay as gift wrap.

JACKIE. True, true. How is Donnie?

SHELLY. Getting on my nerves. The Golden Boy // will be here tomorrow with his husband.

JACKIE. // You still call him that? Adam right?

SHELLY. Yes, Adam. They got married.

JACKIE. This summer. I know.

SHELLY. I know you know. You didn't show. MOM YOU DONE?

JACKIE. I was out of the country.

SHELLY. You suddenly had to go to Mexico. I watch your Twitter feed girl. You planned that trip in twenty-four hours.

JACKIE. Shelly, I couldn't.

SHELLY. I wasn't going to bring it up. He was hurt but I thought that was your business. MOM???

DOTTY. (*Offstage.*) I'm doing my business!

SHELLY. (*To* DOTTY.) GOOD! (*To* JACKIE.) We got a few more minutes.

JACKIE. I just didn't want to make Adam uncomfortable. Donnie and I were a couple. I didn't want to be a threat.

SHELLY. You were not going to be a threat to anybody! It was FIRE ISLAND! Gay Disney with booze! Wasn't nobody thinking about you! He and Adam got married on the beach and everybody wore white. Jason is nine and he loved it. Kids these days benefit from exposure.

JACKIE. That's nice. That's really good for them. I wish them the best.

SHELLY. You still carrying that flame.

JACKIE. Of course not. We were teenagers. (*Tsk.*) Flame.

SHELLY. You turned him gay.

JACKIE. No I didn't and you don't turn anyone gay.

SHELLY. You did!

JACKIE. I didn't.

SHELLY. You were his last girlfriend and then POOF!

JACKIE. You really think you are funny.

SHELLY. You still need to work things through with him. It's been what? Twenty years now.

JACKIE. I don't need to work ANYTHING out! I've worked it out! (*Tsk.*) Flame.

(SHELLY *removes the trash from the bin.*)

SHELLY. I don't even want to talk about him right now because his ass is on my last. He hasn't returned my calls in about three weeks. All he does is text. I got too much to say that requires picking up a phone instead of texting. He and Averie both! Donnie needs to give up on that newspaper career and get a real job and Averie needs to do a little better than working BACK down at the "PRICERIGHT"! Because they both have to help out in a big way and that requires adult strategies. Am I right?

JACKIE. Preach!

SHELLY. Who am I talking to? You are on the run with a bun in the oven.

(SHELLY *takes the trash outside.*)

JACKIE. You got me. Guilty as charged. But wait, doesn't Donnie make a good income? He writes for newspapers and magazines.

SHELLY. That is a thing of the past! You know nobody is reading those things anymore. I don't remember the last time I read a newspaper, period. I get my news on Facebook.

JACKIE. Same here.

SHELLY. And his husband is working for some Rainbow Alliance or something or other. NON-PROFIT which equals NO MONEY!

JACKIE. Oh okay. I see. But what about Averie? Didn't she make a lot of money from being a YouTube sensation?

SHELLY. GONE! I told her to put all that money away that she got from all those interviews and appearances at clubs. But you know that term "Nigga Rich"? Hmph! That's what I'm saying. She's living in my basement.

JACKIE. Oh, I thought you were living here again.

SHELLY. No, but I am here most of the time. It's a good thing because Averie is a lot!

JACKIE. She had those commercials running—

SHELLY. I don't consider a 1-800-Bad-Credit or a 555-We-Do-Hair legitimate commercials. She had the nerve to get herself an agent and a manager. Actually—they came after her! Agents and Managers! Agenting and Managing WHAT?! She was suddenly a celebrity! Ain't that some shit? Hmph, these bootleg people that she had running her newfound career took most of her money and now she is back at the "PRICERIGHT," cashiering.

JACKIE. Well that's good. She's got a job!

(SHELLY *shoots* JACKIE *a look of death.*)

Don't hate me, but I played that YouTube clip like a hundred times. After she chased down that robber and got that old lady's purse back.

SHELLY. Caught on a cell phone.

SHELLY and JACKIE. "You would rather run through hell in kerosene-soaked drawls than to raise your hand at me!"

SHELLY. She ain't got a thin dime now. But she and my brother are going to have to get some money together so we can get Mom some permanent care because I am going berserk! I sound like such a bitch. I don't feel like myself. This isn't me. I am much more positive than this. Right?

    (*Silence.*)

JACKIE. It's the holidays. Everyone is just a bit more wound up. Can you make me a Watermelon Vodka drink thing?

SHELLY. You want a cigarette, too? What is this, the 1950's? You're pregnant! NO!

JACKIE. But, wait, I don't know if I'm keeping it.

SHELLY. Well then, NO, until you figure it out!

JACKIE. Right now my life looks like a lost episode of "Sex and the Shitty."

SHELLY. I'll make you a Nutri Bullet. I got some fresh kale. This is the only thing that gives me life!

    (SHELLY *begins the art of making a fresh juice.*)

JACKIE. I'm just taking a moment to breathe down here and then I can regroup and think about what this single, forty-year-old Jewish woman is going to do.

SHELLY. Who's Jewish?

JACKIE. Me!

SHELLY. Since when?

JACKIE. Um, FOREVER.

SHELLY. And you think you know somebody. JEWISH! I just always thought you were the white girl whose family didn't run out of this neighborhood in the white flight of the seventies.

JACKIE. My parents were hippies.

SHELLY. Jewish hippies?

JACKIE. Jewish hippie musicians that raised me around the people that they loved. Black folks.

SHELLY. Back when we were Afro-American! You still trying to pass?

JACKIE. I had those cornrows once!!!

SHELLY. I don't care how many white girls come back from Jamaica with their hair cornrowed! You ain't fooling nobody girl!

JACKIE. (*Laughing.*) I wasn't trying to pass, I just wanted to have black hair. You can do so much with it. Watching Karl Chambers part and grease your hair!

SHELLY. Yes. His fingers would play me like he played that bass.

JACKIE. Music pouring all over this neighborhood. He and his brother Roland.

SHELLY. Roland played me like he played those drums for Philly International. Banged the—

(DOTTY *comes into the room.* SHELLY *and* JACKIE *do not see her. She just stands there looking confused.*)

JACKIE. When I am in that house I can put my hand on my old bedroom wall and feel all that history. That music. If I am going to have a child, I would want that child to have all that soul. Right here.

SHELLY. (*Lost in a sexual memory.*) Hmph. Roland.

JACKIE. Listen, I know. I wasn't smart.

SHELLY. Nope! But, I'm not going to judge you.

JACKIE. Sounds like judgment but okay, thank you.

SHELLY. You're welcome.

JACKIE. I told you too much. Please don't tell anybody. Oh my God, I hope your mom hasn't heard any of this.

(DOTTY *exits back towards the bathroom.*)

SHELLY. If she did, she won't remember.

JACKIE. Really?

SHELLY. It's Alzheimer's. Mom? You alright? I'mma have to go in there in a minute if she doesn't come out.

JACKIE. My problems seem so insignificant. These are things I can at least control in one way or another. Although I have no idea what I am doing.

SHELLY. Honestly, neither do I. I'm just trying to keep us afloat.

(SHELLY *pulls out a very nice brochure.*
Sotto voce.)

I found a pretty good assisted living community out on City Line Avenue. (*She looks over and glances at the paper that she asked* DOTTY *to sign earlier.*) And thankfully I got her to sign for me to get power of attorney so I can make this shit happen if she slips into a more deteriorated state. I can't wait for any other plan. Fidel is all I can afford right now—(*She realizes.*) SHIT!!! She didn't sign!!!

(DOTTY *enters.*)

DOTTY. FIDEL is from Kazakhstan! Always on the SKYPES to call his mother since he doesn't have the internet where he lives.

SHELLY. MOM! You didn't sign! The power of attorney—

DOTTY. Oh really? What time is it?

SHELLY. Ten Something!!! Okay! BEDTIME!!! Sign later!

DOTTY. At ten a.m.?

SHELLY. P.M.!!!

DOTTY. But it's still light out.

JACKIE. Shelly…

SHELLY. AURORA BOREALIS!

DOTTY. What?

SHELLY. THE NORTHERN LIGHTS.

DOTTY. In West Philly?

SHELLY. GLOBAL WARMING.

DOTTY. But I'm about to have my breakfast!

SHELLY. Well, take it upstairs with you for dessert. Let's get you to bed.

(SHELLY *moves* DOTTY *toward the stairs.*)

DOTTY. Well…good night everybody!

SHELLY. Goodnight.

DOTTY. I'm not even tired.

SHELLY. I am.

DOTTY. When are you going to take care of that brassy hair?

SHELLY. Tomorrow. Come on, MOM, BRUSH YOUR TEETH AND TUCK YOURSELF IN!

DOTTY. SHELLY!!! STOP TREATING ME LIKE A CHILD! I AM YOUR MOTHER!

(*Silence.*
Silence.
Silence.)

DOTTY. It's Christmas in a few days.

SHELLY. I know, I'm picking up your tree.

DOTTY. What do you want for Christmas?

SHELLY. Nothing Mom, I don't want anything.

DOTTY. Everybody wants something.

SHELLY. Mom, I don't need anything.

DOTTY. What do you want Jackie?

(JACKIE *bursts into tears.*)

You alright?

JACKIE. I'm fine Mrs. Shealy. My emotions are just all over the place. Christmas coming and all.

DOTTY. You look pregnant.

JACKIE. I'm just a little overwhelmed that's all.

DOTTY. And pregnant. Mark my words. You might wanna get one of them little box tests. Shelly you got any?

SHELLY. What?

DOTTY. You and Averie used to keep a whole case of 'em under your bed.

SHELLY. Goodnight!

DOTTY. Your sense of humor must have been burned out with that hair color!

SHELLY. I'm about to be on the news tonight Jackie!

DOTTY. The boys are coming in tonight, right?

SHELLY. Yes. Tonight. LATE. Your boys are coming in late tonight. Donnie said that he and Adam can't come in until about midnight. You will see them in the morning. Them and the Blue Spruce!

DOTTY. I'll wake up to a Blue Spruce on Christmas Eve morning.

(DOTTY *comes over and kisses* SHELLY *on the head.*)

Good night.

SHELLY. Good night.

JACKIE. Uh. Good night.

(DOTTY *goes up the stairs.*)

Aurora Borealis?

SHELLY. AURORA BOREALIS!!! Yes. AURORA BOREALIS. You're lucky! Your mother's gone already! Mine is here and gone at the same time! AURORA BOREALIS! I gotta go pick up a Blue Spruce, take care of this brassy ass hair and get ready for Christmas!

(*The kitchen light goes dim as* JACKIE *and* SHELLY *leave out of the front door. Lights shift. Late at night.*)

A DETOX

DONNIE, *40, African American, handsome, masculine and fit is sneaking down the back stairs into the kitchen. He wears J. Crew loungewear. Opens a cabinet. Reaches to the far back. Retrieves oatmeal cookies. Gorges. Then turns off light. Turns back on light. Pulls a roast chicken from the fridge. Eats from underneath. Pulls out lemonade. Drinks heartily. Closes fridge. Footsteps. He shoves everything in the fridge. Pulls out a glass and fills with water.* ADAM, *40, a Caucasian, Latin, or Arab buff specimen of a man, appears. Most of this conversation takes place sotto voce until* DOTTY *enters.*

ADAM. What are you doing?

DONNIE. Water.

ADAM. There were a lot of cabinet openings and closings for water.

DONNIE. I was looking for an Advil.

ADAM. Come here.

(*They begin to circle the kitchen table.*)

DONNIE. Why?

ADAM. I wanna kiss.

DONNIE. No.

ADAM. Why?

DONNIE. I don't feel like it. It's late. My breath stinks.

ADAM. Like what?

DONNIE. I don't know, like stink.

ADAM. Like food of some sort. I swear—

DONNIE. (*Laughs.*) No.

(*They stop circling.*)

No! Really. No.

ADAM. Because we are on day four of the Juice Cleanse, it would be a shame if you didn't follow through.

DONNIE. That shit is expensive, of course I'm following through.

ADAM. We have just one more day and then we need transitional raw and vegan meals.

DONNIE. Whose idea was it to do a juice cleanse before the holidays.

ADAM. Yours.

DONNIE. I just put it on the calendar. I forgot what day it was.

ADAM. How can you forget five days before Christmas?

DONNIE. People forget. I forgot.

ADAM. You forgot?

DONNIE. Anyway, I know, we are going to feel so much better. Right? This is great! Yesterday was rough but today I…I feel good. How do you feel?

ADAM. I feel good.

(*Silence.*)

DONNIE. What?

ADAM. Nothing.

DONNIE. Am I too fat for you?

ADAM. What?

DONNIE. This "fast"?

ADAM. Come on! It's about staying healthy.

DONNIE. Oh really? Tell Molly.

ADAM. THAT WAS ONCE!!!

DONNIE. YEAH, ON OUR WEDDING NIGHT!!!

ADAM. I haven't done it since. Get over it.

DONNIE. Really? What about Vann and George?

ADAM. I don't know if they do? Okay, yeah, I'm sure they do.

DONNIE. Right.

ADAM. But this is me. Come on, I'm tired of this, give me a kiss.

DONNIE. Oh. What? Is it gonna lead to sex? I forgot what that was.

ADAM. Okay. I think this fast is getting the better of you. What the fuck are you talking about? We had sex LAST MONTH!

DONNIE. Make-up sex.

ADAM. I guess NOT!!!

DONNIE. Well…somebody was a little too drunk to—

ADAM. Hey not here.

DONNIE. Well, we don't talk at home.

ADAM. Well, you know what? It's hard to have sex with someone who is always so fucking angry and negative.

DONNIE. I'm negative?

ADAM. If the shoe fits. You are just so angry all of the time!

DONNIE. Do you read the news? I have EVERY FUCKING RIGHT TO BE ANGRY.

ADAM. I know. I know. I'm angry too but we have to find the light. Remember the light?

(*Silence.*)

I'm going back up while you pretend to drink your water.

(ADAM *heads for the stairs.*)

DONNIE. Why didn't you hold my hand?

ADAM. What?

DONNIE. When we were at your *"friend"* Robert's Christmas party last night?

ADAM. Why do you say it like that? *"Friend."*

DONNIE. I hate those guys. Those circuit boy queens that live from one party to the next.

ADAM. They like to have FUN. So what? Is it a crime to have FUN???

DONNIE. Dressing alike in those high top sneakers and tank tops, backwards baseball caps // and look down on gays that are not clones just like them and have no idea of the history of who stonewalled for them! Cackling like little girls who think life is just one big sex, Andrew Christian, and Molly buffet.//

ADAM. // You know, I'm not going to listen to you bitch about my friends. (*Beat.*) Maybe if you got your head out of your writing and got some "friends" of your own you'd feel a little better. And stop being so insecure. Acting like an OLD MAN! Is that why you are still wound up? // The Molly??? I tried it once! ONCE!!!

DONNIE. All you did was criticize the way I did things or the way I was dressed.

ADAM. You were way too dressed up!

DONNIE. We shouldn't have come.

> (*Silence.*
> *Silence.*
> *Silence.*)

ADAM. Mom's not... We need to be here with our family. It's Christmas. Christmas at the Shealys'.

> (ADAM *goes halfway up the stairs, thinks and then comes back down.*)

You know I don't like going to sleep mad. Kiss me.

DONNIE. I don't feel like it.

ADAM. Do you not want to make things better? Kiss me. Kiss me gatdamnit!

> (DOTTY *enters.*)

DOTTY. Kiss him!

DONNIE. MOM!!! Did we wake you?

DOTTY. Momma's sweet thing! Gimme a kiss.

> (*They slowly circle the kitchen table.*)

DONNIE. NO.

DOTTY. Been in the cookie jar, hunh?

DONNIE. No!

DOTTY. You puttin' on a little weight!

DONNIE. I haven't seen you in months and this is the first thing out of your mouth?

DOTTY. Adam, what are you feeding my boy?

ADAM. I'm not feeding him anything.

DONNIE. I'm on a cleanse.

> (*They stop circling.*)

DOTTY. A what?

ADAM. A Juice Cleanse.

DOTTY. What in the world are you gays doing now? Why can't you just put on chaps and call it a day?

ADAM. (*Laughs.*) Chaps? Mommy Dotty, you crazy.

DOTTY. I told you, that's the way I like my gays! Handlebar mustaches and chaps. I think that's sexy.

ADAM. I do too. Tell Donnie.

DOTTY. Y'all are way too conservative for my taste. Whatchu wearing, J. Crew or something? Come on now, if you gonna be gay, BE GAY!!! I think I got an old boa in the basement.

> (DOTTY *goes to the cabinets in search of a snack or tea or something. Pulls many things out and leaves them in disarray. She eventually finds a bag of nuts and takes them with her to the table.*)

ADAM. We only do that on Fire Island!

DOTTY. Fire Island! I love it! Are you getting that house in the Pines again next year?

ADAM. We are not going to get the house ever, EVER, again.

DOTTY. Why?

ADAM. Donnie—

DONNIE. Doesn't want to! What are you doing up Mom?

DOTTY. My sleep is all over the place. I don't know. Wait, wait, wait, I'm focused. Why aren't you gonna get the house? You get it every year. It's become your tradition. You gotta hold up your traditions.

DONNIE. I'm not doing it anymore! I don't need that tradition. Case closed!

DOTTY. Donnie what's wrong?

DONNIE. Nothing Mom, I'm just tired. It's late, we should all get some sleep.

DOTTY. I felt like I slept all night and day yesterday. That "Aurora Borealis."

> (DOTTY *cracks the nuts.*)

ADAM. Aurora Borealis?

DOTTY. The Northern Lights.

DONNIE. The Northern Lights?

ADAM. The Northern Lights?

DOTTY. Shelly told me that—

ADAM. Here?

DONNIE. In West Philly?

DOTTY. The Northern Lights are now in West Philly. Global warming.

DONNIE. (*Sotto voce.*) Fuck. (*Shrieks.*) SHELLY!!!!!

ADAM. (*Steps in front of* DONNIE *and tries to calm.*) Donnie.

DOTTY. Son, why are you yelling at three o'clock in the morning?

DONNIE. (*Whispering to* ADAM.) I'm gonna kill her. She had her sleeping all day again.

ADAM. (*Whispering.*) What's that smell on your breath? Smells like chicken and cookies.

DONNIE. What?

ADAM. Chicken and cookies.

DONNIE. (*Yelling.*) SHELLY!!!???

    (SHELLY *enters down the kitchen stairs. Her hair color is now red.*)

SHELLY. What's wrong with you? Why are you shrieking my name?

DOTTY. Don't y'all get started. It's almost Christmas Eve. Why is your hair red?

SHELLY. Leave it alone. Why is all this stuff out here?

DOTTY. It seems like, every time I go to sleep, I wake up and you have another hair color!

SHELLY. It was too brassy, remember?

DONNIE. You got her sleeping all day again?

SHELLY. Yes I do. I'm stressed! I got my hair colored but the queen fucked it up. I ain't going to him no more.

DONNIE. (*Sotto voce.*) Answer me! Why you got Mom sleeping all day?

SHELLY. (*Sotto voce.*) Why you worried about it? You ain't here! Hey Adam. You looking buffed up. You been working out?

ADAM. I have. Thank you for noticing. I like the red! Very Jessica Rabbit.

SHELLY. Thank you! I had a do-over.

ADAM. Looks good. I'm sorry, are we too loud? Where's Jason?

SHELLY. Sleepover.

DOTTY. Who was sleeping all day?

DONNIE and SHELLY. NOBODY!

DONNIE. (*Sotto voce.*) I thought you said that it was only for emergencies.

SHELLY. (*Sotto voce.*) Every day is an emergency.

DONNIE. She's fine.

DOTTY. Shelly did you get the tree?

SHELLY. I got it Mom, I got it! I "Paul Bunyan-ed" it. It's in there.

DOTTY. Yes Lord!

    (DOTTY *goes into the living room.*)

SHELLY. (*Yelling into the living room.*) It's a Blue Spruce. Nine feet, just like you asked for!

DOTTY. (DOTTY *screams at the top of her lungs as if she is being stabbed.*) Look at it! Shelly you *did* THAT!!! Adam, Donnie look at what my daughter did!

    (DOTTY *runs offstage to the living room.* ADAM *goes into the living room.* DONNIE *begins to go and* SHELLY *stops him.*)

SHELLY. Look! It's getting worse every day and before I take a bullet to her head and mine, I thought I'd cheat the clock gatdamnit!

ADAM. (*Offstage.*) Wow, that's ginormous! How did you get it in here?

DONNIE. She's not that bad. She just forgets.

SHELLY. And forgets and forgets. Wake up "Golden Boy"—

DOTTY. (*Offstage.*) Let's break out the decorations!

DONNIE. Golden Boy???

ADAM. (*Offstage.*) It's kinda late, Momma Dotty.

SHELLY. Daddy's Golden Boy. Fingers made out of gold.

DONNIE. Stop calling me that, I don't want to be called that—

SHELLY. Why? What's wrong with that? Why you so touchy?

DOTTY. (*Offstage.*) Don't tell me you gays aren't into decorating anymore?

DONNIE. I just don't—

SHELLY. Donnie, she's getting worse every single day.

ADAM. (*Offstage.*) Oh no we still decorate. Butch, leather or flaming queen! We still decorate. Let's decorate! I'm not sleepy anyway!

DOTTY. (*Offstage.*) Neither am I! That Aurora Borealis!

ADAM. Did you smell something on Donnie's breath, Mom?

SHELLY. What kind of money you got?

(DOTTY *and* ADAM *re-enter and head to the basement door.*)

DONNIE. What kind of money I got? How about…HI??? Good to see you little brother! Merry Fucking Christmas.

DOTTY. Donnie, watch your mouth. You can express yourself better than that. We all need to learn to stop this gatdamn cussin. Come on Adam, down in the basement I've got decorations that would put Martha Stewart to shame.

SHELLY. WAIT! WAIT! HOLD UP!!! What y'all doing?

ADAM. Decorating the tree.

SHELLY. It's the middle of the night!

DOTTY. I'm up!

ADAM. She's up!

DOTTY. I'm up!

DONNIE. She's up!

SHELLY. She's up, I'm up, we're all fucking UP!

DOTTY. Language!

SHELLY. Go head, go head!

DOTTY. I wasn't asking you Shelly! What's wrong with you Donnie?

DONNIE. Nothing Mom.

ADAM. Nothing is wrong with him Mom.

DOTTY. Y'all fighting? Let's deal with it!

SHELLY. Family meeting! I'll start a list.

DONNIE. No, Mom, no!

DOTTY. Your father always called a family meeting so that we could nip //
it all in the bud! Don't let things fester! Eats up a family. Nip it!

DONNIE. // Mom, Dad always wanted to nip things in the bud before people
could really process what they were feeling. He outed me before I could. Telling
everybody at the dinner table that I was gay. // I was 16. I didn't really know yet.

DOTTY. // But he was fine with it. We all were. He just called a spade a
spade. And you ARE gay.

SHELLY. You are Donnie! You *really* are.

DOTTY. Give him a kiss.

DONNIE. No!

DOTTY. Give my Adam a kiss!!!

DONNIE. No!

(DOTTY *holds* DONNIE *around his arms from behind!*)

DOTTY. Get him! Get him!

(ADAM *kisses* DONNIE. *More like tastes his lips. It is not a romantic kiss.
It is purely informational.*)

ADAM. Chicken, two oatmeal cookies, and lemonade!

(DOTTY *and* ADAM *high five!*)

DONNIE. No! Chicken! THREE oatmeal cookies and lemonade!

ADAM. The fast is over. Donnie!!! Damn!

SHELLY. Language.

DONNIE. I'm sorry.

ADAM. (*To* DOTTY.) I'm sorry.

DONNIE. No, I'm really sorry.

ADAM. That was expensive, Donnie.

DONNIE. We shouldn't have scheduled it right before the holidays.

ADAM. I can't believe you couldn't hold out a few more days.

DONNIE. IT'S CHRISTMAS! I'm hungry.

DOTTY. You have always been hungry.

ADAM. It's okay.

DONNIE. I'm sorry. We'll do it again after New Year's.

ADAM. No worries. I knew you couldn't stick it out.

DONNIE. Oh really. You got to give some to get some.

SHELLY. What's that supposed to mean?

ADAM. Come on Mom! The DECORATIONS!!!

(ADAM *and* DOTTY *exit down the basement stairs.*)

SHELLY. Okay, we'll put a pin in that conversation. I need your help Donnie. We gotta deal with Mom's condition.

DONNIE. Can we please talk about this in the morning, when we can all think straight. We can get Averie over here in the morning. It's late.

SHELLY. Okay. Fine.

(*Silence.*)

Whatchu doing up anyway?

DONNIE. I'M FUCKING STARVING!!!

SHELLY. Okay. Unhinged.

(*Offstage laughter from* DOTTY *and* ADAM.)

DONNIE. Adam and I have been on a Juice Cleanse.

SHELLY. Why the fuck you doing that?

DONNIE. To CLEANSE! RESET! DETOX!!!

SHELLY. You doin' drugs or something?

DONNIE. No, no, no, I'm trying to get more healthy. You know, like you are supposed to, when you turn forty.

SHELLY. Well we need to get very healthy in the way that we deal with Mom's reality! In the morning we will talk about how everybody, meaning you and Averie, are going to have to figure out a way to cough up some money.

DONNIE. I told you last month that my money is funny and my change is strange.

SHELLY. Well then you have to make some hard financial choices.

DONNIE. I'm chasing money. I'm a writer!

SHELLY. Even I know that THAT is not a lucrative career!

DONNIE. PAUSE!!!

SHELLY. You are so smart.

DONNIE. PAUSE!!!

SHELLY. You got into Wharton.

DONNIE. Let's not beat that old horse.

SHELLY. You have the brains to do something that ACTUALLY turns an income.

DONNIE. I turn an income—it's just more precarious than one would hope.

SHELLY. I still don't understand how you can make money being a…what do you call what you do?

DONNIE. I'm a musicologist Shelly.

SHELLY. Someone who loves music and gets paid for it. I don't understand.

DONNIE. I love music! I am an archivist.

SHELLY. And…

DONNIE. I am freelancing right now, there are no staff positions for music critics.

SHELLY. Why?

DONNIE. I don't know!!! I am a dying breed! Print media is under attack from the ravages of social media and any dimwit who can create a blog and bolster his uninformed opinions // to his list of followers and spread it like a—

SHELLY. // This sounds a little too political for this time of night. (*Beat.*) This is what I get for opening up Pandora's Box. Go ahead baby brother. Unleash! (*Beat.*) I have nothing else going on in my life. (*Beat.*) Give me your tired, your poor, your huddled masses yearning to breathe free, the wretched refuse of your teeming shore.

DONNIE. // THAT'S THE WHOLE POINT! I am trying to salvage our cultural history by being an archivist of our music. If we don't record our history we are doomed. It is not only in our basslines and song stylings but it is in the swagger in our walk. The rhythm of our talk. We need the griots of our time so that we know who we are. Raise up the youth and let them walk tall, pants up and eyes forward! No more (*Sounding like the lyrics of the "Good Times" anthem.*) Shuckin' and-a-ST-R-IVIN'!

(*Silence.*)

SHELLY. So you don't have any money?

DONNIE. No, not right now. I am doing some freelance work.

(*Offstage laughter from* DOTTY *and* ADAM.)

SHELLY. Maybe you can get a steady job at like Costco or something!

DONNIE. (*Squeals.*) WHAT?!!

SHELLY. I've been looking at brochures and there are some good care facilities not too far. I don't want to put her in some bootleg one where she will die in a year because they ain't monitoring her heart medication // or something.

DONNIE. // What's wrong with her heart?

SHELLY. She's got a heart condition.

DONNIE. WHAT?

SHELLY. You act like I've never told you.

DONNIE. (*Squealing.*) YOU NEVER TOLD ME!

SHELLY. Yes I did. I told you. Shhh, quiet!

DONNIE. I would remember you telling me that Mom had a heart condition!

SHELLY. Okay, well, she does! I'M OVERWHELMED!!! Okay???? I am EXHAUSTED!!! I need a break. (*Beat.*) Maybe you and Adam can move down here.

DONNIE. Unh, Unh! That is not possible!

SHELLY. You ain't got a steady job, so why not?

DONNIE. You've got to be kidding. I create for a living.

SHELLY. Well, sort of.

DONNIE. I. Have. A. Life. In. New. York. It. Is. Not. Possible!

SHELLY. I. Don't. Have. A. Life. Here. In. Phila. Del. Phia! We gonna have to MAKE it possible. Somehow!!! Well at least until… Mom's gonna kill herself.

DONNIE. (*Shrieks.*) WHAT?!???

SHELLY. I know, I know, it's HORRIBLE, but she's planning it. I think that's what she is plotting with Fidel.

DONNIE. WHAT??? What are you saying???

SHELLY. Am I speaking Chinese? They are plotting!

DONNIE. Shelly, what the fuck are you talking about?

SHELLY. Shhh, shhh, Fidel, Fidel! She said that she didn't want to be a burden and she was going to go when she was ready.

DONNIE. That doesn't say that she is going to kill herself! She's not that bad. She's in the early stage.

SHELLY. The early stage has passed little brother. You see it. You can't deny it anymore. We are in the middle. I've watched it, with my own two eyes. I live in this city and I am over here most of the time! Her disease is crashing all around us. I'm sorry I couldn't fit that into a TEXT!

DONNIE. IT'S THE 21ST CENTURY!!!! I TEXT!!! WE ALL TEXT!!!

SHELLY. Not me. Not about stuff like this.

DONNIE. I'M HUNGRY!!!

SHELLY. Boy, eat something!!!

(*Offstage laughter from* DOTTY *and* ADAM.
DONNIE *slams open the fridge and pulls out a chicken leg and devours it. They sit.* SHELLY *puts her hand on her brother's hand.
We hear laughing from* DOTTY *and* ADAM *in the other room.*)

SHELLY. I'm sorry to be so…HARSH. Donnie, brother, she is slipping fast and her plan for killing herself might be a thought that will pass. (*She snaps her fingers.*) Like this! So, the obvious plan would be to get her into a care facility.

DONNIE. She won't go for that! We can't put her into a home.

SHELLY. It's not a home. It's care.

DONNIE. She won't go for that.

SHELLY. She will have to. She is no longer the mother that we once had that is so fully in control of everything. She forgets to eat, to take her meds, where the bathroom is, who I am—

DONNIE. Okay! OKAY!!! Please STOP! Just…

(*Silence.*)

I just need a minute.

(*Silence.*)

SHELLY. You alright?

DONNIE. You talk to Averie?

SHELLY. We're not speaking.

DONNIE. She lives with you now.

SHELLY. I let her stay in my basement. That is about as sisterly as I can get with a woman who refuses to get her life together.

DONNIE. (*Under his breath.*) Like you are any better.

SHELLY. What?

DONNIE. I didn't say anything.

SHELLY. We just stay out of each other's way. She's good with Jason, I will give her that. She is entertaining to him.

DONNIE. You two need to cut it out. You're just alike, that's the problem.

SHELLY. (*Terse.*) I am nothing like your sister!

(*Silence.*)

DONNIE. Okay, whatever.

(*Silence. Offstage laughter from* DOTTY *and* ADAM. *A record comes on.*)

SHELLY. Are they playing music?

(SHELLY *begins to head towards the living room.*)

DONNIE. Leave it. Leave it.

(SHELLY *sits back down.*
Silence.)

DONNIE. So you got a tree for Mom.

SHELLY. Yeah, after I dropped Jackie off around the corner.

DONNIE. What?

SHELLY. She's back. Came by earlier to borrow sheets.

DONNIE. She has finally emerged. Texting me that she couldn't make it to our wedding was the last I heard from her.

SHELLY. She's on the run.

DONNIE. From what?

SHELLY. She's pregnant.

DONNIE. Girl, who?

SHELLY. Jackie.

DONNIE. Really? With who?

SHELLY. Some married dude. Don't tell her I told you.

DONNIE. Some married dude? What is she doing with some married dude?

SHELLY. She was his side piece.

DONNIE. What? That is not like her. She is such a traditionalist. She always dreamed of the husband, two kids and driving a family van.

SHELLY. No she dreamed of YOU, the two kids and driving a family van.

DONNIE. That was twenty years ago.

SHELLY. She's not over it.

DONNIE. What?

SHELLY. Sometimes it's not easy for women to move past trauma. It shows up one way or another. I know, I'm a woman! And just by being a woman, I'm in trauma!

DONNIE. No, you choose to be in trauma.

SHELLY. No, YOU choose to be in trauma.

DONNIE. I'm a black man in America. I OWN trauma.

(*Silence.*)

SHELLY. You win.

DONNIE. Is she gonna keep it?

SHELLY. Is she gonna keep it? She's forty! Forty ain't no time to be having no baby. She should be putting extra money in her IRA. She is headed for the *Guinness Book of World Records.*

DONNIE. That is not too old.

SHELLY. For who? No, no, no, no too many possibilities for complications besides the fact that she is pregnant by a married man, thank you very much.

DONNIE. You are one to talk.

SHELLY. No, no, no—

DONNIE. A married man???

SHELLY. Getting some man to stick it in you without a condom and running across state lines and making sure he never knows, is what I did. He was good-looking, smart, and healthy and I was ready to be a mother. Case closed.

DONNIE. Jason is nine, does he ever ask about his dad?

SHELLY. Case closed.

DONNIE. He is nine now he needs to know something.

SHELLY. No he don't. I'm his mother and his father.

DONNIE. He must ask.

SHELLY. I squashed it last week.

DONNIE. What do you say?

SHELLY. Immaculate Conception! It worked for Jesus. He didn't go around Jerusalem talking about "where's my father?"

DONNIE. Because he was the son of God.

SHELLY. Case closed!

(*Silence.*)

DONNIE. So my high school sweetheart is having a baby?

SHELLY. Well…it's nice to know that somebody has been having sex. Good ole Jackie.

DONNIE. Tell me about it!

SHELLY. It's a damn shame when you can't even remember the last time you had sex.

DONNIE. She is finally getting what she wanted. Well, sort of.

SHELLY. Wait a minute, you ain't havin—

DONNIE. No. (*Beat.*) We just started speaking a few days ago after moving around the house without speaking to each other after a fight about a pair of skinny jeans. It was stupid, I don't really want to talk about it.

SHELLY. Gay.

DONNIE. I'm afraid that we are growing apart and I thought we finally got married after seven years and that he would be ready to have a family. I want more than just me and him.

SHELLY. Really? I've never heard you say that. I thought gay boys were more selfish than that.

DONNIE. (*Dry.*) Fuck you Shelly.

SHELLY. (*Drier.*) Fuck you Donnie.

(ADAM *and* DOTTY *emerge from the basement with decorations.* DOTTY *has her arms filled with garland.*)

DOTTY. Shelly, where did you put the key to that trunk?

SHELLY. I don't know where that key is Mom.

DOTTY. I'm gonna need that key.

SHELLY. Mom, I don't know what you do with things.

DONNIE. Shelly, don't be so short. Mom what do you need?

DOTTY. The key, the key to the trunk where I put my gifts—I guess I hid it from myself this time.

SHELLY. Fidel must have put it somewhere.

DOTTY. Okay. Okay. I'll wait for Fidel. He's got the key.

ADAM. Did you still want to decorate the tree?

DOTTY. The tree?

(*Silence.*)

Yes. Yes.

(*Silence.*
No one moves.)
We need garland, right?

ADAM. In your hands Mom.

DOTTY. I know…I know…

ADAM. Let's decorate the tree.

(ADAM *and* DOTTY *exit into the living room.*)

DONNIE. She's not well.

SHELLY. No, she's not.

(*Silence.*)

This morning before breakfast Mom told me that she is so worried that Daddy stays in bed all day and doesn't get up. She said, she kisses and hugs him and lays under his arm and he doesn't get up.

(DONNIE *sobers. He understands.*)

In and out, in and out, in and out. But something inside her stays right there. Right at that moment. Trauma.

DONNIE. (*Muffles his scream.*) AAAAAAHHHHHHHHHHHH!!!

SHELLY. You good now?

(SHELLY *lays a comforting hand on her brother.*)

DONNIE. I think so.

SHELLY. Mom's Alzheimer's has progressed and we can't stop the inevitable. Like Christmas, or illness, or Averie's coming in the morning!

DONNIE. No fighting. I can't take it. Girls don't fight fair.

(SHELLY *pretends to take off her earrings, put Vaseline on her face and swing like rough Ghetto Girl fighting.*)

SHELLY. Let's go and help decorate this Blue Spruce. That's something that we CAN do!

(*She pinches or punches* DONNIE *playfully. We hear another burst of laughter from* DOTTY *and* ADAM.)

DONNIE. What time is it?

SHELLY. If you ask me that question one more time, I will gut you in the neck!

DOTTY. Donnie, Shelly come on!!!

SHELLY. I think I'm gonna need a pill! I'mma check Mom's medicine cabinet. You want one?

DONNIE. ABSOLUTELY!!!

(*They run up the back stairs. Blackout.*)

End of Act One

TURN IT ALL OVER

We hear the sounds of Nat King Cole's "The Happiest Christmas Tree." It is playing on the record player. The next morning. Living room. Tasteful and well lived-in. There is a baby grand piano with photos of family members adorning it. It is well preserved and polished. There is a proper living room set of furniture including a "breakfront," sofa, love seat, recliner, coffee and side tables. It is a house that has raised many children. The nine-foot-tall Blue Spruce is decorated to perfection. There is a desk with a computer on it. DOTTY is on the couch going through a shallow box. FIDEL, a good-looking Central Asian guy of 28 years old is stringing Christmas lights around the window. It is 9 a.m. DOTTY is wide awake.

DOTTY. I found these last night when we were going through all the… (*To* FIDEL.) Fidel, don't string the colored ones up there. String up the white ones. Save the coloreds for the front yard! I want the colored ones to stop traffic! (*Back to the box.*) What's this? I have been trying to get these pictures organized for years, for my grandson Jason. You know how you just toss the envelopes from the Foto Mat in the drawer and they just stack up for years? Wait a minute, they don't have Foto Mats anymore! (*Laughs.*) They sure probably never had 'em back in um, in um…

FIDEL. I'm not sure. I don't think so.

DOTTY. Where did they all go? Like aliens just came down and swooped them all up. (*Shows* FIDEL.) Look at the Blue and White stripes. The booths were that color too. And you would just pull over to one and drop your pictures off. Foto Mat! Matte or glossy finish and they had a little place for negatives. Donnie used to love to look at the negatives. He would just stare at them for hours. Said that the world looked so different in the negatives and that he thought that they should be called positives. He was always saying stuff like that.

(FIDEL *just looks at* DOTTY. *Confused.* DOTTY *chuckles to herself.*)

Play that song you like. We need some music in this house. Wake 'em up.

(FIDEL *smiles. And runs to the record player. He plays Barbra Streisand's "So Many Stars."*)

Look at this. You know what this is?

(FIDEL *looks at the photograph and shakes his head no.*)

DOTTY. That, there, is the Royal Pavilion. It's in Brighton, England. Just the most beautiful place that Richard and I have been. The Royal Pavilion. Made for this King. I think his name was George. The third? Fourth? Third. No Fourth! Fourth! That's right the fourth! George the fourth. Wait!

(DOTTY *reaches for a recorder and hits record.*)

Little Jason—George the fourth. He was the Prince of Wales. He was fascinated with the Orient. Can I say that now? Orient. Well that's what it was called. The Orient. Such a beautiful name.

FIDEL. It is.

> (*Silence.* DOTTY *stares at* FIDEL.)

Royal Pavilion. (*Beat.*) You were telling me about the Royal Pavilion. (*Beat.*) Tell me about the Royal Pavilion in Brighton, England. Who took you there?

DOTTY. Richard. Richard my husband.

FIDEL. Really?

DOTTY. Nobody was going to places like London around here in the 1960's. But Richard and I went. I married well. Richard is…was an ear, nose and throat doctor. Went to Howard University. Then on to the University of Pennsylvania. That's where we met. Right? The University of Pennsylvania. I was working at the University, in the cafeteria, as a cashier. Richard came to my line every day for two months before I said to him, point blank, "When you gonna take me to a picture show and buy a girl a drink?"

> (FIDEL *laughs.*)

We were married a year later and Richard showed me the world outside. Showed me that Royal Pavilion slapped down in the middle of town. Domes and towers. Who sings this?

FIDEL. Bar-bar-a.

DOTTY. Barbara?

> (DOTTY *has lost her thought.* FIDEL *looks confused. Then he picks up on this story.*)

FIDEL. Remember? Domes and towers.

DOTTY. What's that honey?

> (FIDEL *turns off the record player and begins to mime as* DOTTY *becomes enthralled like a child watching a storyteller.*)

FIDEL. Domes and towers. The Pavilion. Husband.

DOTTY. My husband?

> (DOTTY *stares intently.* FIDEL *does his best girly girl impression.*)

FIDEL. Buy a girl a drink?

> (DOTTY *smiles.*)

Orient.

> (*The alarm on* FIDEL'*s phone goes off.*)

DOTTY. Oh that thing scares me!

FIDEL. Sorry.

DOTTY. You gotta get a better ring for that thing.

FIDEL. Sorry.

(*He goes into the kitchen.*)

DOTTY. What am I looking for?

(FIDEL *returns.*)

FIDEL. Medicine.

DOTTY. (*Frustrated with herself.*) What am I looking for???

FIDEL. Medicine.

(FIDEL *begins the task of getting the right pill out for* DOTTY.)

DOTTY. (*Quietly frustrated.*) What, what, what?????

FIDEL. I get Ms. Shelly for you?

DOTTY. No. No. Sit. Sit with me. (*They sit quietly for a long moment.*) Can I tell you something?

(FIDEL *nods and waits.*)

Do you know what cognitive…cognitive…I keep forgetting the last word of it, is? It's like decline or something. It's got worse. I forget things I just said or did. I cannot pick up my clothes. Get organized. I lose everything. I forget appointments even after I write them down. And the worst thing is that I can't remember people's names, the way they look to me and more and more I am having trouble finding the right words to say.

(DOTTY *thinks.*)

FIDEL. You can say it.

(*Silence.*)

DOTTY. (*Simply.*) I'm scared.

FIDEL. Okay.

(*Silence.*)

Okay. You said it. It's okay.

(*Silence.*)

DOTTY. Thank you.

(*Silence.*)

Do you understand me?

FIDEL. Yes.

DOTTY. Do you understand…us?

(FIDEL *thinks.*)

FIDEL. Sometimes…no.

DOTTY. You get confused?

FIDEL. Yes. Sometimes. The rules of English language don't make sense.

DOTTY. To me either. (*Then.*) I'm getting confused all the time.

(FIDEL *sits next to* DOTTY. *She looks intently at* FIDEL. *He holds* DOTTY's *hand.*
Silence.
Silence.
Silence.)

FIDEL. You okay?

(DOTTY *stares into nothingness.*)
Medicine?

DOTTY. You got the cutest little accent. What is medicine in Russian?

FIDEL. Leekarstva.

DOTTY. Lik-ars-vka.

FIDEL. Leekarstva.

DOTTY. Leek-harv-sta.

FIDEL. Medicine.

DOTTY. Medicine. I guess that is my Russian word of the day. (*Laughs.*) Doesn't that make your brain hurt?

(FIDEL *and* DOTTY *share a little laugh.* DOTTY *leans in conspiratorially.*)

DOTTY. (*Sotto voce.*) Fidel, remember to gather those gifts up for me and help me to set it up for Christmas. You are going to help me right?

FIDEL. (*Sotto voce.*) Right. Gotcha!

DOTTY. (*Sotto voce.*) I got you squared away. I scratch your back—

FIDEL. (*Sotto voce.*) And I scratch mine.

DOTTY. (*Sotto voce.*) We gotta stick together. You and me.

FIDEL. (*Sotto voce.*) Yes. Yes. One Donepezil.

DOTTY. (*Sotto voce.*) One Donepezil. Bottoms up!

(DOTTY *begins to down the pill. The front door opens sneakily and it is* JACKIE. DOTTY *chokes or spits the pill out.*)

JACKIE. Mrs. Shealy!

DOTTY. Shit! What the hell? Scared me half to death!

JACKIE. Oh, I am so sorry!

DOTTY. You can't just be walking in doors around here!

JACKIE. I'm sorry! I was just returning the linen that I borrowed.

DOTTY. If I still had my .32 I would have blown your head off.

JACKIE. I wasn't thinking. I just thought I'd leave them right here inside the door.

DOTTY. You can't be sneaking in doors! This is the hood! THE HOOD!

JACKIE. I am so sorry. I'm going back to New York.

DOTTY. Wait a minute, wait a minute. Fidel I think I need another round. I can't eat this pill from up off of the floor.

(FIDEL *looks confused.*)

More Leeky.

(FIDEL *looks even more confused.*)

Leeksharvis. Medicine. More sweetie.

(FIDEL *understands and runs into the kitchen.*)

JACKIE. I am so sorry.

DOTTY. It's alright. I was just in the middle of my Russian word of the day.

JACKIE. What was it?

DOTTY. Honey, I wish I knew.

JACKIE. Mrs. Shealy. I'm going back to New York. I have this Zipcar out there and I am sure that it is now costing me a fortune in late fees and I have to make some decisions and those will require me to actually deal with what I have going on in New York.

DOTTY. Sit down. You're confusing me.

(JACKIE *is looking around to make sure no one is watching.*)

JACKIE. I really should go. (*She sits.*)

DOTTY. Whose baby is it?

JACKIE. You know. Shelly told you?

DOTTY. I just know. Women know other women. I've known you all of your life.

JACKIE. Some asshole. Bad choice. Baaaaaad choice.

DOTTY. (*Simply.*) He's a dick.

JACKIE. He's a dick. I gotta go back to New York and face my truth.

(FIDEL *enters with the medicine.*)

DOTTY. I'm starting to face mine.

JACKIE. I'm sorry Mrs. Shealy. I didn't know.

FIDEL. One Donepezil.

DOTTY. One Donepezil. Bottoms up.

(DOTTY *downs the Donepezil and drinks the full glass of water.*)

The doctor says that it improves the symptoms and slows down the progression. (*Earnestly.*) It's Alzheimer's. I should have told you. I probably forgot.

(*She laughs.*)

JACKIE. That's not funny.

DOTTY. It's hilarious. (*She sobers.*) My doctor said it is better to come from me. To have no shame. No shame about it. It's Alzheimer's.

JACKIE. (*She cries.*) Oh, Mrs. Shealy, I am so sorry.

DOTTY. This is EXACTLY why I don't tell people. What am I supposed to do with this?

JACKIE. I'm sorry.

DOTTY. It's alright, it's alright. Stop all this. It's Christmas Eve. I'm not dead.

JACKIE. Shelly says that you want to kill yourself.

(*Silence.*)

Is that true?

(*Silence.*)

DOTTY. Ask anyone who is living with this and be prepared for the answer.

(*Silence.*)

JACKIE. Do you need anything?

(*Silence.*)

DOTTY. I do. My mind.

(*Silence.*)

What do you need?

JACKIE. Just a hug and assurance that everything will be alright in the world.

(DOTTY *hugs* JACKIE.)

DOTTY. I guess we all need that.

JACKIE. Life is just not turning out the way we hoped it would, right?

DOTTY. We are all in the same boat.

JACKIE. Don't you feel mad? I mean what the fuck??? Alzheimer's???

DOTTY. I do. I'm mad one minute, sad the next.

JACKIE. Me too. I just want some peace, you know.

DOTTY. Me too. It gets so noisy in here. (*Points to her head.*)

JACKIE. Me too.

DOTTY. Fidel plays music for me. It helps. (DOTTY *gets up and puts the Barbra Streisand song back on.*)

JACKIE. I should go now before everyone wakes up.

DOTTY. You can't leave without saying Merry Christmas.

JACKIE. But—

DOTTY. Adam is here too. Adam. His husband.

JACKIE. I know. I met him the last time I was here. Actually, walked in on them.

DOTTY. Were they…you know?

JACKIE. No, no, they were just kissing. I'm fine with him being gay, I just didn't need to see it. We used to kiss on that couch.

DOTTY. You know, I always knew he was gay? Even as you two were running around here after each other. Always knew. A mother ALWAYS knows. Even if she tries to look the other way, like Marquis' mother, Lena, down the block. That boy wears more make-up than I do and she still tells me how all the women are always after him at church. Hmph—after him to see what kind of foundation he is wearing! (*She laughs and hoots.*) Even though you don't love the same, you can still love. He had to be what he had to be.

JACKIE. I know.

DOTTY. Do you need someone to go around and check on the house 'til the next time you come home?

JACKIE. I think it will be fine. I still trust this neighborhood. The hood, the HOOD.

DOTTY. Don't. That big beautiful house lies dead in between two crack houses. This neighborhood is something. People drive by and all they see is what WAS. What used to be! A middle class inner city neighborhood that has now caved in on itself.

JACKIE. But the heart is still here, right?

DOTTY. It's doing the best that it can with what it's been given. (*Beat.*) There was a promise that we made to this neighborhood. Your parents. Me and my husband. We were determined to not run out of this place in search of the suburbs. We could have. But if we left, what would that be saying about our community? A community of strivers. People that wanted big glorious dreams for their children. To be the first black president. For women to be paid well for what they do. For all people to be free and live in harmony. But then at some point most of the folks we knew, well, couldn't take it and fled or many of the older folks died off and left their houses without a plan. No legacy. No inheritance. Left these young men and women that have been spit out by the system to do what they could. Drugs and whatever else they need to do to keep the lights on. No one is even aware of the history of this neighborhood.

JACKIE. I am. I'm proud of where I come from.

DOTTY. It's all wrapped up in a memory now. We gotta move forward. Whatever that means. (*Beat.*) But I tell you what, I'm gonna record as much as I can hold on to.

JACKIE. I will do the same. Pass it on.

FIDEL. (*In very broken English.*) Can I call home?

DOTTY. What's that?

FIDEL. Home. Phone home.

DOTTY. Sure E.T.

(FIDEL *goes over to the computer and speaks softly under this.*)

E.T. Phone home. (*Laughs.*) That was some movie. He was so cute. I wonder what ever happened to him. E.T. What did that stand for?

JACKIE. Extra-Terrestrial.

DOTTY. Extra-Terrestrial. E.T. Ain't that something. Reaching his little finger out, pointing to home. Home. Everybody is always trying to get back there. We search the whole world over trying to make and remake our lives, searching. If E.T. came out now in the cineplex, would he text home? Nawwww. E.T. knows. It's not the same as the sound of a warm voice. Calling you home. (*She reaches out her finger to* JACKIE *and* JACKIE *does the same.*) Reaching out that finger hoping that someone is reaching out a finger to you. (*Very E.T.*) Phone Home.

> (*Silence.*)

Did you find my keys?

JACKIE. What keys?

DOTTY. The keys to that trunk in the basement.

JACKIE. I don't know anything about keys, Mrs. Shealy.

DOTTY. Mrs. Shealy? Oh we are awfully proper today aren't we Ms. Shealy. You always been uppity after we sent you to those private schools. I told Richard not to put y'all in those fucking schools. I went to public school and look at me.

JACKIE. Unh hunh.

DOTTY. Jack and Jill socials. Trying to turn you and your sister into Grace Kelly or something.

JACKIE. Mrs. Shealy, it's me Jackie. Jackie.

> (DOTTY *stops and thinks.*)

DOTTY. I know Jackie. Jackie I know who the fuck you are!

JACKIE. Mrs. Shealy!!! (*She yells.*) Shelly!!!

> (FIDEL *takes off headphones and looks up from Skype on the computer.*)

FIDEL. Everything Okay???—

JACKIE. I think we need Shelly—

DOTTY. No, I'm—

JACKIE. Mrs. Shealy needs a glass of water—

DOTTY. NOTHING! MRS. SHEALY NEEDS NOTHING. Stop treating me like a child! I am your mother.

JACKIE. Mrs. Shealy please. I don't mean to upset you. It's me Jackie. Jackie.

> (FIDEL *runs off and grabs a glass of water from the kitchen.* DOTTY *stares at* JACKIE.)

I didn't mean to upset you—

DOTTY. It's me—FUCK!!! FUCK ME. FUCK. FUCK. FUCK.

(*Silence.*
Silence.
Silence.
FIDEL *returns with the glass of water.*)

DOTTY. I'm sorry. Thank you Fidel. Tell your momma I said hi. Hi momma.

FIDEL. Okay.

JACKIE. No, no, it's fine, it's fine.

DOTTY. No. It's not. It's… (*She points to her head.*) Whooo! Bette Davis said it best, "Getting old ain't for sissies!"

FIDEL. Я в порядке мама. Я в порядке. Я собираюсь встретиться с несколькими юристами. Все будет fine. There то, что называется Pro Bono, // где они могут помочь мне бесплатно. [*Translation: I'm fine Mom. I'm fine. I'm going to meet with a few more lawyers. Everything is going to be fine. There is something called Pro Bono // where they can help me for free.*]

DOTTY. When my doctor told me it was Alzheimer's. The first thing I thought was, I wanted to die. But I have children. And they need me. And I'm a grandmother. And I am responsible to them. I can't be selfish and give up. I have to fight this. For them. But it is a losing battle. And I am losing. I am losing Jackie. Tell my children. They don't want to hear it from me.

JACKIE. Mrs. Shealy, have you talked to them and told them this.

DOTTY. They know it but they don't know how to deal with it. They are my children. They only see me as a mother and not as a woman. (*Beat.*) What time is it?

JACKIE. It's 9:20 in the morning.

DOTTY. What day?

JACKIE. Christmas Eve.

DOTTY. Christmas Eve dinner is at five. Five. You coming? Bring your mom. There is a place for you all at the table.

JACKIE. I am actually leaving. The Zipcar—

DOTTY. But y'all come every year. Y'all come here at five. Tell your momma to bring her lemon pound cake. I'm gonna make my 7 Up cake and beat her at our yearly Christmas Eve bake off. Tell her I think I found out her secret! Lemon zest!!!

JACKIE. Okay. Okay. I will. I will be here at five.

DOTTY. What a nice family. This community is wonderful.

JACKIE. Okay.

DOTTY. See you at five?

JACKIE. See you at five.

(JACKIE *exits.*)

FIDEL. //Бесплатно. Я собираюсь получить мое убежище и, когда это будет сделано, я буду в состоянии вернуться домой, чтобы увидеть тебя. Следующего Рождества. Не плачь, мама. Я должен идти. Я на работе. Я позвоню тебе позже. Bye Bye. [*Translation: For free. I'm gonna get my asylum and when that is done I will be able to come home to see you. Next Christmas. Don't cry Momma. I gotta go. I'm at work. I will call you later. Bye Bye.*]

    (FIDEL *is trying to hold back tears.*)

DOTTY. Fidel. You alright?

    (SHELLY *comes down the stairs. And the pace picks up again, messy and noisy.*)

SHELLY. Where she at?

DOTTY. Who?

SHELLY. Averie.

DOTTY. She ain't here yet.

SHELLY. I thought her broom would have arrived by now.

DOTTY. Wait a minute. Fidel?

SHELLY. Fidel did you give her, her pills? Medicine?

    (DONNIE *and* ADAM *come down the stairs.*)

FIDEL. Yes.

SHELLY. Mom, why you got all these pictures out?

DONNIE. Morning.

SHELLY. Morning.

ADAM. Morning Mom, Shelly.

DOTTY. Morning.

DONNIE. Morning Mom. Are you looking for something?

SHELLY. Why is the tape recorder on?

DOTTY. I was looking through these photos. Right Fidel?

    (*He exits into the kitchen.*)

DONNIE. The negatives.

SHELLY. You are so strange. You look at the pictures, fool, not the negatives.

DOTTY. (*Looking at photos.*) Places, things, relatives. Cousin Cypherdean.

ADAM. Cypherdean?

SHELLY. I haven't had breakfast yet. Don't bring up Cypherdean. // (*Yells.*) Fidel! Coffee!

DOTTY. // Cypherdean was a mess. He was 6-foot-4 and wore a beaded gown // to Uncle David's funeral. Remember that?

DONNIE. // No one ever talked about him, he was always shrouded // in mystery.

SHELLY. // I've got my list for the market. // I've got to pick up a few things.

DOTTY. // Cypherdean walked up to the casket and fell over in it. It took me and your cousins Mudee and Sudee // to get him out of it.

ADAM. // Mudee and Sudee?

DONNIE. Nicknames for Martha and Sarah.

SHELLY. Cloves for the ham, // cinnamon sticks, eggnog, got to have eggnog. Mom—

DOTTY. // He fell OUT! He would always wait until he was the last to arrive at any family event. He always wanted all eyes on him.

DONNIE and SHELLY. That's your cousin Geoffrey but he calls himself Cypherdean.

SHELLY. Mom, do you want anything special from the market? //

DOTTY. I didn't know if you were asking me anything. You've been telling me.

SHELLY. What?

ADAM. // Cypher means zero. It also means a person or thing of no importance. A non-entity.

DONNIE. I never thought about that. He called himself a non-entity.

ADAM. It also means a coded message. // He was a coded message.

SHELLY. // Cranberries, oranges, mini marshmallows

DOTTY. // A coded message with tears and more drama than an episode of *Knots Landing.* (*She reveals a photo.*) Here he, um, she is.

(*They all gather around.* FIDEL *enters with coffee service for all.*)

ADAM. Oh my.

DONNIE. For a non-entity, she made a statement. A pioneer.

SHELLY. He wasn't settling the West! Where's my keys?

ADAM. No, he was settling his historically conservative black neighborhood of the East, that was still reeling from the shock of the 1960's.

DOTTY. The sixties changed everything!

ADAM. With his bold footsteps that he paved for all of us. We stand on his shoulders. Gay marriage and all. We owe a lot to the Cypherdeans of the world. We can be our own creation.

(*Everyone just stares at* ADAM.)

DOTTY. That's my gays! Know your history.

DONNIE. Then let's be our own creation because it seems to me that we are now just carbon copies of one another. Our community.

ADAM. If you dared to stop JUDGING the whole community, you would see that if you scratch the surface everyone is just trying to STILL find themselves. Creating and recreating. That is healthy.

DONNIE. I DON'T BUY IT!!!

SHELLY. HEY, HEY!

ADAM. (*Trying to be extremely positive.*) Fine, are we going to open gifts tonight or tomorrow in the morning?

DONNIE. Christmas morning. Tradition.

ADAM. Why don't we try something new? Open one gift tonight?

DONNIE. We don't do that!

ADAM. I'm just trying to lighten the mood!

SHELLY. Adam, we don't do that. We do it all about five o'clock in the morning. Jason will get up first, and he will have barely slept. Bug me to go downstairs because Santa Mom has come.

DONNIE. You told him about Santa?

SHELLY. He was getting too old for all that. My credit cards have my name on them not St. Nicholas.

ADAM. Point taken.

SHELLY. And then we all go down, coffee is brewing, breakfast starts being made and the wrapping paper covers the floor! Christmas at the Shealys'. You can't mess with tradition. So, I'm out. Watch Mom. Back in a few!

DOTTY. Put on that Judy Garland song, Richard.

DONNIE. Richard? Mom?

DOTTY. Happiness is just a thing called—

SHELLY. Mom that's Adam.

DOTTY. It's right there on the side of the record player.

ADAM. Okay.

DONNIE. Adam.

(ADAM *puts on Judy Garland's "Happiness is Just a Thing Called Joe." We hear the flourishes of the intro.*)

DOTTY. Oh I love this intro. Listen.

(*We hear the opening lyrics.*)

Although your name is Richard. Dick. My Dick.

(DOTTY *sings the opening lyrics with Judy.*)

Kids in bed. Bringing me red roses every Friday night.

ADAM. Tradition.

DOTTY. A dream.

ADAM. A dream.

DONNIE. (*Whispers.*) Adam please. I don't think it's healthy to play into this.

SHELLY. Mom—

ADAM. It's not hurting anybody.

DOTTY. Well, are you going to ask me to dance?

ADAM. Can I have this dance?

DOTTY. I thought you'd never ask.

> (ADAM *holds out his hand.* DOTTY *curtsies and* ADAM *does an elaborate bow.* DOTTY *folds herself into* ADAM's *arms. They begin to dance cheek to cheek.* DONNIE *and* SHELLY *watch.*)

Where have you been? I couldn't get you out of bed for a while. For a long time. Laying there, COLD.

ADAM. I've been here. I'm always here. In this house that we made. Me and you.

DONNIE. Adam, what are you doing?

ADAM. Shhh. Me and you.

DOTTY. Shhh. Our kids can be so nosy. I haven't hugged you in what feels like years. Y'all sit down and watch your mommy and daddy dance. You can learn a lot about love just by watching us dance. The way your daddy puts his hand on the small of my waist. The way he looks me in the eye and whispers something in my ear that makes me laugh.

> (ADAM *thinks and then whispers something in her ear.* DOTTY *laughs and then lays her head on* ADAM's *shoulder.*)

I love this song. Take me for a turn around the room.

> (*We hear the musical break. They dance! It is dreamy and romantic.* ADAM *leads* DOTTY *around the room in this sweeping dance.* DOTTY *is as lithe and buoyant as she was at 38 years old. This is just a moment.*)

I miss you so much. I thought you'd never wake up. Me lying under your arm. You as cold as ice. I didn't know how I would make it without you. Raising these kids. I'm pretty strong but you took care of me. Gave our children the best of everything. (*She looks over to her children.*) Now use your gifts. You all have gifts. Use your gifts! That's all I ever want from you! Me and your daddy. This life can be a dream my Michellene, my ballerina! Donatello, my pianist! And my Averie? Where is Averie?

DONNIE. (*Trembling.*) She's coming Mom.

DOTTY. Averie, my First Lady of song.

> (AVERIE *comes in the door, loaded down with Priceright bags. She wears her uniform apron and a pink bubble jacket.*)

AVERIE. Hey Y'all!

SHELLY and DONNIE. Sssshh.

AVERIE. Why y'all shushing?

DONNIE. SHHHHHH!!!

> (FIDEL *goes over to help* AVERIE *with the bags.*)

AVERIE. What is going—

DONNIE. Shhh—

DOTTY. My mind is playing tricks on me Adam.

ADAM. I know.

AVERIE. MOM! WHY ARE YOU DANCING ALL UP ON DONNIE'S MAN WITH THE BLINDS ALL OPEN???!! THAT DON'T EVEN LOOK RIGHT!

SHELLY and DONNIE. AVERIE!!!

AVERIE. WELL SOMEBODY HAD TO SAY IT! JUST CLOSE THE BLINDS! YOU KNOW HOW THESE NEIGHBORS ARE!!! ALL UP IN THIS HOUSE!!! MERRY MERRY ERRBODY—I brought CHITLINS— THEY WERE ON SALE! HAHA!!!! WE GONNA HAVE A MERRY GATDAMN CHRISTMAS!!!

> (*She roars with laughter.*
> *We hear the sound of Lou Rawls' "Christmas Is." We jettison to later in the day with a flurry of movement in the house.* DOTTY *is taken upstairs by* ADAM. FIDEL *puts away the groceries.* AVERIE *bangs pots and pans in the kitchen.* SHELLY *sets the table.* DONNIE *sits.*)

SL(AVERIE)

Lights up on the dining room. You can see the kitchen now upstage and a bit of the living room off stage right. AVERIE *is center stage. Everyone else in silhouette, either in the kitchen or in the living room.* AVERIE *is curling her hair, putting on new earrings, and changing out of her Priceright apron.*

AVERIE. Y'all can talk about chitlins all you want but you know you love 'em! Yes, they may stink up the house for a good 48 hours but they are a delicacy. That is all the slaves could eat. Everything that the slave masters didn't want and threw away and our people had to make something out of it to survive. Fatback, snouts, ears, neck bones, feet, and intestines, given to the slaves. You gotta take lemons and make some shit out of it. And if you don't…well…I don't know what to tell you. My new agent called me today and said that I am up for Celebrity Mud Fight. I know what y'all are going to say, but let me tell you, it's a good opportunity. To make some real money!!! CELEBRITY MUD FIGHT! Every week we would mud fight to stay in the house. And no there is no prize money but it is a chance that would lead to financial opportunities. No need for the side-eye Shelly. Ask Donnie! He knows all about a brand. Writing those critiques about soul music and treating it like he is making anthropologic discoveries with socio economic undertones and wearing those glasses and speaking so intelligently! It's branding. And I am about to get mine on! I have taken the scraps up off the floor and made lemonade out of it. Me and…what's your name again?

FIDEL. Fidel.

AVERIE. Fidel Castro here, and I cleaned those suckers 'til they stopped squealing! Right Fidel?

FIDEL. Yes—

AVERIE. I taught Fidel how to soak and rinse those bad boys until they were squeaky clean. Got all that extra fat—

FIDEL. Right—

AVERIE. undigested food—

FIDEL. Yes—

AVERIE. and bits of fecal matter off of 'em!

FIDEL. We sure did—

AVERIE. Clean 'em, boil the hell out of 'em with a little baking soda and salt. Season 'em up and what? Delicious! Lynnie Poo down the street, even goes so far as to throw them in the washing machine for the final rinse. Now that's crazy! She also makes bath soap out of pot liquor from collard greens but that's another story! We gonna have some Pork Chitlins, not Chitterlings, for Christmas, because Momma said she missed her momma's chitlins and that's what she's gonna get. And no, they didn't come from no Whole Foods, Donnie, and they are not organic, Adam. We are having regular ole chitlins for Mom and I am proud of my slave heritage. (*Sings.*) *We are survivors, I ain't gon give in!!!* We do what we got to do!

> (*Lights up on the rest of the house. Everyone is setting up and the place is a flurry of energy of setting the table and putting food out.*)

SHELLY. Where do you get this very odd modern day slave narrative from?

AVERIE. From LIFE! From LIVING! I may not have gone to college like the two of you but I've got LIFE and the knowledge of history.

SHELLY. That explains why you are living in my basement.

AVERIE. Oh are we gonna go there? //

> (ADAM *comes down from the stairs.*)

ADAM. // She's resting.

SHELLY. // I'm just stating the facts!

DONNIE. // Thank you Adam.

AVERIE. And you ain't got no man!

ADAM. Of course.

SHELLY. // I don't want no man! And you don't need no man! You need some guidance!!!

DONNIE. // Hey!!!

AVERIE. // Why you mouthin???

SHELLY. // I'm not MOUTHIN! Whatever that means!

AVERIE. // Un hunh, Un hunh, I THOUGHT not!

DONNIE. // Don't start, you two.

AVERIE. *Static!!! Don't start none, won't be none!*

SHELLY. *STATIC!!!*

AVERIE. *No static.*

(She does the cabbage patch dance.)

SHELLY and AVERIE. *STATIC!!! NO STATIC!!!*

DONNIE, AVERIE, and SHELLY. Don't start none, won't be none!

SHELLY. That was my jam!

DONNIE. *Static!*

AVERIE and SHELLY. *STATIC!!!*

(They all fall over laughing.)

SHELLY. Now, about those chitlins. I made a turkey and a ham. So we don't need any slave food.

AVERIE. Mom asked for them.

SHELLY. When?

AVERIE. Last week she said she had a taste for her mother's chitlins. I make 'em just like Grandmom. I HOLD ON TO OUR FOOD HERITAGE! Someone has to. And…I could make the giblet stuffing from the drippings of your fancy turkey, too, thank you very much.

ADAM. I'm sorry Averie, we are not having carbs.

AVERIE. What?

DONNIE. Or gluten.

AVERIE. Say what, say what now?

ADAM. Or dairy.

AVERIE. Or anything that brings JOY! PURE UNADULTERATED JOY!!!

ADAM. You know modern agrarian practices—

AVERIE. Y'all about to get on my nerves! All this talk about carbs, gluten and dairy. You think those children in those Save the Children campaigns in Africa or South Central L.A. are thinking about their carb, gluten or dairy intake? UM…NO! They are just trying to EAT. Period. Food. PERIOD.

ADAM. Sugar is poison.

DONNIE. Don't egg her on.

AVERIE. Everybody kills me these days. All this shit people won't eat. Oh I'm sorry, Mom said we can't cuss in the house. SORRY MOM! Fuck. Just eat but don't be a pig about it. Everything in moderation. Right Fidel. Fidel over here eats EVERY DAMNED thing. Why, cause he is from a third world country and people can't afford to have specialty diets. Right Fidel?

FIDEL. I eat meat.

AVERIE. SEE!

DONNIE. Okay fine, Averie. Just put the chitlins on the table as a slave food option.

AVERIE. Oh, I was.

(DOTTY *comes down the stairs.*)

DONNIE. Mom, I thought you were resting.

DOTTY. I can't rest. I've got things to do. It's Christmas Eve. What's that smell?

SHELLY. Mom, we got this. Everything is under control.

AVERIE. (*Yells.*) I cooked the chitlins!

DOTTY. Chitlins?

AVERIE. Just like Grandma used to make!

DOTTY. I haven't had chitlins in years.

SHELLY. Mom, I don't think you can even have chitlins. All that pork ain't good for your diet. Clogging up arteries—

AVERIE. They don't clog up nuthin! Not the way that I cleaned 'em. I cleaned the fuck—

ADAM. Language.

FIDEL. We sure did.

DONNIE. Mom, sit down.

DOTTY. I don't need to sit. I'm fine.

ADAM. You sure, Momma Dotty?

DOTTY. I'm sure, I'm sure. I need something to do. Is the turkey dressed?

SHELLY. Did it.

DOTTY. Well what about the yams and the collards.

SHELLY. Done and ready.

DOTTY. DAMN!

ADAM. Yes, did it, so you can just take it easy.

DOTTY. The sweet potato pies didn't get made did they?

DONNIE. You cooked them last night after you decorated the Christmas tree.

DOTTY. What Christmas tree?

SHELLY. Mom I know what you can do. Since we've got this under control would you mind getting Jason's gifts from down in the basement?

(DOTTY *looks around at everyone. It looks like she is trying to focus intently.*)

DOTTY. It's Christmas Eve. Christmas Eve.

(DOTTY *looks like she can't focus. She is desperate in her attempt to focus on the room. Then—*)

I got to organize those pictures for Jason—Fidel where did I put that box?

(DOTTY *goes down the basement stairs.* FIDEL *is quick on her heels.*)

FIDEL. I'll get the box. The box with photos.

SHELLY. Shit. Okay. Family Meeting. NOW!

(SHELLY *goes over to the basement door and locks it.*)

DONNIE. Now?

SHELLY. You know a better time?

AVERIE. You are locking a woman with Alzheimer's and her illegal caregiver in the basement?

SHELLY. Just for a few minutes. We all need to talk.

ADAM. Well—I'll just go upstairs and check some emails—

SHELLY. You too Adam. You are a part of this family. And since I can't reach you both in a timely manner—we have to lock a woman with Alzheimer's and her illegal caregiver in the basement. I have a list.

(SHELLY *pulls out a list and everyone moans and groans. Expletives and all.*)

AVERIE. Not the list!

DONNIE. We are not going to have time for a list Shelly.

SHELLY. A list will help us stay on track and get things done efficiently.

AVERIE. Girl, just talk! Ain't nobody got time for your list—

SHELLY. One! We need to prepare for putting Mom in an assisted living situation and that costs.

AVERIE. She is not HARDLY going to go for that! And neither will I. WE DON'T DO THAT!!!

SHELLY. In like five minutes, she won't know.

AVERIE. Don't matter. We ain't white people. No offense Adam.

ADAM. None taken.

AVERIE. That's what white people do!

SHELLY. You got a better plan?

AVERIE. If you get down off the cross and listen to me like I told you before we could get her signed up over at the church, for the sick and shut in // prayer ladies, that go by houses on the daily.

SHELLY. // Sick and Shut in prayer ladies? Some random church ladies? With no certification whatsoever to care of my mother.

AVERIE. There you go—YOUR MOTHER!!!

SHELLY. You know what I meant.

AVERIE. Yeah I know what you mean. Which is why you are OVERWHELMED!!!

SHELLY. You have no idea what you are talking about.

DONNIE. This isn't helping.

AVERIE. YOU ARE WORSE THAN CASTRO!

ADAM. What does Fidel have to do with this?

SHELLY. WHAT?

AVERIE. THE DICTATOR! FIDEL CASTRO.

ADAM. Oh—

AVERIE. All you want is your way or the freeway—

SHELLY. Wrong expression and NO. I. DON'T. All I try to do—

AVERIE. If you really want a FAMILY decision, you really have to involve the FAMILY. Not just dictate and then get mad because you feel so put upon!

ADAM. Averie is right!

AVERIE. HA!

ADAM. We should SHARE in these decisions. We should ALL have the information needed to assess these family matters.

SHELLY. YOU TWO DON'T PICK UP PHONES!!!

DONNIE. So you get back at us by withholding information??? // THAT'S FAIR?

SHELLY. // I don't withhold information!

ADAM. When you OVERWHELM yourself you do. And that's not fair.

DONNIE. You do and that's not fair! YOU DO! And it's SPITEFUL.

(*Silence.*)

SHELLY. The thing we should deal with is the fact that she is planning on killing herself.

ADAM. (*Shrieks quietly.*) What???

DONNIE. Shelly said it but I don't believe it.

ADAM. Oh my God!!! You ALL withheld!!!!

AVERIE. She doesn't mean it.

SHELLY. What do you mean she doesn't mean it? Do you know what's going on in her head?

(*Pounding on the door.*)

AVERIE. I don't need to know. That's not the point. Just comfort her, give her what she wants, while she still knows WHO THE FUCK WE ARE!!!

DOTTY. Fidel, just turn the knob. Just turn it.

FIDEL. I'm trying.

DOTTY. Is it locked?

ADAM. We should open the door.

DONNIE. Hold on Mom.

SHELLY. Damn. I'mma give her a pill later so we can finish this conversation. (*Pounding on the door.*)

FIDEL. Hello?

AVERIE. Stop giving her sleeping aids so that YOU can get rest.

(ADAM *opens the door.* FIDEL *and* DOTTY *enter loaded down with Christmas gifts.*)

DOTTY. Why was that door locked?

SHELLY. It was just…

DONNIE, SHELLY, AVERIE, and ADAM. STUCK!

SHELLY. Mom what you are doing with those?

DOTTY. I want to give these out now.

DONNIE. Now? Mom. We always wait until Christmas Day.

AVERIE. I can help you get those under the tree Mom.

DOTTY. I need to give these out now.

(*The doorbell rings.*)

SHELLY. Who's that?

AVERIE. (*She goes to answer door.*) Christmas caroling crackheads!

DONNIE. Mom, let me help you with those.

DOTTY. I don't need help. I want you to have these.

SHELLY. MOM JUST LET US TAKE CARE OF IT!

DOTTY. I'VE GOT THIS!!! I'VE GOT THIS, GATDAMNIT!!!

(*Door opens.*)

JACKIE. MERRY CHRISTMAS SHEALY FAMILY!!!

ALL. MERRY CHRISTMAS!!!

JACKIE. HEY!!! DONNIE!!!

DONNIE. HEY!!!!

AVERIE. Look what the cat dragged in! Hey gurl!

JACKIE. Merry Christmas! Hi! I brought an Entenmann's! Hi!

DONNIE. Oh my God you look great!

JACKIE. Stop lying, I look terrible.

ADAM. Hi!

JACKIE. Hi. We met briefly! A couple years ago!

ADAM. We did?

DONNIE. This is my partner Adam.

ADAM. Husband.

DONNIE. Husband.

JACKIE. Adam! Hi!!! You two were into some heavy petting the last time.

ADAM. Hunh?

JACKIE. On the couch.

DONNIE. What are you talking about?

JACKIE. Heavy petting on the couch a couple of years ago. Thanksgiving. It was awkward.

AVERIE. I hope you ain't still carrying that flame!

ADAM. What is she talking about?

JACKIE. I would have met you but you guys were, you know? On the couch.

AVERIE. Burn it.

ADAM. I don't know what you are talking about?

DONNIE. Wait a minute. Is that why you ran out of here and never showed back up here to eat?

ADAM. (*To* DONNIE.) Who is this?

DONNIE. This is the Jackie that was my high school sweetheart.

ADAM. (*High.*) Oh!!! (*Low.*) Ohhhh… Nice to finally, really, meet you.

JACKIE. High school sweethearts.

ADAM. I know, you missed a fabulous wedding. You broke his heart.

JACKIE. I think it was the other way around. OVER IT!

DOTTY. SIT Jackie. We are about to open presents. It's Christmas.

SHELLY. Christmas Eve.

DOTTY. Whatever. SIT.

JACKIE. I hope I'm not imposing. Your mom asked me to join you all for dinner.

SHELLY. I've got to go pick up Jason.

DOTTY. Get him later. FIDEL—

SHELLY. Mom—

DOTTY. Fidel hand out my gifts please!!!

(FIDEL *does this very quickly and awkwardly. Everyone stands with gift boxes.*)

FIDEL. с Новым годом [*Translation: Happy New Year.*]

AVERIE. What did you say?

DOTTY. Open your gifts.

AVERIE. Open the gifts!!!

(*They all unwrap the gift boxes.*)

DONNIE. Goggles?

SHELLY. Headphones?

AVERIE. Latex gloves? Tape? Pebbles? Mom what kind of freaky deaky stuff you getting into?

DOTTY. Shut up, Averie. Explain it Fidel.

FIDEL. She wants to put your shoes in her feet.

SHELLY. What?

ADAM. You mean our feet in her shoes.

FIDEL. I guess so. Your shoe?

DONNIE. My shoe?

ADAM. Take off your shoe. I think I saw this before.

JACKIE. I think I did, too.

AVERIE. WHY ARE THE WHITE PEOPLE SO WELL-INFORMED?

SHELLY. Spoken by the YouTube sensation.

AVERIE. But yes, I am a sensation.

DOTTY. Shut it. Put them on. (*Referring to the gloves.*) You do it for me son. You are the man of this house.

DONNIE. Do what?

DOTTY. It's an exercise for you and your sisters.

AVERIE. Do it Donnie. Do whatever she says.

DOTTY. Fidel will take you through it.

AVERIE. What's supposed to happen Fidel?

    (FIDEL *takes the tape from* AVERIE *and uses it to tape together two fingers on each hand of* DONNIE'*s. He then gets the pebbles.* FIDEL *puts a few pebbles into* DONNIE'*s shoe.* ADAM *puts it back on* DONNIE.)

FIDEL. And the headphones.

DONNIE. What am I doing?

DOTTY. Read those instructions for me Fidel.

AVERIE. Can he read?

DOTTY. Yes he can read. He's foreign, not stupid.

SHELLY. I barely hear the boy speak.

DOTTY. He can read. He's just shy.

ADAM. Go on Fidel.

FIDEL. (*Reads.*) This is twelve minutes that will change your life!

AVERIE. Twelve minutes?

SHELLY. I've gotta pick up Jason!

AVERIE. That's all?

DONNIE. Food's gonna get cold Mom!

AVERIE. I would have asked for that a long time ago!!!

DOTTY. WILL EVERYBODY PLEASE SHUT THE FUCK UP AND LISTEN TO FIDEL??!!!

>*(A beat.)*

AVERIE. *(Sotto voce.)* Language.

FIDEL. This exercise is designed to give you an idea of what someone with Alzheimer's is dealing with.

DONNIE. I can't do this—

AVERIE. He CAN read!

FIDEL. Most people think because I am foreign, I am dumb. I can hear too, I just don't understand your accents sometimes enough to respond.

AVERIE. He told me!

FIDEL. These tools will help. Goggles which help to simulating glaucoma, cataracts or a blur in vision that is very common in later years. Latex gloves—

AVERIE. Latex gloves???

FIDEL. —and tape for fingers to make your hands feel arthritic, clumsy and hard to bend. A substance is put inside shoes to make it hard to walk. Earphones that emit an incessant gabbering—

SHELLY. JABBERING—

FIDEL. Jabbering—Thank you—which patients say is constant. They say they are hearing all this stuff and they can't turn it off.

DOTTY. Yes. That's right. Go on Fidel.

FIDEL. Give this person five tasks and they only have twelve minutes to accomplish them.

DONNIE. I don't think this is the right time!

SHELLY. He's right Mom, it's Christmas Eve! We can do this later!

DOTTY. I DON'T HAVE TIME TO WAIT!!!

>*(Silence.*
>DONNIE *puts on the headphones.)*

Thank you for being game.

FIDEL. Give the person five tasks. Simple things to do.

AVERIE. Like, what, go to the closet and find a blue sweater?

FIDEL. Yes.

DONNIE. What?

AVERIE. GO TO THE CLOSET AND FIND A BLUE SWEATER.

SHELLY. I'm not playing this game.

>(SHELLY *retreats.)*

AVERIE. You are such a killjoy!

DONNIE. I can't hear you?

JACKIE. FIND A BLUE SWEATER IN THE CLOSET!!!

ADAM. PUT THE WRAPPING PAPER ON THE TABLE.

AVERIE. What else?

SHELLY. POUR ME A GLASS OF WINE!

AVERIE. Oh, you playin' now? How many is that?

FIDEL. THREE.

DONNIE. A TREE?

AVERIE. No THREE! Ignore that. FIND A BLUE SWEATER IN THE CLOSET, PUT THE WRAPPING PAPER ON THE TABLE, POUR DRUNK SHELLY A GLASS OF WINE…FIND THE SNOWMAN ON THE TREE AND…

DOTTY. PLAY "HAVE YOURSELF A MERRY LITTLE CHRISTMAS" ON THE PIANO.

DONNIE. WHAT??!

DOTTY. PLAY "HAVE YOURSELF—

DONNIE. I HEARD YOU…I HAVEN'T PLAYED IN YEARS.

AVERIE. YOU GOT IT?

SHELLY. Let's get this show on the road. I've got to pick up my boy and Christmas Eve dinner is going to get cold.

AVERIE. GO!

FIDEL. GO!

DONNIE. FIND A BLUE SWEATER IN THE CLOSET, PUT THE WRAPPING PAPER ON THE TABLE, POUR SHELLY A GLASS OF WINE…FIND THE SNOWMAN ON THE TREE AND…PLAY "HAVE YOURSELF A MERRY LITTLE CHRISTMAS" ON THE PIANO. Okay. I got it.

> (AVERIE *has pulled out her phone and takes a photo of* DONNIE *with the flash on.*)

AVERIE. Donnie! Smile.

FIDEL. GO!

> (DONNIE *begins the task of walking towards the closet. Turns out to be the front door.* ADAM *jumps in to help navigate him away from the front door.*)

ADAM. Front door.

DONNIE. The door looks the same.

> (*He opens the closet door and begins his search for the blue sweater.*)

What am I looking for?

ADAM. The—

JACKIE. Shh, you're not supposed to help.

ADAM. Right.

DONNIE. A blue sweater.

>   (*He struggles to find this.*)

This is black. A black coat. I need a sweater. Blue. A blue sweater.

>   (*He finds his mother's blue cardigan.*)

I got the blue sweater.

>   (*He holds the sweater and then thinks of the next task.*)

Now I was supposed to do what now? Snowman. A snowman on the tree. I'll put this here. Do I need to keep it? Or put it down or something.

>   (*No one answers. They begin to get wrapped up in the exercise.*)

I'll put it down.

>   (*He looks around for the best place to put it down. He goes over to the table and pulls out the chair and puts it down. He bumps into the furniture. The sweater is now on the floor.*)

Ow, shit. Oh my God I can't hear myself think. What was I doing?

>   (*He picks up the sweater and then puts it on the table. He begins to get very annoyed and panicky. He goes over to the closet and looks in it. Looking for something but he is not sure of what?*)

Snowman. Snowman. THIS NOISE IS DRIVING ME CRAZY!!! Okay. Okay. Alright. Alright. FUUUCK!!!

>   (*He pulls out some coats and boots and things.*)

Where did I just put the sweater? The blue sweater. I found the blue sweater. Now the snowman. No the snowman would be on the tree.

>   (*He starts putting the coats and boots and things away. Then gets the blue sweater and puts it away in the closet.*)

Now what?

SHELLY. POUR ME A GLASS OF WINE.

AVERIE. Shhh—

DONNIE. Right.

>   (DONNIE *stumbles around the dining room.*)

Wine. Wine. This isn't wine. Is this vinegar? Wrong. I can't find it. Is there wine in here or in the living room? Is it on the table?

>   (*He comes back into the living room.*)

Did I get the snowman on the tree? I'll get that and then I will worry about your wine. I can't THINK!

>   (*He goes over to the tree. And almost brings it down.*)

JACKIE. Be careful! The TREE!!!

DONNIE. WHAT??

(DONNIE *stares at* JACKIE. *He is now confused and can't think. He is getting flushed. He looks at his mother. They stare at each other. This is an unspoken agreement.* DOTTY *stands.*)

DOTTY. You see.

(*Silence.*
Silence.
Silence.
Silence.
Silence.)

ADAM. Donnie you alright?

DONNIE. (*Soberly.*) I'm fine. I'm fine.

(*He's heard his mother say this a lot especially after she looks very confused and lost.* DONNIE *rips the headset off of his head and the tape, latex gloves and kicks off his shoes. He looks longingly at* DOTTY. *He NOW understands the trauma, the REALITY of what his mother is going through or what she WILL go through. He goes over to the dining table to make himself a plate.*)

DONNIE. When is dinner time?

ADAM. Donnie are you okay?

DONNIE. Are we going to eat soon? I need to eat!

SHELLY. I have to get Jason and then we'll eat.

AVERIE. HOLD UP! Donnie. You alright?

(DONNIE, *quietly unhinged, grabs a plate and quietly, methodically, starts piling food on his plate.*)

ADAM. Donnie you alright?

AVERIE. You sweating.

DONNIE. I don't know how you are getting through each day.

DOTTY. You understand. He understands.

DONNIE. It's horrible. I'm starving.

(DONNIE *continues to pile food on his plate.*)

SHELLY. IT'S NOT TIME YET!!!

DONNIE. IT'S TIME! The bell has gone off! I'M AWAKE. I get it.

AVERIE. What the fuck?

ADAM. DONNIE CALM DOWN. YOU'RE HAVING ANOTHER ANXIETY ATTACK!!!

SHELLY. Donnie put that down—

AVERIE. Stop controlling people.

DOTTY. You understand.

(DOTTY *turns on the recorder. She is very still with a serene smile on her face, taking in this pandemonium.*)

DONNIE. I'm terrified for you.

FIDEL. Your feet are in her shoes.

SHELLY. Donnie you are ruining dinner!

DONNIE. I shouldn't have come home! Watching you like this Mom tears my heart apart.

DOTTY. JASON!

SHELLY. Jason is not here Mom.

ADAM. Everything is fine.

DONNIE. Everything is not fine.

ADAM. So let's do the work.

DONNIE. I'm so scared.

ADAM. Me too. It's okay.

DONNIE. We have to get her what she needs.

SHELLY. Finally things are starting to make sense around here.

AVERIE. You alright Mom? Why is the tape recorder on? Mom?

(DOTTY *doesn't acknowledge her daughter.*)

DONNIE. Everything is in danger of vanishing. You, me, all of us.

ADAM. It is!!! And that's LIFE!

AVERIE. Mom?

SHELLY. Mom I'm taking you upstairs.

DONNIE. Stop bossing us around!!!

AVERIE. Yeah, you ain't the boss of me!

SHELLY. (*She flips her wig.*) I'M JUST TRYING TO GET SOME SANITY IN THIS HOUSE!!!!!!!!!!

JACKIE. I should go.

AVERIE. Bye, girl, bye!

ADAM. Donnie, stop it with the food.

DONNIE. Why, because I am so fucking old and obese?

ADAM. I NEVER SAID THAT!!!

DONNIE. YOU DID.

ADAM. NO, I DIDN'T!!!

AVERIE. Who gives a shit! There is a woman with ALZHEIMER'S IN THIS HOUSE you selfish fucks.

(*The sound of a text message on* AVERIE'*s phone comes in. She checks her phone excitedly.*)

DONNIE. When I was 13, I thought I would be my best at 40! Didn't we Jackie?

JACKIE. Ummmm?—

DONNIE. We looked forward to 40! Knowing more. Right?

JACKIE. I'm a mess.

DONNIE. I want to grow gray hair and wear AGE APPROPRIATE clothes. No! I don't want to do Tina, or Molly, or some other drug that sounds like your best white girlfriend!

JACKIE. (*Whimpers.*) I USED TO BE YOUR BEST WHITE GIRLFRIEND!!!

(JACKIE *runs into the kitchen.*)

DONNIE. I WANT TO BE A DADDY!

ADAM. Is this what is going on with you? A mid-life crisis???

(DONNIE *eats!*)

AVERIE. You alright Mom? She's not answering me y'all? Mom you alright?

SHELLY. (*Soberly.*) Take her upstairs!

(AVERIE *has pulled out some hair grease and is parting and greasing her mother's head.*)

DONNIE. I don't want to put her to sleep!

SHELLY. I don't want to put her to sleep either. She's fading away, can't you see!

DONNIE. You can't control everything Shelly!!!

ADAM. I'll get the Xanax!!!

(ADAM *charges upstairs.*)

SHELLY. I know I can't control everything. It's happening.

(DOTTY *just smiles and stares off into space. They all finally notice. Silence.*)

SHELLY. I've watched it every day.

AVERIE. (*Whispered.*) Mom?

SHELLY. This doesn't get better.

AVERIE. (*Whispered.*) Mom?

SHELLY. In and out, In and out, In and out. 'Til one day it's just out.

AVERIE. (*Whispered.*) Mom do you hear me?

(*Silence.*
Silence.
Silence.
DONNIE *goes over to the piano and bangs on the keys.*)

DOTTY. Play it Son. Play it for Grandma.

(DONNIE*'s banging turns into "Have Yourself a Merry Little Christmas."*
AVERIE *calmly continues to cornrow her mother's hair.*
JACKIE *bursts into a quiet flood of tears and runs into the kitchen.*
FIDEL *tries to clean up with* SHELLY.)

DOTTY. Grandma always wore white for some reason. Her hair in big Indian braids.

AVERIE. Mom? Why are you talking about Grandma.

DOTTY. What? (*She laughs.*)

AVERIE. Mom?

DOTTY. Richard was too hard on you all. I'm sorry he whooped y'all so much and I did nothing. He whooped me too. When he drank. He was in pain. This life. This world. Drank himself to death. In my arms. Cold as a stone. He said, the world was set up against him and it made him sad and bitter. He cried in bed at night. I would hold him and tried to pick him back up. Race. He said it was race and inequality. When that lady sued him for malpractice and won, he said the system was trying to break him. He drank and I held him. I held on to him. A black man in America.

>   (*Silence.*)

AVERIE. Mom?

DOTTY. Yes?

AVERIE. Do you know who I am?

DOTTY. Why you asking me that? Of course I do. Yes, you're my baby.

AVERIE. Yes, I'm your baby, Mommy.

DOTTY. (*Referring to SHELLY and laughing.*) Who's that cleaning lady? I don't know her.

>   (*This hits SHELLY like a ton of bricks.*)

AVERIE. That's Shelly Mom.

DOTTY. Shelly?

AVERIE. And that's Donnie.

DOTTY. (*To DONNIE.*) Looking just like your father. Descendants of the Masai.

>   (DONNIE *plays tenderly.*)

AVERIE. Come on Mom, let me take you upstairs.

DOTTY. Who put the stairs over here? Did we move?

AVERIE. No Mom. We're still here. A little raw and open but we're still here.

>   (FIDEL *goes over to help* AVERIE *get* DOTTY *upstairs.* DOTTY *looks over to* DONNIE *playing.*)

DOTTY. Richard.

>   (FIDEL *and* AVERIE *take* DOTTY *upstairs.*
>   DONNIE *continues to play.*)

SHELLY. (*She begins to crack.*) I'm the cleaning lady. I'm the cleaning lady.

>   (SHELLY *goes down to the basement.*)

WRAPPING IT ALL FOR JASON

DONNIE *continues to play the piano in the living room. The scene transitions to late that night. Everything is cleaned up. Blue Spruce glitters in all its glory. There is a dim light on in the kitchen.* ADAM *comes down the stairs and just watches* DONNIE *playing.*

ADAM. (*Lovingly.*) You coming up?

(DONNIE *doesn't answer or look at* ADAM. *He just plays.* ADAM *waits for a bit, then decides to go, but—*)

DONNIE. It's something, the way your hands remember something that you thought was lost long ago. Locked deep in your memory. I haven't played in years. I didn't know that I could anymore.

(*He plays the piano with his back to* ADAM.)

My dad made sure that I had lessons. It was very important to him that I did beautiful things with my hands. When he was a child he said he worked with his father sanding hardwood floors and he watched his father break his back and his spirit. He told me that his father told him not to do any hard labor but either heal or do beautiful things with his hands.

ADAM. You told me how much of a respected doctor he was.

DONNIE. He wasn't. He was a broken man. His drinking got in the way of his practice. This world broke him. He became abusive. Not physically but you know…mentally. Although I know he loved me. Instilling values and ideals and…I don't know what I'm saying…but with so much volcanic passion. I played the piano for him.

ADAM. How come you never told me you played piano?

DONNIE. It was too attached to him, I guess. But I do. I haven't played in years.

ADAM. Not bad.

DONNIE. We would have these family gatherings where we were our own little musical evening. Shelly doing some dance from Swan Lake, Averie singing her heart out and me on piano. At the best of times we appeared to be a perfect little middle-class family. Then…when Dad died…suddenly, that just sent us all reeling. Trying to patch up the hole that he left in this family a long time ago. He was a sad man. I only really played for him. He made me. Watched me with such pride in his eyes. We were his dreams for this neighborhood.

ADAM. I think you all made good on his dreams.

(ADAM *puts on a recording of "Have Yourself a Merry Little Christmas" on the record player.* DONNIE *finally stops playing.* DONNIE *still keeps his focus off of* ADAM.)

Sometimes I forget. We all forget. The origins of love or...trauma. You know? But it is marked all over ourselves and we are always carrying it. Trauma. At times it rears its head when we least expect. And that's okay. It's okay. I think being family, we have to know that and be patient with one another. And trust that if there is enough love there that we will keep finding a way in to one another. Especially if you know their heart. I don't care about anything more than YOU. You hear me?

DONNIE. I don't want to be like that guy...that guy who wrote that book. *The Right Side of 40? The Complete Guide to Happiness for Gay Men at Midlife and Beyond?*

ADAM. I didn't read it.

DONNIE. He was all about 40 being the new 30. He killed himself at 48 and there was a note that he left that said "It's a lie based on bad information" with an arrow pointing towards the title of the book!

ADAM. Wow.

DONNIE. Yeah, wow.

ADAM. I don't know—maybe I am having a little bit of a midlife crisis but honestly I think it just takes some gays longer to finally express themselves and POSSIBLY we do revert to these high school archetypes because, let's face it high school was TERRIBLE for us. I was a nerd. And so were you! And now we're 40 and we can afford to have the things that we missed out on but we are just trying it on for size. But that stuff doesn't last. I know this! I want a family. I want what you want. And I don't care if you've got a little around the middle! I just want us to be healthy. (*Suddenly deeply emotional.*) Because I want you and I to be around for a long time.

(DONNIE *finally gives in and looks at* ADAM.)

You're my best friend. Be patient with me. I love you chipmunk.

(ADAM *kisses* DONNIE *sweetly.*)

DONNIE. And I did look good in those skinny jeans!

ADAM. But all I was saying was that I had the same pair—get another color!

(JACKIE *appears from the kitchen.*)

JACKIE. I don't know how long I can lay on the floor of your kitchen. I should go home. It's late.

DONNIE. I'm sorry for the little floor show tonight.

JACKIE. Don't be sorry. Are you okay?

DONNIE. I think so.

JACKIE. It's the holidays. (*Beat.*) Well good night.

ADAM. We should walk you home.

JACKIE. I'm fine.

DONNIE. No, you can't walk out there at this time of night by yourself.

JACKIE. It's actually almost time for the sun to come up. It's quiet. I like this time of night or…day.

DONNIE. James Baldwin says that four a.m. is the most devastating hour.

JACKIE. Why?

DONNIE. Because you have a choice to stay in the darkness or prepare for the light. Because there will always be light.

JACKIE. I like that. There will always be light. I will hold on to that.

ADAM. That contemporary black writers course we took together really paid off.

DONNIE. Shelly told me that you are pregnant.

JACKIE. I told her not to tell you.

DONNIE. Then why'd you tell her?

JACKIE. You got a point. I don't know. I needed some perspective, I guess. On this messy thing called life.

DONNIE. It's messy as fuck.

JACKIE. And I am WINNING!!!

DONNIE. You'll be alright.

JACKIE. You know, you fucked me up for any other man.

DONNIE. Don't be silly, we were kids.

JACKIE. You were my first. And you were so nice. And sweet. And funny.

DONNIE. And gay.

JACKIE. Gay boys make the best husbands. They do you know.

DONNIE. You are so crazy.

JACKIE. I know. (*Beat.*) When did you know? Did you know even when you were with me?

DONNIE. We are not having this conversation. We were together over twenty years ago.

JACKIE. I never got a chance to ask.

(*Silence.*)

DONNIE. Well…I fought it, you know? It wasn't like it is now when kids can identify with another gender and it is widely accepted. Little Christina can be Chris and no one bats an eye. I had no role models of what being gay was. We came into our sexuality in the mid-80's. And our pioneers were dying off. I certainly did not want to be gay. So…I was with my closest friend. The crazy girl from around the corner that I laughed the most with. Trying to be "normal." Until I could not try to be whatever normal was any more.

(*Silence.*)

JACKIE. So…I didn't turn you gay?

DONNIE. You can't turn somebody gay, stupid.

JACKIE. Aww you called me stupid. Like old times.

(JACKIE *kisses* DONNIE *on the lips. Silence.*)

Nothing? Really. Nothing?

(*They laugh.*)

But you look so STRAIGHT! You look good!

DONNIE. That's how the gay boys do it. Gotta stay healthy and fit! I want to be around for a long time. I got a lot to stay around for.

JACKIE. Well…for now I have a late Zipcar. They are going to be in my ass.

DONNIE. You drove a Zipcar down here?

JACKIE. I was on the lam.

ADAM. From who or where?

JACKIE. From New York. From A Hot Latin Married Man. Me. My choices. Probably stemmed from the loss of my parents, having a gay high school sweetheart, and being a white girl who grew up in an all-black neighborhood. You process a lot on a kitchen floor late at night.

DONNIE. Or having a full-on meltdown in front of your family on Christmas Eve.

JACKIE. That was full out.

DONNIE. I just got off of a fast.

JACKIE. A detox will fuck you up.

DONNIE. Trying to make healthy choices will do that.

(ADAM *has been getting coats and boots for* DONNIE *and* JACKIE *and himself to walk her home during this.*)

ADAM. We know you feel safe and you want a quiet walk but we would feel better if you'd let us walk you home.

JACKIE. Okay. Okay. It's the hood, THE HOOD!!! (*Beat.*) I heard you two making up. I am glad you can do that. Nice to see when a couple can work it out. I'm telling you. It's dark out here! You have to fight for one another. Not that I know, I'm chronically single! But from what I see out here, that is the best kind of love. The love when you fight to love each other. Fight to hold on.

(SHELLY *comes up from the basement with a trunk.*)

SHELLY. She has been fighting to hold on for a while.

JACKIE. I told you that there is no carrying of a flame whatsoever.

SHELLY. Not you Jackie. Our mother. This old trunk filled with family albums, report cards, newspaper clippings of when Clinton won, Obama won, family reunion t-shirts, cassette tapes… Trying to hold the memories.

Locking them in a box. Fighting to hold on. (*Beat.*) She has been doing this for a while. For me. For you. For all of us. For this neighborhood, For Jason.

(AVERIE *comes down the stairs.*)

AVERIE. I went and picked him up from your neighbors after I put Mom to bed. He is sleeping in my old room. I thought you needed some time to yourself down there. I mean, you got me and Jason at home, Mom over here, you work all the time. You're welcome.

SHELLY. Well…thank you. Is Mom alright?

(*Silence.*)

AVERIE. I don't know. But we should sit down and talk rationally and see what needs to happen. But most importantly we have to involve her. We can't talk AROUND her Shelly.

DONNIE. She's right.

SHELLY. She is. Oh my God. You're RIGHT. I'm a pain in the ass.

DONNIE. Language.

SHELLY. And so are you.

DONNIE. Me?

AVERIE. Yes, you're a pain in the ass.

DONNIE. I know.

SHELLY. Especially to him.

ADAM. I'm a pain in the ass too.

AVERIE. You're perfect for each other.

ADAM. We are.

AVERIE. Shelly, I'm going to move in here for a while if it's okay with Mom—

SHELLY. Okay—

AVERIE. Get out of your basement and help out more, like I should—

SHELLY. Okay—

AVERIE. That's what I can do right now. Until I can make some REAL money—

SHELLY. Fine.

(FIDEL *comes down the stairs.*)

Fidel what are you still doing here??? You should have gone home.

FIDEL. It's okay. It's good to be here. I don't mind.

SHELLY. Don't you got your own family you should be spending Christmas with?

FIDEL. In Kazakhstan.

SHELLY. Oh okay.

AVERIE. THAT'S how you pronounce it!

ADAM. When's the last time you've been home?

FIDEL. Nine years ago.

DONNIE. Nine years ago!!!

AVERIE. Did he say nine years ago?

SHELLY. Is there an echo? He said nine years ago. Why?

FIDEL. I have been trying to get my asylum. Political asylum. You can be hurt if you are political activist in my country. I tried to make a difference for people in my country. But I was against the establishment. That is a no no. My family was scared for me and helped me get into this program where I came to this country to help handicapped adults at a camp in California. I stayed and taught myself English by watching the movies *Poetic Justice* and *My Best Friend's Wedding*. You know those?

AVERIE. Regina King is the truth.

FIDEL. I watched them over and over again. And lots of TV. You learn so much more than English. You learn behavior. Um, how can I say this? African-American people are just like Kazakhs. Just another color. You are very colorful.

AVERIE. Colorful?

FIDEL. Especially you. Remind me of my sister. Everyone has a sister like you at home.

AVERIE. I even blew up in Kazakhstan! Woop Woop!

FIDEL. I have been able to figure out how it all works here but it is hard but I try. It's better than home. Although I miss my home.

SHELLY. Don't you have an immigration attorney?

(DOTTY *comes down the stairs.*)

FIDEL. I had three. My case is now at ninth circuit of appeals and I am hoping that the new law office that has my case will help this to be my last time in court. If I win, I can stay and get green card, if I don't I—

SHELLY. What new law office?

FIDEL. Bailey Banks and—

SHELLY. Goldstein???

FIDEL. That's it!

SHELLY. That's my office.

DOTTY. That's right!

(*Everyone says something to the tune of "Mom you alright?" "Mrs. Shealy you okay?"*)

I'm alright. I'm alright. At least right now. (*Beat.*) I'm here. I put some copies of his papers in a folder on your desk in your office.

SHELLY. What? Why? Is that what that was?

DOTTY. I want you to help him.

SHELLY. I am a public defender.

DOTTY. The trunk! // You found the key!

SHELLY. // I was just looking around in it Mom. I found the key. I forgot I had it. I forgot!

DOTTY. I've been preserving these for you all. For the next generation.

SHELLY. I see Mom.

DOTTY. You can help Fidel.

SHELLY. I don't know anything about immigration.

DOTTY. You can figure it out. We look to you for that.

SHELLY. You do?

DOTTY. We always have.

AVERIE. That's true. In spite of myself, it's true. You're no Iyanla, but you do try to fix my life.

SHELLY. Fidel, I'll see what I can do.

(FIDEL*'s alarm goes off! It is a Christmas melody.*)

FIDEL. It's time Mrs. Shealy.

DOTTY. It's time!

SHELLY. Time for what?

DOTTY. Did you forget? It's Christmas! Plug in all the lights! Eat the cookies that were laid out for Santa.

(*Everyone does so.*)

AVERIE. Ahem! I'd like to sing a little carol if you don't mind. I got a text from my agent last night in the middle of Donnie's fit, that I got an audition for "America's Singing They Ass Off" or something like that! Donnie?

(DONNIE *gets on the piano and plays.* AVERIE *sings "Have Yourself a Merry Little Christmas."*)

SHELLY. (*Whispers.*) Mom? Your tape recorder.

DOTTY. What do you want me to do with that honey?

SHELLY. Just speak into it.

DOTTY. What time is it?

(SHELLY *turns on the tape recorder.*)

SHELLY. This is for Jason.

DOTTY. Who's Jason?

SHELLY. Your grandson.

DOTTY. I'm too young to have grandkids.

SHELLY. Then I will tell you a story. Okay? We will record it.

(DOTTY *sings "Have Yourself a Merry Little Christmas."*)

SHELLY. Jason. This is the moment before you come down. Your family is all here. It's Christmas Day.

DOTTY. (*Suddenly.*) The moment we are born we are taking steps to get back home. Like E.T. Phone Home.

SHELLY. Even if our future is not what we had in mind. We just have to believe that there is a reason for it all. (*Beat.*) You are our future. Hold it. Hold the stories of our neighborhoods. Our families. Our hearts. This is what your grandmother is trying to tell you. This is the last Christmas that we are all here. For the most part. She wants you to know what you are made of. We will try to record it all. It may sound like a jumbled mess but someday I hope that you will make lemonade out of it.

(DOTTY *looks at* SHELLY.)

SHELLY. (*To* DOTTY.) Ready?

(DOTTY *just smiles wide and looks around at the lights and people. She is delighted and a little confused. What is happening? Where is she? How did she get there?*)

SHELLY. (*Whispers into the tape recorder.*) Remember this. Remember all of this. Pass it on. (*Then—*) Jason it's time!!! Merry Christmas!!!

(*Everyone yells for Jason to come down!!! We hear the sound of Donnie Hathaway's "This Christmas" to send us home.*)

End of Play

THE GLORY OF THE WORLD
by Charles Mee

ABOUT *THE GLORY OF THE WORLD*

This article first ran in the Limelight *Guide to the 39th Humana Festival of New American Plays, published by Actors Theatre of Louisville, and is based on conversations with the creative team before rehearsals for the Humana Festival production began.*

On Fourth Street in downtown Louisville, in the middle of a busy corner, stands a remarkable plaque—a marker commemorating not a historical event or building, but an epiphany experienced by Thomas Merton, the Kentucky-based Trappist monk, activist, and prolific writer of more than 70 books. In his *Conjectures of a Guilty Bystander*, Merton recounted the 1958 revelation recognized on the plaque, a discovery which led him to question his monastic separation from the world and to engage in social justice causes: "In Louisville, at the corner of Fourth and Walnut, in the center of the shopping district, I was suddenly overwhelmed with the realization that I loved all those people, that they were mine and I theirs, that we could not be alien to one another even though we were total strangers... There is no way of telling people that they are all walking around shining like the sun."

During his first several years living in Louisville, Actors Theatre Artistic Director Les Waters walked past this spot every day, and marveled that a memorial to a metaphysical revelation existed on a bustling urban sidewalk. When he read more about Merton, a leading figure in 20th-century spiritual thought who spent 27 years at the Abbey of Gethsemani near Bardstown, Kentucky, Waters' fascination grew—alongside a keen interest in producing work about subjects with local resonance. He was also planning to embark on a project with longtime friend and frequent collaborator Charles Mee, a Humana Festival veteran whose provocative, wide-ranging writings and collage techniques have been a groundbreaking force in the American theatre over the past several decades.

Realizing that 2015 marks what would have been Thomas Merton's 100th birthday, Waters and Mee decided to collaborate on a play about Merton, and Mee accepted a commission to write it. ("I said, 'Sure,' because I'm crazy about Les—I love how he thinks about the theatre—and I love the Humana Festival, so that was easy," Mee reports.) The piece that grew out of that conversation is distinctly not a docudrama or neat biographical narrative, but rather a wildly theatrical exploration of the myriad points of view on Merton the spiritual and political writer, priest and poet. And at its heart, this play— aptly titled *The Glory of the World*—is a huge birthday party. An event that Merton would have enjoyed, if you will.

Merton's was a life lived both in quiet meditation and the noise of the world, and Mee's play adopts a structure that reflects those dualities, beginning in silence and evolving toward cacophonous celebration. It unfolds as a series of toasts that erupt into a raucous party. The giver of each toast is eager to claim Merton for his own school of thought. Was Merton primarily a Catholic, as his vows indicate? A Zen Buddhist, where his spiritual interests led him later in life? A pacifist whose anti-war advocacy was well known? A Communist? A mystic, bohemian, or adventurer? "I was writing—thrown into the middle of a birthday party, imagining what these people would say—and it just happened," says Mee of the play's dialectical flow. But its multifaceted perspectives on Merton also speak to the seeming contradictions of a man who valued solitude and social activism, whose thinking was too expansive to fit into a linear, easily-explained story. "I think, fundamentally, that our lives are more complicated than that," Mee muses. "It's not A causes B causes C causes D. It's really like this: A causes B causes C causes 236 causes purple causes everybody to dance. At least, that's more how my life has been."

Speaking of dance, *The Glory of the World*'s action spans the extremes from quiet listening to exuberant physical spectacle. Waters credits Mee with encouraging his own interest in "things that go from absolute stillness to noise and chaos," and in the electricity that results from juxtaposing contrasting elements. Mee explains his own instinct thus: "I love everything that can happen in the theatre—music and dance and movement and text and everything else." Accordingly, this is a play and production that tangles with big philosophical quandaries through a vibrant and constantly changing visual world. Without spoiling too many surprises, let's just say that there's some drinking, some dancing (choreographed by SITI Company's Barney O'Hanlon), singing and more, as the perspectives on Merton tumble forth and his birthday party rages on.

The piece's progression also allows Mee to pose some of the biggest questions of existence that Merton grappled with, through ruminations on the necessity of love, the quest for happiness, and seeking a kind of heaven on earth. "I threw myself into the material in the way that I imagine Merton threw himself into his wandering meditations," the playwright says of his journey through various sources to create the play's shifting arguments. At one point, the play posits the act of writing itself as a kind of life everlasting, a way for a consciousness to permanently live on. Through the accumulation of all these hopes, *The Glory of the World* is a truly joyous, rollicking party of a play that considers how we can live fully in all our contradictions, and leap into the unknown.

—Amy Wegener

BIOGRAPHY

Charles Mee has written six plays that have premiered at the Humana Festival: *Big Love*, *Limonade Tous les Jours*, *bobrauschenbergamerica*, *Hotel Cassiopeia*, *Under Construction*, and *The Glory of the World*. Mee's plays have been performed at Signature Theatre, BAM, New York Theatre Workshop, The Public Theater, Lincoln Center for the Performing Arts, Steppenwolf Theatre Company, American Repertory Theater, and other theatres around the country as well as in Berlin, Paris, Amsterdam, Brussels, Vienna, Istanbul, and elsewhere. All his plays are available on the Internet at www.charlesmee.org. Among other awards, Mee is the recipient of an Obie and the Lifetime Achievement Award in drama from the American Academy of Arts and Letters.

ACKNOWLEDGMENTS

The Glory of the World premiered at the Humana Festival of New American Plays in March 2015. It was directed by Les Waters with the following cast:

ALBERT	Bruce McKenzie
BENNY	Andrew Garman
CAMERON	David Ryan Smith
CONRAD	Conrad Schott
ROBERT	Aaron Lynn
ROLAND	Eric Berryman
ARNOLD	Ramiz Monsef
BOBBY	Barney O'Hanlon
A MAN	Les Waters
ENSEMBLE	Josh Bonzie, John Ford-Dunker, José Leon, Joe Lino, Max Monnig, Collin Morris, Brian Muldoon, Blake Russell, Lorenzo Villanueva

and the following production staff:

Scenic Designer	Dane Laffrey
Costume Designer	Connie Furr Soloman
Lighting Designer	Mark Barton
Sound Designer	Christian Frederickson
Media Designer	Philip Allgeier
Production Stage Manager	Paul Mills Holmes
Assistant Stage Manager	Jessica Kay Potter
Dramaturg	Amy Wegener
Casting	Zan Sawyer-Dailey
Fight Director	Ryan Bourque
Movement Director	Barney O'Hanlon
Properties Master	Mark Walston

Assistant Director..John Rooney
Assistant Dramaturg ....Ariel Sibert

The Glory of the World was commissioned by Actors Theatre of Louisville and was developed at the 2014 Perry-Mansfield New Works Festival in Steamboat Springs, Colorado. Commission supported by the 50th Anniversary Theatre Forward/Ford Foundation Fund for New Work.

CHARACTERS

ALBERT
ARNOLD
BENNY
BOBBY
CAMERON
CONRAD
ROBERT
ROLAND
CHORUS
A MAN

Ramiz Monsef, Collin Morris, Barney O'Hanlon, Joe Lino,
Lorenzo Villanueva, and David Ryan Smith
in *The Glory of the World*

39th Humana Festival of New American Plays
Actors Theatre of Louisville, 2015
Photo by Bill Brymer

THE GLORY OF THE WORLD

A MAN *is sitting at a table with his back to us, listening, and his thoughts are projected on the walls.*

Listen, it's raining

> (*SILENCE.*)

All of this ambient and low, all of it far away

> (*SILENCE*
> *SILENCE*
> *SILENCE*
> *SILENCE*
> *SILENCE*
> *SILENCE.*)

There is a bubbling—metallic—behind me

> (*SILENCE*
> *SILENCE*
> *SILENCE.*)

Something whispers, slithers and then stops

> (*SILENCE*
> *SILENCE*
> *SILENCE*
> *SILENCE.*)

Crunch of shoes on sidewalk
Like sound of peanuts being cracked

> (*SILENCE*
> *SILENCE*
> *SILENCE*
> *SILENCE*
> *SILENCE.*)

Door clicks behind very near

> (*SILENCE.*)

Door slam to the left
Door slam to the left
Car starting up on the left
Car driving away

> (*SILENCE*
> *SILENCE.*)

Sound of a bike or an insect

(*SILENCE*
SILENCE
SILENCE.)

Very faint yelp, first voice of any kind
It's a screeching sort of bark

(*SHORT PAUSE.*
And then some guys enter, holding glasses of bourbon, looking happily at one
another.)

EVERYONE SINGING. Happy Birthday to you
Happy Birthday to you
Happy Birthday, dear Thomas
Happy 100th birthday to you.

(*It is the most varied cast ever seen on a stage—varied by race, age, personal*
grooming, hairstyles, costume, behavior—but all men:

ROLAND
ROBERT

ALBERT
ARNOLD

BENNY
BOBBY

CAMERON
CONRAD

and
a swimmer in a swimming suit
a basketball player
an electrician
a football player
a policeman
a truck driver
a waiter
a doctor
a couple guys with rifles
etc.
etc.
etc.

And one of them proposes a celebratory toast.)

ALBERT. I'd like to propose a toast.
To the great Thomas Merton.
I mean, the reason I'm here

the reason I've come to this 100th birthday party for Merton
is because Thomas Merton was such a guy for me
for my life
for how I've spent my entire life ever since
always thinking of him as I went forward
with his deep, deep commitment to peace
his adamant anti-war stance
his forthright engagement with the
great, profound, everlastingly important cause of world peace
his pacifism
which remains forever
an inspiration to us all.
So:

To Thomas Merton.

>*(All drink,*
>*and*
>*here in the beginning*
>*even though they may disagree from time to time*
>*everyone is being sociable and agreeable*
>*for the sake of a nice party.)*

BENNY. I would like to propose a toast, too, if I may.
And, if I may,
I would propose a toast not to Merton's pacifism
I mean that's OK,
that's totally OK, but
I don't think Thomas Merton was
fundamentally
a great pacifist.
I'm here today because,
as a Buddhist,
he's been a great inspiration to me, too—
not for his commitment to worldly things
outside in the noise
well, the politics of the world
but for his commitment to solitude and meditation
to simply sitting in a room
and letting his mind and spirit roam
through thought and feeling
for being at peace with himself.
An impulse that drew him in to an engagement
with his deepest, most profound, quiet, isolated self,

and which, of course,
I acknowledge
if we all did the same
would result,
secondarily,
in pacifism.

To Thomas Merton.
ALL. To Thomas Merton.
CAMERON. If I may, I would like to propose a toast, too.
As with all of you,
Thomas Merton has been a great inspiration to me
for my entire life
and that is why I have come today,
to pay tribute to that.
And so I would like to offer a toast to Merton
not Merton the pacifist or the meditator in solitude—
which I think are not things that speak to his essential being really
but really,
if you want to get fundamentally to his fundamental heart and soul
underlying all he felt and believed and did
we really are speaking of the elements that actually precede
such things as pacifism and meditation
we are speaking of an engagement with the deep
underlying fundamentals
that are the cause of things that finally come to disturb
someone who also desires peace and quiet and meditation
that is to say
we are speaking of fundamental rightness
and goodness and justice in the world
in the air we breathe
and the culture we live in
and so
I would like to offer a toast
to Thomas Merton
the Communist.

CONRAD. Because, as Merton himself said,
"The peace the world pretends to desire
is really no peace at all.
To some men,
peace merely means the liberty to exploit other people
without fear of retaliation or interference.

To others,
peace means the freedom to rob brothers without interruption.
To still others,
it means the leisure to devour the goods of the earth
without being compelled to interrupt their pleasures
to feed those whom their greed is starving.
And to practically everybody,
peace simply means the absence of any physical violence
that might cast a shadow over lives
devoted to the satisfaction of their animal appetites
for comfort and pleasure."

CAMERON. And so,
I would like to drink
to Thomas Merton, the Communist.

CONRAD. To Thomas Merton, the Communist.

ALL. To Thomas Merton, the Communist.

ROBERT. Well…
I mean…
Communist…
I mean…I guess…
briefly…

CAMERON. As George Bernard Shaw said:
I am a Christian.
And that obliges me to be a Communist.

ALBERT. Yeah. Well.
Or, as H.L. Mencken said:
The only trouble with Communism is the Communists,
just as the only trouble with Christianity is the Christians.

CONRAD. Or, as Jenny Holzer said:
If you behaved nicely,
the Communists wouldn't exist.

CAMERON. And then, too,
as Albert Einstein said:
The world is a dangerous place to live,
not because of the people who are evil,
but because of the people who don't do anything about it.

ROLAND. As Lenin said:
Communists have become bureaucrats.
If anything will destroy us, it is this.

ROBERT. As Ronald Reagan said:
How do you tell a Communist?

Well, it's someone who reads Marx and Lenin.
And how do you tell an anti-Communist?
It's someone who understands Marx and Lenin.

ALBERT. As Mae West said:
Between two evils, I always pick the one I never tried before.

ARNOLD. As Leslie Moak Murray said:
There are two kinds of people in the world:
Communists,
and those who love chocolate.

CAMERON. To Thomas Merton, the Communist.

ROLAND. I think, in all our toasting
if we are going to be respectful of the truth
we should not forget to say
that Merton was, after all,
fundamentally fundamentally
a devout Catholic
who believed in God.
He would not want us to forget.
And so
I would like to offer a toast to Merton the Catholic

ALL. To Merton the Catholic

ROLAND. and a toast to God.

ALL. To God.

ROBERT. Well, and not just any Sunday Catholic
but to a seven day a week monk and a priest.
We are toasting someone who was
fundamentally
a monk and a priest.

ROLAND. A faithful Catholic
who believed in Catholicism.

BENNY. I think we have to say, too,
and not just because I'm a Buddhist:
Merton was also fundamentally a mystic!
A great mystic.
One of the great mystics of all times.
And I would offer a toast to Merton the mystic!

BOBBY. And a proponent of interfaith understanding!

CONRAD. And a Communist!

CAMERON. A Communist!

CONRAD. To Thomas Merton, the Communist.

ALBERT. And a hitchhiker!

ARNOLD. And a drinker!

ALBERT. Well,
a party lover
really.
So yes,
a drinker!

ARNOLD. And so,
of course,
a writer!

ALBERT. I think of him as the patron saint of writers!
Writing more than 50 books

ARNOLD. more than 70 books!
10,000 letters
and I don't know how many words

ALBERT. Well, yes,
and a poet!

ARNOLD. A man!!!!
I mean
that is to say
at the same time
both a lover
and the father of an illegitimate child.

ALBERT. Yes.
Right.

CONRAD. Sometimes I think you see
in the world
the kind of real, deep, committed, constant love
that you see when you spend time with
the cicadas in the south of France.
And you remember
there was a time long ago, in prehistoric times
when cicadas were human beings
back before the Muses were born.
And then when the Muses were born
and song came into being
some of these human creatures were so taken by the pleasure of it
that they sang and sang and sang.
And they forgot to eat or drink
they just sang and sang
and so,

before they knew it,
they died.
And from those human creatures a new species came into being
the cicadas
and they were given this special gift from the Muses:
that from the time they are born
they need no nourishment
they just sing continuously
caught forever in the pleasure of the moment
without eating or drinking
until they die.

This is the story of love.
If you stay there forever in that place
you die of it.

That's why people
can't stay in love.

But that's why we all want to be cicadas, really.
Someone who can give themselves to another
entirely
the sort of person who
if they were betrayed in love
would throw rocks
through the window of the person who betrayed them
because the rock thrower was the kind of person
who called up all their old lovers
when they got together with their new love
and said they were no longer available
            (*Turning to* CAMERON.)
but you
you
you insisted your family was your family
and your friends were your friends
and there was no reason to drop family and friends
because it had nothing to do with love affairs
and friendships don't have to end when you stop sleeping with someone
and when I told you I felt jealous
however irrational that was
you said you couldn't be controlled by my irrationality
and you would continue to see your friends
what if I didn't

that was my choice
so when I said then I would see my old lovers
you said, why would you do that, you said you didn't want to
I said I will do it if you do
you said that was infantile
I was doing it just to get back at you
whereas you were doing it because you wanted to do it
and I said then I want to do it, too, I always wanted to do it
and you said you never wanted to do it
I said I got the idea from you, I think it is a good idea
I will do it, too
and you said, if you do, I will leave you without thinking twice about it

you will leave me, I said
you will leave me?
yes, you said,
because you are an adolescent
and I only want a relationship with an adult, you said,
so I said, fine, fine, forget it
see whoever you want
forget it!!!!

> (*He turns abruptly away from* CAMERON
> *and faces in another direction.*
> *Everyone else is awkwardly quiet for a moment,*
> *not knowing quite what to do*
> *until* BOBBY, *looking at* CONRAD,
> *and then at* CAMERON,
> *and then at the crowd,*
> *saves the moment by saying:*)

BOBBY. To Thomas Merton, our hero!

SEVERAL CHORUS MEMBERS. To Thomas Merton!

> (*A guy comes forward with a mike*
> *and starts singing a song*
> *and a couple guys join him for backup.*
> *They sing*
> *sing*
> *sing*
> *sing*
> *sing*
> *sing*
> *sing*
> *sing*

sing
sing
sing
sing
sing
sing
sing.
Another guy listens to the singers for a minute
and then goes out
and comes back in with a big wooden box.
He turns,
takes hold of a bourbon bottle,
turns back,
and
happily
with a big, triumphant smile,
throws it into the wooden box,
and we hear the bottle shatter.
He turns
and finds more bottles and glasses
which he also throws into the box,
shattering them all.

No big deal.
It's happy, raucous party behavior.

Some of the CHORUS MEMBERS *might call out*
"Yeah!"
"All right!"

Another guy watches him throw the first bottle into the box
and the second bottle
and a third bottle,

and then this second guy throws himself to the floor.
Happily.
Smiling.
He gets up and throws himself to the floor again.
And again.

No big deal.
Just his own version of raucous party behavior.

And another guy joins in,
throwing himself to the floor, too.

CONRAD,
watching the guys throw themselves to the floor,
joins in enthusiastically,
and throws himself to the floor, too.
Over and over again.

So the bottle throwing
and the three throwing themselves to the floor
and the singing of the song
are all happening at the same time.

CAMERON *watches* CONRAD *throw himself to the floor.*

In time,
the guy who brought in the box
stands on his head in the box
for a couple of minutes
and emerges a few moments later with a few cuts on his head
and blood all over his face.

Another guy drags the box out.

CONRAD *is now lying on the floor*
exhausted,
not getting up.

CAMERON
leans down and locks lips with CONRAD
and raises him from the floor into a dance.

More music.
With lips permanently locked in a kiss
they keep dancing.

And, in the midst of all the dancing,
has one person sat down on the floor,
and gone into a deep meditation?

And someone else into a series of yoga maneuvers?

CONRAD *stops,*
steps back gently
and tells CAMERON—*sweetly—*
that he is dancing the wrong way,
he should put his hand here,
around CONRAD*'s waist.*

The other dancers all stop to watch CONRAD *and* CAMERON—

and to make sure they are doing the same thing.

CONRAD *and* CAMERON *lock lips and dance again,*
and all the other couples resume dancing, too.

CONRAD *stops for just a moment to correct* CAMERON *again—sweetly—*
how to hold CONRAD*'s hand,*
just where to put his left foot when he first moves,
—moves they both make
and that the other couples imitate.

And then CONRAD *and* CAMERON
are in a respectful conversation
about how to dance properly,
which naturally segues into observations
by everyone, about proper behavior.)

ROBERT. Proper behavior is always proper.

ROLAND. And always correct.

ROBERT. And always correct.

BENNY. And as such
in its own way
though everyone always mocks propriety
and I myself do, too,
as a sort of upper class snobbishness
nonetheless, in its way
it is a kind
of considerateness.

ROBERT. Which is good.

BENNY. A kind of thoughtfulness.

ROBERT. Compassion.

BENNY. Empathy.

ROBERT. An understanding that
in human relationships
there is no innate privilege
that rests on one side or the other.
And so
you could say
propriety
is a form of truth.

CHORUS. And we like the truth.

CHORUS. Truth is good.

CHORUS. If ANYTHING can be said to be true

truth is good.
CHORUS. Right.

ALBERT. I'd like to offer a toast to our little truthful party here itself
and I think Thomas Merton would approve
because a party is a celebration
of the events and qualities of life
life itself
and of happiness itself
and I think that deserves a toast

ARNOLD. Certainly I would drink to happiness
I think Merton was a happy man
Oddly
When you think of all the time he spent alone
you would think he was gloomy or depressed
or just withdrawn
or sort of suspended in nowhereland
but I think with all his engagements
with all his things
he was enormously active
and happy
and I would drink to happiness.

ALBERT. And just simply to fun.
There is nothing wrong with fun.
I like to have fun.
People like to have fun.
Fun is a good thing to have.
It should really be thought of as a virtue
because it does celebrate the gift of life itself.
It takes pleasure in being alive.

Human life.
A thing that some people think
was a gift of God.
I mean
I know
other people—
like myself—
think it evolved from little mucky
one-celled mollusks or something in the ocean
or little blobs in the mud
but even if that was the case
it's not something to be despised

it is rather something to be thought about
contemplated
and enjoyed
—and toasted!

ARNOLD. Being alive is good.
I drink to being alive.

BENNY. And even if you are not living in a nice
middle-class home in the suburbs
or you're not an investment banker
or someone with all the comforts
of a well-financed life in a nice living room
but someone who has chosen
an unconventional life
a life not of an investment banker
but of a florist
or a pastry chef
or someone who runs a Mexican restaurant
this is not an evil or contrary thing to have done
it is simply another avenue of pleasure
potential joy
the relishing of being alive
which is a form of flattery of life itself
a form of flattery of Darwin or God
or whoever else is responsible for where we are
even acknowledging that we have difficulties
with war and with some people who really need help
and more help than we are giving them
still
the alternate life can be the good life, too,
the pastry chef
the balloon manufacturer
the Disneyland ticket taker
the guitar-playing bohemian

ALBERT. I know a lot of people who would like to be bohemians
although they mostly would like to have
five or six million dollars in the hands of a really good
investment manager
so they could be a bohemian and live in the East Village
without worrying
and take walks every day in Tompkins Square Park
where Allen Ginsberg used to hang out
and Jack Kerouac probably

ARNOLD. and everyone still does if they do drugs
and they're homeless

ALBERT. and I love to take a walk there
and think
right
these are the winners
these are the living legacy
of the great beatniks
who showed us
that the way things are
is not the only way they have been
or the only way they can be

ARNOLD. life is full of impossible possibilities
and Tompkins Square Park is the memorial
to possibility

ALBERT. although it is true
that even sitting in the park
letting the time go by
like everyone else
you wish you would have five or six million
in the hands of a good investment manager
so you really know you don't have to worry
you can be at peace
with yourself and with the world
and set an example of how to be—
or just live in a monastery
where you have a roof over your head
and your meals are free

ARNOLD. and your clothes

ALBERT. and you don't have to worry about anything
and then you can hate capitalism
like all the other bohemians
and have contempt for jobs
and for all the conventions of daily life

ARNOLD. Certainly Merton was a bohemian
who lived a bohemian life
and more lives than that
many lives in one really
because also he was an adventurer

ALBERT. a wonderful adventurer in the biggest sense
an explorer

which is the sort of thing we admire
and praise
and name buildings after
and make statues for public parks
to remind the rest of us
to explore the universe ourselves
to be not afraid to leap into the unknown

BENNY. And also,
into a mental
or a spiritual place

BOBBY. A place where you find yourself alone

BENNY. In solitude

ROBERT. With God.

ROLAND. As Robert Schuller said:
Any fool can count the seeds in an apple.
Only God can count all the apples in one seed.

CHORUS. As the poet said, "Only God can make a tree"—
probably, as Woody Allen said,
because it's so hard to figure out how to get the bark on.

CHORUS. As Saint Augustine said:
God is not what you imagine or what you think you understand.
If you understand you have failed.

CHORUS. As Isaac Bashevis Singer said:
Life is God's novel. Let him write it.

CHORUS. As the Reverend Jerry Falwell said:
I feel most ministers who claim they've heard God's voice
are eating too much pizza before they go to bed at night,
and it's really an intestinal disorder, not a revelation.

CHORUS. As Mary Crowley said:
Every evening I turn my worries over to God.
He's going to be up all night anyway.

CHORUS. As Chuck Palahniuk said:
All God does is watch us and kill us when we get boring.
We must never, ever be boring.

BOBBY. When you think about God
sometimes I think:
okay,
heaven.

Well, I don't need to wait till I die
to go to heaven.

I have some heaven right here on earth,
spending time with friends
afternoons on the beach
or just having lunch on the terrace
overlooking all the hills and the beautiful grass
BENNY. or going to the south of France
BOBBY. or to Paris!
I mean, honestly,
I think this is better than the heaven people talk about.
And I think so who needs heaven.
Although
then
of course
I have some hell on earth, too.
BENNY. Really horrible times
not just joking about it
or covering it all up with these unemotional generalizations
like horrible.
BOBBY. And then of course
I might wish I would just be in heaven all the time.
Although I think the times of hell on earth
make me love so much more the times of heaven on earth.
I feel it so much more intensely.
And I think the heaven everyone talks about
in the afterlife
doesn't it get a little boring?
Just going on day after day in that bland sort of heaven
or even if it is ecstatic heaven all the time
wouldn't you need a break
and a little change of pace
just to really remember to enjoy it
to relish it deeply?
So I'm not really eager to go to heaven in the afterlife
and honestly
I think heaven in the afterlife was just made up
by people who don't quite know how to enjoy it on earth
or, probably more tragically,
who are not well to do enough
to have a lot of heaven in their daily lives.
And I'm truly sorry about that.
And I wish there would be a heaven in the afterlife
for all those people.

But unhappily I can't quite get myself
to believe in heaven in the afterlife.

CHORUS. As Woody Allen said:
God is silent.
Now if only man would shut up.

> (*A guy turns front and takes a dance posture—*
> *keeping his mouth firmly closed—*
> *putting one shushing finger over his lips—*
> *and so, because his other arm is free,*
> *he flexes his bicep in his free arm.*
>
> *Music.*
>
> *The guy flexes his bicep to the music.*
>
> *Music.*
> *Music.*
> *Music.*
> *Music.*
> *Music.*
> *Music.*
> *Music.*
> *Music.*
> *Music.*
> *Music.*
> *Music.*
> *Music.*
> *Music.*
> *Music.*
>
> *5 guys join him in a bicep flexing dance*
> *bicep flexing dance*
> *bicep flexing dance*
> *bicep flexing dance*
> *bicep flexing dance*
> *bicep flexing dance*
> *bicep flexing dance*
> *all in unison*
>
> *and then they all do a hip thrust*
> *hip thrust*
> *hip thrust*
> *hip thrust*
> *hip thrust*

hip thrust
hip thrust
hip thrust
very macho

then turn upstage and wiggle their butts
wiggle their butts
wiggle their butts
wiggle their butts
wiggle their butts
wiggle their butts
wiggle their butts
wiggle their butts
[not SO macho]

they move through other male display dance moves
finger snapping, etc.

then three others step up
three others
three others
three others
three others
three others
three others
three others
and do the same display moves.

Some guys enter with lawn sprinklers and set them off so the stage is drenched
in water.
One or two of them dance among the lawn sprinklers.

The rhinoceros enters
while the dancing is going on,
and the rhinoceros looks around at the dancers and
then slowly crosses the stage.

While this is going on,
a guy appears in a wacky outfit,
carrying a gigantic birthday cake.

He puts the birthday cake down on a table.
Looks around to see if anyone is going to do anything
with the cake.
Sees that no one else is interested,
and leaves.

A few moments later
he returns
wearing a red shirt and white undies
with a dozen party hats
that he puts on the table.

And then
he turns and leaves.

He returns wearing a white shirt and tie and glasses
—as though he has been trying out acceptable party clothes.

This time he also has a bowl of ice cream.

And now 3 others come in,
wearing only underpants
with plates and bowls and forks and spoons
for the cake and ice cream.

3 naked men sit at the dinner table
with one in evening clothes:
a snapshot of society.

[If a birthday party seems too obvious and simple-minded
for the occasion
then people can just bring in hors d'oeuvres and glasses of bourbon
and have a more elegant dinner party—
though they all still go through several changes of clothes
to get in the proper attire.]

The first man returns
this time only in white underpants.

The elegantly dressed man sings solo.

solo
solo
solo
solo
solo
solo
solo
solo
solo
solo
solo
solo

solo

A rack of clothes is brought on
and everyone dresses in dinner clothes.

It is as though they had stripped down to the essentials
or "desocialized" themselves
and now they "resocialize" themselves.

Everyone now sits or stands around the cake,
wearing their party hats,
and eating cake and ice cream.)

ALBERT. I think of Merton.
I think: my family
my aunt was a nun
and my other aunt was the mother
of three priests and another nun
so, growing up,
I thought
that's enough Catholics in the family
I'm going swimming
I'm getting out of here
I'm going to get some fresh air
I'm going to be an atheist
but then I just lapsed into a life of thinking
and then writing things down
and now I think
I want a place like Thomas Merton had
and a life
reliable
forever
quiet
sitting in a room
alone
mulling
writing
permanent
everlasting
finally, it may be,
filled with sorrow
since I know
departure is inevitable
but, meanwhile,
it feels like it is lasting forever.

To have a writer's life
it is like having a monk's life
or it could be
to have a monk's life
that means you can have the perfect writer's life
that you can't have any other way
a place to write
to be alone
quiet

CHORUS. As Pascal said:
All men's miseries
derive from not being able to sit in a quiet room alone.

CHORUS. As Franz Kafka said:
You do not need to leave your room. Remain sitting at your table and listen. Do not even listen, simply wait, be quiet still and solitary. The world will freely offer itself to you to be unmasked, it has no choice, it will roll in ecstasy at your feet.

CHORUS. As Stevie Wonder said:
I can't say that I'm always writing in my head but I do spend a lot of time in my head writing or coming up with ideas. And what I do usually is write the music and melody and then, you know, maybe the basic idea. But when I feel that I don't have a song I just say, God, please give me another song. And I just am quiet and it happens.

CHORUS. As Lady Gaga said:
I was very depressed when I was 19… I would go back to my apartment every day and I would just sit there. It was quiet and it was lonely. It was still. It was just my piano and myself. I had a television and I would leave it on all the time just to feel like somebody was hanging out with me.

CHORUS. As Napoleon Bonaparte said:
The best cure for the body is a quiet mind.

CHORUS. As Alan Watts said:
I'll tell you what hermits realize. If you go off into a far, far forest and get very quiet, you'll come to understand that you're connected with everything.

CHORUS. As Christina Applegate said:
My dream is to have a house on the beach, even just a little shack somewhere so I can wake up, have coffee, look at dolphins, be quiet and breathe the air.

ROBERT. A quiet place
that's what I want

ROLAND. Everlasting on earth
that's what I want

BENNY. Me, too

ROBERT. Everlasting forever

BOBBY. Some solitude
some time and quiet to think
just to wallow in it all

ROLAND. For myself, I have only one desire
and that is the desire for solitude.
To disappear into God.
To be submerged in his peace.
To be lost in the secret of his space.

ALBERT. And, at the same time,
let's not forget
Thomas Merton's lover
and their illegitimate child
because, in the middle of all the solitude
and all the meditation
and the removal from the world
he acknowledged, too,
the attraction of life on earth
the things of daily life
the contradictory feelings we have
frankly, the personal and intimate love
we can feel for another person
and he didn't despise that
or judge it wrong
or take a strict negative moral view
but rather he understood
and he embraced it
as I hope to do.

CHORUS. As Oscar Wilde said:
Keep love in your heart. A life without it is like a sunless garden when the
flowers are dead.

CHORUS. As Mahatma Gandhi said:
Where there is love there is life.

CHORUS. As Lao Tzu said:
Being deeply loved by someone gives you strength, while loving someone
deeply gives you courage.

CHORUS. As Mother Teresa said:
I have found the paradox, that if you love until it hurts, there can be no more
hurt, only more love.

CHORUS. As Thomas Merton said:
Love is our true destiny. We do not find the meaning of life by ourselves
alone—we find it with another.

(And now,
when they disagree from time to time
they aren't quite able to be as agreeable as they were
in the beginning of the party
because they have begun to irritate one another
with their different opinions of who Merton was,
and so they begin speaking with irritation
emphatic conviction
and even anger.)

ROLAND. Still, nonetheless,
let's not forget
let's remember to toast
above all
again and again
Merton the Catholic
Merton the Catholic monk and priest!

BENNY. Well, you say he was a Catholic,
but no, really he was a Buddhist.

CHORUS. As Björk said:
I'm no Buddhist, but this is fu**ing enlightenment

CHORUS. As Cameron Diaz said:
You haven't partied until you've partied at dawn in complete silence with
Buddhist monks.

CHORUS. As Regina Brett said:
Wouldn't it be great if health care plans
included a list of Buddhist monks among the network providers?

CHORUS. As Buddha said:
Do not dwell in the past, do not dream of the future, concentrate the mind
on the present moment.

BENNY. He was a Buddhist.
Don't forget
at the end of his life
he went to Thailand
and most people think it was finally to become
a full-time Buddhist

ROLAND. I don't think so

BENNY. And he died by stepping on an electric wire
and he was electrocuted
and some people think his murder
was arranged by the Pope!

ROLAND. Murdered by the Pope!
By the Pope?!?!?!?!?!?!?!?
I don't think so.
All this talk of his being murdered by the Pope
and having an illegitimate child
these are all lies
by people trying to destroy his memory

ROBERT. and destroy the Catholic Church

ROLAND. and destroy the Catholic Church, yes

BOBBY. I don't think so.
I think this is an effort merely to speak the truth.

ROBERT. To lie is a sin.
Do you forget that to lie is a sin?

BOBBY. I am not lying!

ROLAND. That's a lie!

ROBERT. Merton was a Catholic!
He believed in Catholicism!

BENNY. Merton was a Buddhist.
In the end he was becoming a Buddhist!

ARNOLD. He was a bohemian!
If you want to know above all
Above all he was a bohemian.

CHORUS. As Brigitte Bardot said:
I'm a girl from a good family who was very well brought up. One day I turned
my back on it all and became a bohemian.

CHORUS. As Marge Piercy said:
Long hair is considered bohemian, which may be why I grew it, but I keep
it long because I love the way it feels, part cloak, part fan, part mane, part
security blanket.

CHORUS. As Lenny Kravitz said:
My dream is to become a farmer. Just a bohemian guy pulling up his own
sweet potatoes for dinner.

CHORUS. As Wittgenstein said:
When we can't think for ourselves, we can always quote.

CHORUS. He was, above all,
an adventurer,
an explorer
someone not afraid of stepping into the unknown
the great unknown

brave
fearless
strong
exciting
not simple minded
not simple
not reducible to this or that or the other
but willing to throw himself
defenseless
into the strange, the unfamiliar
the mysterious
the infinite

He was a Taoist, finally
at bottom, a Taoist

CHORUS. Taoism is: shit happens.

CHORUS. And Buddhism.
Buddhism is: If shit happens, it isn't really shit.

CHORUS. Zen Buddhism: Shit is, and is not.

CHORUS. Catholicism: If shit happens, you deserve it.

CHORUS. Protestantism: Let shit happen to someone else.

CHORUS. Presbyterian: This shit was bound to happen.

CHORUS. Episcopalian: It's not so bad if shit happens, as long as you serve the right wine with it.

CHORUS. Darwinism: This shit was once food.

CHORUS. Capitalism: That's MY shit.

CHORUS. Communism: It's everybody's shit.

CHORUS. Feminism: Men are shit.

CHORUS. Chauvinism: We may be shit, but you can't live without us…

CHORUS. Commercialism: Let's package this shit.

CHORUS. Existentialism: Shit doesn't happen; shit IS.

CHORUS. Atheism: What shit? I can't believe this shit!

CHORUS. Nihilism: No shit.

CHORUS. Narcissism: I am the shit!

BENNY. That's not funny
you think that's funny
to make fun of people who believe certain things
but that's not funny
And Merton would not have thought that was funny.

ALBERT. I say it's not funny, it's serious!

BOBBY. And do you think I am funny because I am a Buddhist?

(*And now*
all patience is finally gone.)

ALBERT. (*Shoving* BOBBY *in the chest.*) Who said I'm not a Buddhist?

BOBBY. Wait.

(*Shoving back.*)

I'm not joking.

ALBERT. I'm not joking.

BOBBY. I know an insult when I hear it.

ALBERT. (*Shoving again.*) I'm not a person who insults people!

BOBBY. (*Twisting* ALBERT'*s arm up behind his back.*) No, you just start a fight.

ALBERT. I don't fight.

(*They struggle.*
It might be too messy for everyone to throw cake at each other,
but it could be that just one guy
smooshes his big piece of cake in another guy's face.)

ROLAND. I fight!

I fight!

CAMERON. And so do I.

For the right thing!

(*And the fourth guy shoves the third guy to the ground.*)

CHORUS. What's that?

(*Grabbing* CAMERON *and wrestling him toward the ground.*)

You think it's OK to do some violence?

(*Those five guys continue to struggle*
and fight with one another,
and members of the CHORUS *join in the fighting*
and the shouting and yelling.)

ALL THE OTHERS. Hey!

What!

What are you......

Get the fuck....

Goddammit!

(*Etc.*
etc. etc.
as we finally end up with <u>everyone on stage</u> *in a huge, horrible, knock down*
riotous brawling fight.

And this fight maybe wants a fight choreographer to turn it into a fifteen-minute
brawl like we have never seen on stage before?

And sometimes two fighters will engage in such an amazing, stupendous feat of
physical miraculousness that everyone else will stop and look at their solo or their
duet, and then the group will resume again in the group brawl.

And slowly the fight comes to an end.
Everyone sits or lies on the floor, exhausted.
THE MAN *is still sitting at the table with his back to us,*
listening,
his thoughts
are projected on the wall.
PAUSE.)

What do you mean by contemplation anyway?

> (*SILENCE.*)

Does the silence scare you?

> (*SILENCE.*)

How do I live?

> (*SILENCE*
> *SILENCE.*)

Who could tell where I would have ended?

> (*SILENCE*
> *SILENCE.*)

Is nothing sacred?

> (*SILENCE*
> *SILENCE.*)

Is everything sacred?

> (*SILENCE*
> *SILENCE.*)

What is the question? Salvation, damnation?

> (*SILENCE*
> *SILENCE.*)

Who can explain those things?

> (*SILENCE*
> *SILENCE.*)

Or is the question: What is serious?
What is to be taken seriously?
What is the
meaning of seriousness?
What is to be doubted?
What is to be dismissed as not serious?
Is there anything serious?

Is there anything not serious?
            (*BRIEF PAUSE.*)
Yes, but don't you think…?
            (*BLACKOUT.*)

End of Play

.

THE ROOMMATE
by Jen Silverman

ABOUT *THE ROOMMATE*

This article first ran in the Limelight Guide to the 39th Humana Festival of New American Plays, *published by Actors Theatre of Louisville, and is based on conversations with the playwright before rehearsals for the Humana Festival production began.*

How do people change? Can they transform themselves? Is there a singular moment? Or does change occur as a series of events? Could it be caused by a particular person? Playwright Jen Silverman was inspired by the notion of how and why we evolve: "I've been particularly interested in stories of how people transform themselves, or in people who are drawn or driven to a point in their lives where no choice is left to them but self-transformation." In *The Roommate*, a pair of characters find that the table that's propped up their lives has been overturned. Whether they or someone else pushed it over, what happens next?

Sharon has long since resigned herself to living the version of life she was told to want. She got married, raised a child, and kept a warm home in the heartland of Iowa. In her mid-fifties, she's been "retired" from her marriage. As she's done her whole life, she vows to make the best of it, and advertises for a roommate to help make ends meet. Sharon's careful, though—she specifies that she's seeking another woman in her fifties. That way she'll surely avoid dangerous drug addicts or serial killers and get someone like herself. Or maybe like one of the ladies in her book club.

Hilarity ensues as Sharon gets more than she bargained for when she rents the room to Robyn. Robyn couldn't be more different. She's a lesbian, a vegan, and was most recently living in the Bronx. Perhaps most shocking, she drinks almond milk in the middle of cow country. Within the first ten minutes after Robyn moves in, Sharon finds that this is not the person she imagined as her new roommate. But far from being deterred, Sharon comes to relish her discoveries of their different perspectives, and begins to experiment with Robyn's foreign (and forbidden) ways of life—which, as a sheltered divorcée, she finds thrilling. The problem is that Robyn's looking for a fresh start with a clean slate, and is trying desperately to put her former life away for good.

These opposing views of transformation—Sharon's dictated by the circumstance of her divorce and Robyn's by her drive to forge a new path—are muddied by the fast friendship that forms between the two seeming opposites. Silverman describes the dichotomy between Robyn and Sharon in the play as an illustration of her "warring desires." Both characters embody things Silverman craves. On one hand, admits the playwright, "I'm attracted to Sharon's deep roots and a sense of place that feels like it was made to contain me. But on the other hand, I identify with Robyn's craving for constant adventure and transformation."

In *The Roommate*, Silverman also wanted to create a play for older women, to write the sort of meaty roles she wasn't seeing for actresses past the ingénue phase. "I realized that when I went to the theatre I wasn't seeing roles in which older women were total badasses," she explains. "I was seeing roles where older women were waiting for their children to come home, or older women were watching their husbands sleep with younger women. The audience was being invited to laugh at them in a way that felt kind of suspicious to me. I wanted to give them something to do that I knew they would rock, and that I wasn't seeing them being asked to do." This also informed her choice for the play to focus upon two characters. Silverman notes, "I wanted to see these women at center stage in a way that a large ensemble piece might not allow them to be." Sharon and Robyn, in the writer's words, "have very active, vibrant, and dangerous lives. They make decisions that require a lot of boldness and recklessness, out of both desperation and desire for life." Silverman plays with the stereotype of the sequestered Midwestern housewife by subverting the path you'd expect Sharon to take. Ironically, Robyn accidentally exposes Sharon to a new way of seeing the world, even as she's been trying to find the settled normalcy that was the fabric of Sharon's quiet life.

It's a neat trick that Silverman finds both the comedy and the pathos in Sharon and Robyn's relationship. The playwright describes their closeness as "triggered by humor." As they get to know each other and start letting their guard down, one of them will say something that startles the other and "surprises them into laughing." Despite their purported opposition, the two women share many similarities. They're both mothers with children they wish were closer. They both have a spark in them that ignites that sense of humor and a sense of adventure. Their laughter leads to an intimacy that invites them to find connections and bond. For all of the laughter, as their relationship develops, these two women must grapple with the new directions their lives have taken, and figure out if they're capable of stopping the snowball effect of transformation. Once you've started making changes in your life, how far do you go?

—Kimberly Colburn

BIOGRAPHY

Jen Silverman's work has been produced at Actors Theatre of Louisville (*The Roommate*, 2015 Humana Festival; *Wondrous Strange*, 2016 Humana Festival), Yale Repertory Theatre (*The Moors*), InterAct Theatre Company in Philadelphia (*The Dangerous House of Pretty Mbane*, Barrymore Award), and in New York by the Playwrights Realm (*Crane Story*) and Clubbed Thumb (*Phoebe in Winter*). She has developed plays as workshop productions at the Cherry Lane Mentor Project (*The Hunters*, mentor Lynn Nottage), Juilliard (*Wild Blue* and *Still*), and Playwrights Horizons Theater School (*That Poor Girl and How He Killed Her*, a commission). She is a member of New Dramatists, is a Core Writer at the Playwrights' Center in Minneapolis, and has developed work at the O'Neill National Playwrights Conference, PlayPenn, SPACE on Ryder Farm, Williamstown Theatre Festival, New York Theatre Workshop, Portland Center Stage, The Theatre @ Boston Court in Los Angeles, The New Harmony Project, FUSION Theatre Company in New Mexico, Youngblood at Ensemble Studio Theatre, and the Royal Court Theatre in London, among other places. She's a two-time MacDowell Fellow, and a recipient of the Kennedy Center's Paula Vogel Award in Playwriting, a New York Foundation for the Arts grant, a Leah Ryan Fellowship/Lilly Award, the 2015 Helen Merrill Playwright Award for emerging playwrights, and the Yale Drama Series Award for *Still*. Education: Brown University, Iowa Playwrights Workshop, Juilliard. For more information, visit www.jensilverman.com.

ACKNOWLEDGMENTS

The Roommate premiered at the Humana Festival of New American Plays in March 2015. It was directed by Mike Donahue with the following cast:

SHARON	Margaret Daly
ROBYN	Tasha Lawrence

and the following production staff:

Scenic Designer	Andrew Boyce
Costume Designer	Kathleen Geldard
Lighting Designer	Paul Toben
Sound Designer/Original Music	Daniel Kluger
Stage Manager	Katie Shade
Dramaturg	Kimberly Colburn
Casting	Kelly Gillespie
Properties Master	Joseph Cunningham
Directing Assistant	Sophie Blumberg
Production Assistant	Hannah Barnes
Assistant Dramaturg	Robyn Carroll

The Roommate was developed in part with assistance from SPACE on Ryder Farm (www.spaceonryderfarm.com) and The Playwrights Realm.

CHARACTERS

SHARON: Female, 54.
ROBYN: Female, 56.

TIME

Now.
Summer.

PLACE

A big old house in Iowa City.
The kitchen.
The porch.

NOTE

The spacing is a gesture toward indicating rhythm and how thoughts change, morph, contradict each other, escalate, or get supplanted by other thoughts as we talk. The line breaks often signal either an intensification of, or a shift away, from something. It *doesn't* indicate a beat or pause except where written.

[ ] is unspoken, although the character is thinking it.

( ) is spoken out loud but is a side-thought.

ON MUSIC

Sharon's CD in Scene 3 might be Mary Chapin Carpenter.

"New Music" at the end of Scene 3 might be Patti Smith, especially "Dancing Barefoot."

"World War II London Music" might mean Sidney Bechet.

Tasha Lawrence and Margaret Daly
in *The Roommate*

39th Humana Festival of New American Plays
Actors Theatre of Louisville, 2015
Photo by Bill Brymer

THE ROOMMATE

1.

The kitchen.
SHARON *helps* ROBYN *carry and unpack boxes. So many boxes! One contains weird vegetables from a CSA. Some vegetables are just odd, but others look actively dangerous.*

SHARON. (*A little out of breath.*) And this is the kitchen, it's got a dishwasher
I'm a big cook, I love to cook
You said you cooked?

ROBYN. I cook, sure.

SHARON. Okay! Okay
Well
we can divide up the refrigerator or the pantry shelves depending on
sort of *what* and *when* you cook

ROBYN. I'm a vegan

SHARON. (*Doesn't really know what that is.*) Okay! Okay…

ROBYN. No animal products.

SHARON. Okay!
So like… no meat…

ROBYN. Nope, no meat

SHARON. Or eggs

ROBYN. That would be an animal product

SHARON. Sure! Sure it would
Uh… but like, carrots

ROBYN. Yes carrots are fine

SHARON. I mean, clearly carrots are   [fine]
…but for example, using pans or pots or
knives or
you know, that I've used for meat…
I mean, is that going to be…?

ROBYN. I have my own cooking utensils
in one of the boxes there's

SHARON. Oh! sure sure
yeah we can find
there's some extra cabinet space if we just
move things around a bit

ROBYN. Yeah there's a lot of space
this seems very spacious

SHARON. I mean there's *space*
it's not *palatial* but
I mean, Iowa, it specializes in
corn and *space*

> (*She laughs,* ROBYN *doesn't. Awkward.*)

If you want you can leave stuff on the porch
'til you're all unpacked

ROBYN. Oh no no, I don't want to take up your

SHARON. No no! that's fine
I don't use the side porch that much anyway
it's nice in the summer I guess but

> (*Picking up weird vegetable:*)

What's this?

ROBYN. That's goya.

SHARON. What-now?

ROBYN. Goya. It's a vegetable.
A bitter gourd.

SHARON. Okay! yes. yes. Wow. Well. I see I am going to learn a lot from
having you as a roommate.

> (*She laughs.* ROBYN *doesn't really.*
> *Beat.*)

You must be tired. Driving all the way from… New York, you said?

ROBYN. The Bronx.

SHARON. The—! The Bronx!

ROBYN. Took about two days, by car.

SHARON. I thought…

ROBYN. What?

SHARON. I don't know,
When you said New York, I thought
somewhere Upstate
I didn't think…
Isn't the Bronx…
dangerous?

ROBYN. "Dangerous."

SHARON. And you're— I mean. You're a woman.
I mean. I don't know.
I've never lived in New York.

ROBYN. It's OK. I mean. There's parts. Parts where you don't wanna
late at night, you don't wanna
but it's fine. I stayed there for a little while and nothing ever
SHARON. *(With relief.)* Oh you aren't *from* the Bronx!
    (A slight pause.)
ROBYN. Everywhere has parts like that.
SHARON. Oh it's mostly pretty safe here.
Except for the tornados.
ROBYN. *(Alarmed.)* Tornados?
SHARON. Oh yeah, in the spring mostly
early summer
you just go on down to the basement 'til they pass. It's fine.
ROBYN. *(Even more alarmed.)* There are a lot of tornados here?
SHARON. Not as bad as some places.
ROBYN. Like how many tornados would you say, on average?
SHARON. It's fine! If you hear that big old siren
you just go down to the basement.
Really
it's no scarier than the Bronx.
ROBYN. *(Has to smile.)* I guess not if you're from here.
SHARON. *(Immediately.)* I'm not *from* here. You know. I'm not *Iowan.*
ROBYN. Oh OK
SHARON. I don't know if I said that?
when we talked on the phone, if I said that?
ROBYN. I don't think so, but it doesn't really
SHARON. I'm from Illinois, originally.
ROBYN. Oh!
SHARON. It's actually quite different from Iowa.
ROBYN. I'll take your word for it.
    (Beat.)
SHARON. My son lives in New York.
ROBYN. Oh!
You have a son?
SHARON. I do, he lives in New York.
ROBYN. That's great. In the Bronx?
SHARON. No! No no
He lives
"Park Slope" do you know where   [that is?]

He lives in "Park Slope."

ROBYN. Oh yeah, that's great.

SHARON. He pays way too much for   [rent]
I tell him that all the time, I say
In Iowa you could have a *house* for the money you spend on   [rent]

> (*Laughs a little, stops.*)

He doesn't like it when I say that.
He didn't like Iowa.

ROBYN. The tornados?

SHARON. No he just didn't like it.

> (*Beat. Have they run out of conversation?*
> SHARON *hastens.*)

He's a designer.

ROBYN. Oh! That's great!

SHARON. He's very good, everybody thinks he's very good.

ROBYN. What does he design?

SHARON. (*Doesn't really know.*) Clothes, he mostly designs clothes. For women?

ROBYN. Oh!

SHARON. Everybody thinks he's a homosexual, but he's not.

> (*Where did this come from?? SHARON has surprised herself. A beat.*)

ROBYN. I'm gay.

SHARON. Oh!
You're—?
Oh!!
You're—??

> (*Beat.*)

I mean, I don't have any problem with homosexuals.

ROBYN. Oh good.

SHARON. Nope. Not at all. I think, you know, gay rights! Let them marry!

ROBYN. Thank you.

SHARON. Some of my son's friends are homosexual people. Probably most of them.

ROBYN. Oh.

SHARON. I think most New Yorkers are.

ROBYN. I think actually there are a lot of straight people in New York.

> (*Beat.*)

SHARON. I kissed a girl once in college.

(Beat.)

I'm sorry. I'm nervous.

ROBYN. Why are you nervous?

SHARON. I mean. A roommate! I've never had a roommate.

(This is an admission of failure:)

I'm fifty-four years old.

A roommate!

ROBYN. It's OK. You'll save money.

SHARON. No, I know! I know. I definitely
I will definitely save money.

(Beat.)

You—did you have a lot more boxes in the car?

ROBYN. I've got it.

SHARON. *(Really doesn't want to keep carrying boxes.)* Well if you're sure.

ROBYN. Be right back.

*(She exits back out to the car.
SHARON sits alone in her kitchen with all these new weird vegetables. She
takes a deep breath. OK. It's OK.)*

SHARON. *(Calling after her.)* Today is my reading group!

(ROBYN returns. She's carrying a heavy box.)

ROBYN. What did you say?

SHARON. Oh, I said: today is my reading group.
If you want to come with me.

ROBYN. Your "reading group"?

SHARON. You know, a book club. Only Tanya calls it a reading group—

*(She jumps up to help ROBYN set the box on the table. ROBYN pulls
away.)*

ROBYN. I've got it!

SHARON. —Tanya's the one who runs it, she says everything just a little bit
wrong, it's because she's from Idaho and there wasn't any culture there, so she
didn't get exposed to things until much later in life.

(Beat.)

Is that more vegetables?

ROBYN. No that goes upstairs.

A reading group…

(Beat.)

Isn't that. Kind of. For old people?

SHARON. (*Amazed.*) We *are* old people.

ROBYN. (*Amazed.*) *We* are?

> (*A beat. They study each other.*
> *Each is kind of baffled by the other.*
> *Then* ROBYN *turns away.*)

ROBYN. I'll just take this upstairs. But thanks for the invitation.

SHARON. You're so welcome. You let me know if there's anything you need.

Mi casa es su casa!

> (*Beat.*)

Literally.

ROBYN. OK then.

> (*She picks up the box and almost drops it.*
> *A ceramic doll falls out and smashes.*
> *The box is full of ceramic dolls.*)

SHARON. Oh no!

ROBYN. Stay there!

> (ROBYN *moves quickly between* SHARON *and the shards.*)

SHARON. Are you OK? Do you need help?

ROBYN. (*Sharp.*) I've got this!

Is there a [broom]?

SHARON. Here…

> (*Gets her a broom.*)

Do you want me to…?

ROBYN. No no

I've got it.

> (*As she sweeps – calmer.*)

Sorry. I didn't mean to [snap]

I just didn't want you to get cut.

SHARON. (*Peering into the box.*) What… are all these dolls?

ROBYN. Please!!

> (SHARON *moves away from the box.*)

Sorry. They're—it's personal.

SHARON. I didn't mean to pry.

ROBYN. I made them. I used to be a potter.

SHARON. You were?

ROBYN. They're patterned after these antique South American dolls.

SHARON. Oh! Wow

ROBYN. But then I stopped. So.
It's a little embarrassing.

SHARON. You shouldn't be embarrassed, they're very
  (*She doesn't like them.*)
Evocative.

ROBYN. *Evocative?*

SHARON. They evoke things.

ROBYN. They're actually voodoo dolls.

SHARON. Voodoo??

ROBYN. Kidding.

SHARON. I mean I don't know
They look a little voodoo-y to me.

ROBYN. Maybe they *evoke* voodoo.
  (*A beat. They share a smile.*)

SHARON. I didn't mean that in a bad way.

ROBYN. It's OK. I'm done with all that.

SHARON. Why did you stop?

ROBYN. I stopped because
uh
it wasn't the sort of lifestyle
that...
Being a potter can be very
stressful.
  (*Beat.*)

SHARON. Your boxes are so heavy and you just got here.
Leave them on the porch and put your feet up.
I'll get us coffee.

ROBYN. Is your porch safe?

SHARON. Safe?

ROBYN. Break-ins?

SHARON. This is Iowa.

ROBYN. Yes?

SHARON. No break-ins.

ROBYN. But you lock the doors?

SHARON. I *can* lock the doors.
If that makes you feel comfortable, I can *start* locking the doors.

ROBYN. I feel better with things. Locked.

SHARON. A New York thing?

ROBYN. Sure.

SHARON. A Bronx thing?

ROBYN. A Robyn thing.

> (*Re: the doll box.*)

I'll just take this up to my room…

SHARON. Oh! just up the stairs
immediate left—
would you like me to show you?

ROBYN. I've got it.
Here we go, take two.

> (*She hoists the box with the dolls and exits upstairs.*)

2.

> *Morning. Kitchen.*
> SHARON *on the phone with her son.*

SHARON. (*Excited, sotto voce.*) And here's the other thing!
She's a homosexual!

> (*Beat.*)

Well I don't care OF COURSE, but you asked if anything interesting happened,
and I thought that was interesting.

> (*Beat.*)

Also she used to be a potter
she said she made voodoo dolls but
she was just joshing me.

> (*Beat.*)

When are you going to come visit?

> (*Beat – he's too busy.*)

No… I know… of course, yes…
No, forget it, maybe over the summer.

> (*Beat.*)

Maybe I should come visit you.

> (*Beat – he's trying to get out of this.*)

We always have such fun when I visit you! I love staying with you, your
roommate is so lovely, the tall one, what's his name… Do you know what he
did last time, he did the funniest thing, did I tell you this? He was—

> (*Beat – her son is saying that she has told him this SO MANY times.*)

Oh. Oh yes. I guess I did, didn't I.

(*Beat.*)

She's joined a… local farm. And she just got here! She just picked up some boxes of vegetables on her way here. I mean that's very healthy, she seems very healthy. And she just bought a folding bicycle, like a… like sort of a folding chair, but it's a bicycle.

(*Her son isn't as impressed as she is.*)

Anyway, she seems like a very healthy person with a very sort of *healthy* lifestyle, and I just think this is all going to just be very healthy for me.

(ROBYN *wanders in. She's smoking.*
SHARON *coughs. She coughs pointedly.*
ROBYN *glances at her.*)

ROBYN. Oh! Sorry!

(SHARON *coughs and fans the air.*)

Sorry!

(*She goes out onto the porch and chain-smokes.*
Back to the phone:)

SHARON. (*Intense whisper.*) SHE. IS. SMOKING.

(*Beat.*)

Well I thought I was fairly clear about that when I said I was looking for a woman in her fifties. I thought that sort of ruled out the kind of crowd that… I thought I ruled out junkies!

(*Beat.*)

Are you LAUGHING at me?

(*Beat.*)

I have to go.

(*Beat – he's apologizing but she won't be mollified.*)

No, no it's OK. I have to go. I know how busy you are.

(*She hangs up.*
A beat.
ROBYN *comes back in.*)

ROBYN. Morning.

SHARON. Good morning.

(*Beat.*)

ROBYN. Sorry about that.

SHARON. I didn't know you smoked.

ROBYN. I quit. I'm quitting. I quit.

SHARON. Oh.

ROBYN. I quit right before I moved. So.

SHARON. Oh.

ROBYN. New places stress me out.

SHARON. You weren't stressed out in the Bronx but you're stressed out in Iowa?

ROBYN. I *was* stressed out in the Bronx, which is why I smoked there.
And I am stressed out in Iowa, which is why I just smoked here.
Even though I quit.
I am re-quitting.

SHARON. They have nicotine gum at the gas station.
They didn't used to, but now it's become popular.

ROBYN. The gum is no good, I get hooked on the gum.
I just need to quit cold turkey.
Everything that I do, I just need to DO it, no half-measures. Just jump.

SHARON. (*Impressed despite herself.*) Like moving to Iowa?

ROBYN. Like moving to Iowa.

      (*A warmer beat between the women: a shared humor.*)

SHARON. Do you want some eggs? I was gonna make eggs.

ROBYN. I can't, but thanks.

SHARON. You—?
Oh!
Vegan!

ROBYN. Vegan.

SHARON. Vegan.
Coffee? Without milk?

ROBYN. I'd love some coffee. With almond milk.

SHARON. I don't have almond milk.

ROBYN. I got it from the co-op yesterday.
You can try it.

      (*She gets out the almond milk.*
      A beat.
      SHARON *thinks it's very strange, but:*)

SHARON. (*Very determined.*) OK yes.
Yes, I will.

      (*She lets* ROBYN *put almond milk in her coffee. They drink coffee together.*)

SHARON. It's…

ROBYN. Weird?

SHARON. Weird.

ROBYN. Bad?

SHARON. Not bad.

> (*Beat.*
>
> *The warmth between them becomes awkward again.*)

SHARON. So what do you *do?*

ROBYN. Me?

SHARON. Uh. You.

ROBYN. Well. I do a lot of things.

> (SHARON *waits.* ROBYN *drinks more almond-milk coffee.*)

SHARON. Oh.

Well.

Like what do you do?

For example.

ROBYN. Well.

> (*Beat.*)

I'm a poet.

SHARON. A poet!

ROBYN. Yes, I write poetry.

> (*Beat.*)

SHARON. That's great!

I love poetry!

I was an English major!

> (*Beat – honest.*)

I don't really understand poetry.

ROBYN. I write slam poetry.

SHARON. I don't know what that is.

ROBYN. I write poems and then I perform them.

SHARON. And what do you write… about?

> (*A pause.*)

ROBYN. I do other things too.

SHARON. Oh?

ROBYN. I grow things. I like to grow things.

SHARON. I never had much of a green thumb but
that's wonderful!

What do you grow?

> (*A pause.*)

ROBYN. What do you do?

SHARON. (*Completely off-balance.*) Me?

I mean.

I live here. Obviously.

ROBYN. Yeah…

SHARON. I'm a mother…

ROBYN. Right.

SHARON. I'm retired!

ROBYN. From what?

(*Beat.*)

SHARON. My marriage.

ROBYN. *Oh.*

SHARON. Yeah. So.

ROBYN. I'm sorry?

SHARON. Don't be.

ROBYN. Then I'm not.

(*Beat,* ROBYN *smiles, then* SHARON *does. A shared moment.*)

SHARON. I'd love to hear some of your poems.

ROBYN. Oh. I don't think so.

SHARON. Maybe you could explain them to me.

ROBYN. Poetry can't really… be explained.

SHARON. That's probably why I don't like it. Oh! Sorry! I didn't mean…

ROBYN. No. No no. It's OK. I don't like poetry either.

SHARON. You don't?

ROBYN. I like mine. But I don't have a lot of patience for other people's.

SHARON. I think I feel that way about children.

ROBYN. I think I feel that way about most things.

(*Another shared smile. Beat.*)

SHARON. So… why Iowa?

ROBYN. Why not Iowa?

SHARON. Do you know anybody here?

ROBYN. You.

SHARON. Me?

ROBYN. You now. Now I know you.

(*This pleases* SHARON.)

SHARON. Well

what would you like to *do*
here?
There's the University, there's adult classes
(there's poetry!)
or
hot yoga
on North Clinton
Which I've never taken but I see everybody through the window
when I go by, and they all look so
Healthy and Happy, you sort of want to injure them
but yeah, so, there's yoga…
My son thinks Iowa City is boring but
if he just visited me more often he'd see that
now it's very cultural here, Iowa City is actually very [cultural]
I mean *I* sort of haven't [been involved]
but *you* might want to [be involved]

ROBYN. I thought maybe I'd raise bees.

SHARON. Bees.

ROBYN. And maybe a sheep or
a cow or
something.

SHARON. A… sheep.

ROBYN. I don't know, I imagined
wide open skies, I think and
rising at dawn…
A sort of…restorative manual labor…

SHARON. Oh… hmm…
We could have a garden…?

ROBYN. My grandmother was from Iowa.

SHARON. She was?

> (ROBYN *has surprised them both with this revelation. A moment.*)

ROBYN. I didn't know her.
But.
I heard she was from Iowa.

SHARON. (*Beat – a little wistfully.*) I guess everybody wants to start over. Just burn it all down and start over.

ROBYN. (*A genuine question.*) Do you?

SHARON. I don't know…

ROBYN. You said "everybody." So… don't you?

SHARON. I guess I do. Sometimes.

ROBYN. Maybe you already did. When you… retired… from your marriage.

SHARON. No, that didn't feel like a… glorious blaze. It just feels—
felt
very sad. And cold.
And then there was nobody to talk to in the mornings.

> (*Beat.*)

He retired before I did.
Actually.
From the marriage.
But he didn't tell me that, so I had to find it out myself.

ROBYN. Another woman?

SHARON. No
He just started spending all his money on models of things
airplanes, trains, cars
and he'd spend all his time with those mini-things
instead of with me, in our normal-sized life.

> (*Beat.*)

Ha!
Maybe I'll write a… "slam" poem about that
and you can perform it.

> (*Beat.*)

ROBYN. I've retired from slam poetry.
But you should do it anyway.

SHARON. I've never written a slam poem before.

> (*Beat.*)

If you're no longer a poet
or a potter
what *are* you?

> (*A beat.*
> ROBYN *gets up.*)

ROBYN. It'll probably be bad, all first poems are bad poems.
There's a great liberty in being bad.

> (*She leaves the kitchen.*
> SHARON *stares after her, struck to the heart by this wisdom.*)

3.

Night. A week later.
ROBYN *at the kitchen table, alone.*
Her pot plants are set on the windowsill.
Very carefully, with immense precision, she rolls a joint. SHARON *comes in, phone in hand.*

ROBYN. Hey!

SHARON. (*Startled.*) Oh!

(*Sees.*)

I thought you quit.

ROBYN. It's not tobacco.

SHARON. (*Not kidding.*) Then what is it?

(*A beat.*
ROBYN *looks at her like: SERIOUSLY?*
A beat.
SHARON *gets it.*)

OH.

You—?

Are those—?

Are those drugs?

ROBYN. Sharon.

SHARON. What!

ROBYN. It's medicinal.

Medicinal herbs.

SHARON. I thought it was drugs?

ROBYN. Herbs only become drugs when a capitalist economy gets involved.

SHARON. Oh.

(*A beat. She sits at the kitchen table.*
She can't help her curiosity.)

Is there some—place—here? Where you go? And buy… herbs?

ROBYN. You mean like a long sticky alley, and a black guy with a ski mask is waiting at the end of it?

SHARON. Is that…?

Is that—!

ROBYN. No!

I grew these.

(*Gestures to the plants.*)

I grow my own medicinal herbs, Sharon.

SHARON. *Those* are…?

ROBYN. I thought you knew. You said you liked them!

SHARON. I did like them! I thought they were just… weird… plants.

ROBYN. Oh man, Okay. Well.

> (*Finishes rolling the joint.*)

Outside. Right?

SHARON. Right.

ROBYN. Right.

> (*She gets up.*
> *But* SHARON *isn't ready to be left alone.*)

SHARON. I can't get ahold of my son.

ROBYN. You called him?

SHARON. I've called. I've been calling.

ROBYN. It's a Friday night.

SHARON. I know.

ROBYN. So he's probably out.

SHARON. I texted him too.

ROBYN. Is something the matter?

SHARON. What do you mean?

ROBYN. Well if it's a Friday night and you're texting him and you're calling him, is something the matter?

> (*A beat.*)

SHARON. I just think it's a good thing for us to stay in touch.

For a mother and a son to stay in touch.

Don't you?

ROBYN. Yeah. Yes. I do.

But it might be better to stay in touch on a Thursday. Or in the morning. You know?

> (*A beat.*)

SHARON. (*Completely unconvinced and kind of upset.*) No, sure, of course.

> (*A beat.*
> ROBYN *sits back down.*)

ROBYN. Is he dating someone?

SHARON. Yeah.

I think so?

He doesn't really

communicate

about that kind of thing.

ROBYN. Maybe he's out with his boyfriend.

SHARON. Girlfriend.

ROBYN. Right, sorry. Straight. You said that.

SHARON. Just because he's a designer doesn't mean

ROBYN. You're right, I forgot.
Maybe he's out with his girlfriend, at a nice dinner.

SHARON. I met her once.

ROBYN. That's nice.

SHARON. She's a lesbian.

ROBYN. ...Oh?

SHARON. Not that there's anything wrong with that!!

ROBYN. How long have they been dating?

SHARON. A few years.
She's got that short hair.
You know.
We went to brunch and she mentioned an ex-girlfriend.
Apparently they're friends with her ex-girlfriend.
It's all very confusing.

> (*A beat.*)

ROBYN. I was married to a man.

SHARON. You were??

ROBYN. Yeah.

SHARON. I didn't know that.

ROBYN. I've only been here a week, why would you know that?

SHARON. But then you realized you were gay? And you left him?

ROBYN. No, we were in love. And it ended badly. But we loved each other.

SHARON. (*Amazed and a little scared.*) Are you... a bisexual?

ROBYN. No. I'm just saying
people find specific words for themselves because it's easier than not having words.
You know?
But
it doesn't mean those words are *all* accurate
all the time.
So if she's been with your son for years, she probably loves him.
Which means, your son probably has lots of people who love him.
Which is a good thing.
He's probably out right now with people who love him.
And if you call him in the morning, maybe he'll tell you about it.

(*A beat.*
SHARON *gets up. She goes to the cupboard, gets out some Johnny Walker.*)

ROBYN. Ohhh-kay.

SHARON. You want some?

ROBYN. I'm OK.

SHARON. Just a little nightcap.

ROBYN. I'm sober. But you go ahead.

SHARON. (*Factually, not mean.*) You do drugs.

ROBYN. I medicate myself with medicinal herbs.
But my days with alcohol are over.

(SHARON *sits down but doesn't pour herself a drink. She studies the joint carefully.* ROBYN *gets up.*)

I'm gonna have a smoke on your porch and then call it a—

SHARON. (*Doesn't want to be left alone.*) I've never.
Smoked that.

ROBYN. …No?

SHARON. No.
Not even in college.
I kissed a—
I told you that.
But drugs? I never.

ROBYN. Please stop calling it that.

SHARON. Sorry.

(*Beat.*)

ROBYN. Would you like some?

SHARON. Yes.
Yes please.

ROBYN. Okay.

(*She hesitates, then sits back down. Lights it up. Takes a long drag, then hands it to* SHARON.)

SHARON. How do you…?

ROBYN. You just… like a cigarette.
Have you ever…?

SHARON. Once.

ROBYN. Once. Okay. Like that.
Just drag it in deep, and then hold your breath.

SHARON. This isn't gonna give me cancer, right?

ROBYN. Nope. No cancer.

SHARON. Okay.

> (*She takes a deep drag.*
> *Lets it out, coughing a little, but.*)

ROBYN. Yeah! Nice.

SHARON. I don't feel anything.

ROBYN. Give it a second.

SHARON. What am I going to feel?

ROBYN. Relaxed.

SHARON. Am I gonna hallucinate?

ROBYN. No! no. You'll just feel relaxed.

SHARON. (*Getting more tense.*) I never feel relaxed. I'm not a relaxed person. What if I don't feel relaxed?

ROBYN. You will one hundred percent feel relaxed.

> (SHARON *takes another drag, just in case.*
> *Then gives the joint back to* ROBYN.)

SHARON. I think my son doesn't like me.

ROBYN. I'm sure that's not

SHARON. He *loves* me. I know he *loves* me.
But I think he doesn't like me very much.

ROBYN. Our kids don't have to like us, they just have to survive long enough to become us.

SHARON. Do you have kids?!

> (*Beat.*
> ROBYN *passes the joint back to* SHARON.)

ROBYN. Your turn.

> (*Beat.* SHARON *takes another drag.*)

SHARON. You didn't tell me you—

ROBYN. Sharon.

SHARON. Yeah?

> (*A half-beat. In lieu of saying "shut up":*)

ROBYN. Tell me more about your son.

> (*Half-beat.*)

SHARON. He's very smart.
He's very good-looking.
I know it's strange for a mother to say that about her own—
but it's true. He's a very attractive boy.
And I don't know where he gets that from because his father
Good lord.

That man looked like a potato.

ROBYN. He probably got it from you.

SHARON. Me?

No!

Me?

> (*Beat.*)

Do you think I'm good-looking?

ROBYN. I think you're pretty, yeah.

SHARON. Do you mean that in a lesbian way, or a factual way?

> (*Half-beat.*)

ROBYN. I think I need you to make the distinction for me.

SHARON. Sorry. I'm sorry. Was that—?   [homophobic]

I said it all wrong.

I just meant

Like, there's a way a man would say to me: you're pretty.

And that would mean I was actually pretty.

And there's a way a woman—a straight woman, I guess—would say that to me.

And it would mean that she felt sorry for me.

And I don't really know what it means when a lesbian person says that to me

because I haven't ever really known any lesbian people before, except for—

ROBYN. Your son's girlfriend.

SHARON. Right.

ROBYN. Right.

SHARON. And she didn't like me.

I think she thought I was boring.

And possibly judgmental but I don't think I was judgmental

I didn't feel judgmental I just felt confused.

Am I high?

Maybe I think I'm high?

ROBYN. I think you're just getting relaxed.

Okay. Well.

I said it like: factually, I think you are factually pretty.

And I don't feel sorry for you.

But I'm not hitting on you.

SHARON. Oh! Thank you.

That's very clear.

ROBYN. Good.

SHARON. But nuanced.

ROBYN. Yes.

SHARON. But now it's clear. Thank you.

ROBYN. You're welcome.

(*A beat. They smoke.*)

We should turn some music on.

SHARON. Music?

ROBYN. Yeah.

No?

SHARON. I don't really listen to music?

(*Beat.*)

I have this CD…

My son sent it to me

for Christmas one year

he couldn't come home so

in the mornings I'd make breakfast

and just play that CD.

ROBYN. Let's hear it.

SHARON. Okay.

Okay!

(*She goes and gets a CD player off a kitchen shelf. Gets a CD. It's from the late 70s/early 80s. Something SO TERRIBLE, but also, it kind of moves us a little bit, in ways we will never admit to later.*

They listen to the CD and get high.)

SHARON. I've never

you know   [smoked pot]

with anyone

I mean obviously because I've never   [smoked pot]

but

this is really nice.

No wonder all the kids do drugs.

Oops.

Sorry.

Medicinal…

drugs.

ROBYN. (*Laughing.*) "All the kids" don't

SHARON. Don't they?

ROBYN. Not *all*.

SHARON. Well they should.

All of them maybe should.

Also, I should've been in a band.

ROBYN. A band!

SHARON. Were you ever in a band?
I bet you were in a band.

ROBYN. Sort of, when I was in college.

SHARON. I knew it!!

ROBYN. I told this girl that I was in a band to impress her.
Then she asked me out, and I actually had to be in a band.

SHARON. What did you do?

ROBYN. I made my roommates dress up and pretend they were a band.

(They laugh together, smoke together.)

SHARON. *(Feeling good, enjoying this.)* I had a crush on this boy
(before my husband of course)
(this was in high school)
and I was too shy to talk to him
so I just followed him
whenever he was in the hallway I'd just
you know walk behind him
and if he was walking with someone, I'd imagine that person was me
and then this one time I wasn't paying attention
and I followed him into the bathroom.

ROBYN. The bathroom??

SHARON. It was the worst!

ROBYN. You should've talked to him!

SHARON. What would I have said?

ROBYN. Tell him you were in a band.

(They're laughing. Then:)

SHARON. *(Very gently.)* Where's your child?

ROBYN. What?

SHARON. Or children.

(A beat. ROBYN could say anything. Then she gets up, decisively.)

ROBYN. We need new music.

(She gets her iPhone. She plays some kind of hard, rhythmic music.)

SHARON. …What is that?

ROBYN. New music.

*(She starts to dance.
A beat. SHARON gets up too. She dances.
Both women dance in the kitchen, by themselves, but together.)*

4.

> *Next day. Kitchen.*
> ROBYN, *on the landline.*
> *She looks over her shoulder.*
> *She doesn't want to be overheard.*
> *She takes a deep breath.*

ROBYN. Hello!
Yes, uh
yes I'm calling for Amanda.
Well
when will she be back?
Oh.
Well.
Did she give you any sort of
ballpark idea of—
No no
that's OK
I'll just
I'll try again.

> *(She hangs up. A beat.*
> *A deep breath. Resolve!*
> *She picks up the phone again. Dials.)*

ROBYN. Hi. Yes. I'm calling back.
Yes, for Amanda.
Yes I know you said that
but we both know she told you to say that
and right now she's there
standing behind you
and you're darting her kind of wide-eyed looks
like WHAT DO I DO ABOUT THIS
and she's shaking her head
and biting her fingernails
so you know what
I *do* want to leave a message.

You tell my daughter that I'm doing it.
She thinks I can't do it but I'm doing it.
I'm in *Iowa*
of all places
so.
That's all.

I'm going to hang up now.

> (ROBYN *hangs up.*
> *A beat. Another deep breath.*
> *She goes out on the porch.*

> SHARON *enters the kitchen.*
> *She doesn't see* ROBYN *at first.*
> *She calls her son.*
> *It goes to voicemail.*)

SHARON. Hiii

it's me

your mother

um

it's Saturday morning

I just wanted to make sure you got home OK

from wherever you were

whatever you were doing

with whoever it was

> (*Beat.*)

Also are you still dating that lesbian girl?

> (*Beat.*)

It's OK if you are

> (*Beat.*)

You should visit me!

> (*Beat.*)

Also, I just have been thinking

maybe you don't tell me enough things

about your life

and

maybe you don't want to tell me

(which I guess is OK)

(although I don't know why you wouldn't)

but I *do* want to know.

Because

I care.

So.

> (*Beat – this comes bursting out of her.*)

I smoked marijuana last night.

> (*A frozen moment, she's shocked at herself.*)

Goodbye.

(*She hangs up. A beat.*
ROBYN *comes in from the porch.*)

SHARON. (*Startled.*) Oh!

ROBYN. Just me, again.

SHARON. Good morning.

ROBYN. Morning.

SHARON. How'd you sleep?

ROBYN. Good. You?

SHARON. (*Finds this to be true, as she says it.*) Really good.

(*A warm beat between them.*)

Do you want an   [egg]—?

(*Catches herself.*)

Coffee?

ROBYN. I'd love some.

SHARON. Okay!

(*The phone rings. They both freeze. Then both move to it.*)

ROBYN. It's / for me.

SHARON. (*Same time.*) Oh god.

(*Beat* – ROBYN *is quizzical:*)

I mean, go on.

ROBYN. (*Answers the phone.*) Hello?

(*It's* SHARON*'s son.*)

Oh!

Uh. Hello. Hi.

Oh, this is Robyn, your mother's roommate.

Yeah, nice to meet you as well.

Yeah, your mom is—

(*On a sudden whim,* SHARON *starts shaking her head frantically.* ROBYN
pauses, startled.
Head-shaking continues.)

Your mom is not
available
right now.

(*Beat.*)

Yeah she's busy.

(*Beat.*)

No, I don't know what she's doing, I just know she's…

(SHARON *gestures emphatically:* OUT.)

OUT. She. is OUT. right now.

What?

Well I guess she must've stepped out right after she called you.

(*Beat – he's asking her something.*)

Marijuana?

Your mother?

I have no idea.

You'll have to ask her that.

Okay.

Okay.

You too.

(ROBYN *hangs up.*
A beat. Co-conspirators. Then:)

ROBYN. You told him you smoked pot?

SHARON. I didn't mean to

I meant to say something else

some bullshit Mom thing

stay safe, be careful, don't ride the subway at night

and then I said that. Instead.

(*Beat.*)

ROBYN. He sounds nice.

SHARON. He does?

ROBYN. Yeah.

He had a nice voice.

(*Beat.*)

SHARON. I'm always home in the mornings.

He's going to ask where I was.

ROBYN. (*Shrugs.*) You were out.

SHARON. I don't really *go* out.

ROBYN. (*Teasing her.*) But I hear there's poetry classes and hot yoga and

SHARON. —okay okay—

ROBYN. *cultural* [things]

SHARON. I go to the book club.

And the store. On Thursdays.

ROBYN. The store?

SHARON. I work at a gift shop. Just on Thursdays. It's nice. Maybe I'll say I went in today as well. Early.

ROBYN. Tell him you were on a date.

SHARON. *What?*

ROBYN. Yeah. A date.

SHARON. Noooo

A—!

On a *Saturday morning?*

ROBYN. Breakfast date.

SHARON. Oh man.

ROBYN. You met him online. He asked you to breakfast. What.

SHARON. On*line?*

ROBYN. Don't tell me you never…

(*She sees* SHARON *hasn't.*)

You *never?*

SHARON. There are *serial killers* online.

ROBYN. Oh my god.

Time-out. Time.

You have *never* been on an internet date.

SHARON. No!! Have you??

ROBYN. Yes!

SHARON. Oh!

(*Beat.*)

There aren't any women serial killers though. So that's different.

ROBYN. When was the last time you were on a date?

SHARON. When I got married! And we all saw how well *that* turned out!

ROBYN. Okay.

Okay.

We have to remedy this.

SHARON. No we don't. Nope.

ROBYN. Sharon. You have to stop thinking about yourself as basically dead.
You are actually younger than most U.S. presidents.

You are young enough that, if you were a president, you would be a *young* president.
OK?

So just. Stop mummifying yourself.

(*A beat. This strikes* SHARON *all the way to the heart. After a moment:*)

SHARON. I'd go on a date if you went.

ROBYN. What! Oh no no no

SHARON. Like a double

ROBYN. I am not going on your date with you!

SHARON. Like a double date, what

ROBYN. Awkward! That shit was awkward in college, it's awkward now!

SHARON. Someone with a sister

ROBYN. No! No no

SHARON. We could all get coffee together

ROBYN. No! I will help screen the applicants so that you do not find yourself sitting across from a serial killer, but I'm not gonna come along and have coffee with his sister!

SHARON. You'd help me screen them?

ROBYN. Yeah I could do that.

SHARON. I don't know how to set up a… page. A home page.

ROBYN. A profile.
I could help you do that.

SHARON. How come you know all these things?

> (*A beat.*)

ROBYN. I used to run a lot of businesses.

SHARON. You did?

ROBYN. Yeah.

SHARON. What kind of businesses?

ROBYN. Businesses that helped people with personal things.

SHARON. I didn't know that.

ROBYN. We're just getting to know each other. There's a lot you don't know.

SHARON. (*Doesn't mean to say this.*) I'm glad you're here, Robyn.

> (ROBYN *is moved, and this makes her awkward. A beat. Then:*)

ROBYN. I'll just…
I forgot my glasses.

> (*She leaves the room.*
> *A beat.* SHARON *drinks coffee.*
> *The phone rings.* SHARON *considers.*
> *She considers. She sighs.*
> SHARON *picks it up.*)

SHARON. Hi.

> (*Beat, it's not her son.*)

Excuse me?
No, this is Sharon. Who's calling please?
Amanda, I think you have the wrong number.
No, there isn't anyone here by that name.
Victoria, there's no Victoria—
What?
No, I'm not…

I just *said*, there's no *Victoria* here.
You have the wrong number, dear.
What do you mean she just called you from—
> (*A beat.*)

I don't know what to tell you.
I have to go.
> (SHARON *hangs up.*
> *She sits for a second.*
> *She opens her mouth.*
> *She closes it.*
> *A beat.*
> ROBYN *returns.*)

ROBYN. Did I hear the phone?

SHARON. It was
just
my son.
Calling back.

ROBYN. You picked up?

SHARON. I told him
I couldn't talk.
I was going on a date.

5.

> *Later that morning.*
> *The porch.* ROBYN'*s boxes still stacked.*
> SHARON *goes through her things.*

> *She doesn't know exactly what she's looking for, but she knows there's something.*

SHARON. (*Reading the box labels.*) Kitchen supplies
Odds and ends
books
okay
cookbooks
really?
you don't cook
I've never seen you
winter clothes
okay
Antiques

I like Antiques
Dress clothes

> (*She opens the clothing box.*
> *Looks at* ROBYN'*s clothes. Takes them out.*
> *Beat.*
> *Beat.*
> *Puts on a hat.*
> *Beat.*
> *Puts on a jacket.*
> *Models.*
> *She tries on* ROBYN'*s clothes. She feels powerful in them.*
> *She moves around the porch in them.*
> *Clears her throat. Sort of as* ROBYN:)

I'm a poet.
I write poems.
Here's a poem.

> (*Silently pretends to recite The Best Poem That Has Ever Been Written.*)

Thank you.
Thank you.
An autograph?
Oh my.
I suppose I could.

> (SHARON *keeps going through the boxes.*)

Newspapers
kitchen supplies?
another box of…?

> (SHARON *opens one of the boxes marked Kitchen Supplies. A beat. She*
> *double-takes. A beat.*)

Oh.

> (*She reaches in. She pulls out a fistful of driver's licenses. Beat. Another fistful.*
> *She reads the names, dropping them back into the box.*)

Claire Jones.
Claire Doyle.
Sarah Lucas.
Victoria Lucas.
Robyn Doyle.
Victoria Jones.

> (*Beat, more fistfuls of drivers' licenses, she drops them back without reading*
> *them, beat.*)

Oh.

6.

Evening.
SHARON *sits at the kitchen table.*
She waits for ROBYN *to get home.*
Key in the lock.
ROBYN *enters.*

ROBYN. Oh!
Hey!

SHARON. Hi.

ROBYN. How was your day?

SHARON. Good
how was yours?

ROBYN. I went to the Farmer's Market on
what is that street
the one with the parking garage

SHARON. Gilbert

ROBYN. Yeah, Gilbert! I bought a necklace
there was this woman selling these necklaces she'd made
out of hemp I think, she grew it herself, and these clay beads,
do you know who I'm talking about? Is she maybe in your book club or
something?

SHARON. How come you have so many driver's licenses?

(*A real beat.*)

ROBYN. Excuse me?

SHARON. I asked how come—?

ROBYN. Did you go through my stuff??

SHARON. I was looking for
a peeler

ROBYN. A *peeler?*

SHARON. For apples.

ROBYN. A *peeler* for *apples* in my *stuff?*

SHARON. It said "kitchen stuff."
I thought, maybe Robyn has a peeler.

ROBYN. Okay.
Wow.

SHARON. I'm sorry.
I don't mean it like…
you *shouldn't* have a hundred driver's licenses

but also

why do you have them?

ROBYN. Because.

Because I do. I collect them.

SHARON. They're all you, but with different names.

ROBYN. Right.

SHARON. And different addresses and different birthdays.

ROBYN. I mean did you examine every single one?

SHARON. Who's Amanda?

(*A real beat.*)

ROBYN. Did she call?

SHARON. Yeah.

She asked for Victoria.

Who is she?

ROBYN. Is this 20 questions? Are we doing the roommate get-to-know-you thing, or is this 20 questions, or is this an interrogation?

SHARON. I'm not interrogating—

ROBYN. Do you want me to leave?

SHARON. I'm not asking you to leave!

(*Beat.*)

Should I be asking you to leave?

(*Beat.*)

ROBYN. No.

(*Beat.*)

SHARON. Then I'm not.

(*Beat.*)

Are you hungry?

ROBYN. Am I…?

SHARON. No dairy. No meat. I made vegetables.

ROBYN. What did you make?

SHARON. I just kind of cut them up and cooked them. I don't know. You don't have to…

ROBYN. I'll try some.

(*Beat.* SHARON *gets her a bowl of vegetables.*
They sit. Eventually:)

Have you talked to anyone about this?

SHARON. "This"?

ROBYN. This
me
this

SHARON. No!
Who would I—?
No

ROBYN. Okay.

> (*Beat, re: food.*)

This is good.

SHARON. (*Pleased.*) Thanks.

> (*Beat.*)

What should I not be telling people?

ROBYN. Nothing. There's nothing to not-tell.
I came here for some peace and quiet.

SHARON. Look, I'm not trying to
I don't mean to
I *like* you

> (*This surprises them both, greatly.*
> *A beat.*)

What I mean is
it's nice
to have a friend.

ROBYN. Are we friends?

SHARON. Aren't we?

ROBYN. I thought we were roommates.
House, housemates

SHARON. We are.
But
then you got me high so
now we're friends.

> (*A beat.*)

ROBYN. (*Amused despite herself.*) Is that how it works?

SHARON. That's how it seems to work when the kids do it.

ROBYN. (*Laughs, then sobers.*) All right
if we're *friends*
don't go through my shit.

SHARON. I didn't mean to

ROBYN. Yeah I know you wanted a peeler
if you want a peeler, ask me for a peeler

SHARON. Right

> *(Beat.)*

Is Amanda your daughter?

ROBYN. Jesus Christ.

SHARON. I'm very nosy and I'm very persistent
it's something that has always irritated my son
but inescapable, in our line of work

ROBYN. *(Alarmed.)* What line of work!

SHARON. Being a mother?

> *(Beat.)*

ROBYN. Yes.

SHARON. Yes?

ROBYN. Yes.
You are correct.
Amanda is my daughter.
Yes.

SHARON. Oh.

> *(Beat.)*

What's your name actually?

ROBYN. Robyn.

SHARON. But... Victoria? And Julia? And...?

ROBYN. Those were also my names, actually, when they were actually my names.

SHARON. But what were you born as?

ROBYN. I was born as a malleable, changeable template.

> *(Beat.)*

SHARON. Is that a poem?

ROBYN. No.

> *(Beat.)*

SHARON. I guess what I'm asking is,
Are you doing something illegal?

ROBYN. Right now?

SHARON. Or like... recently.
Or... ongoingly.
Or like... were you?

> *(A beat.)*

ROBYN. Yes.
Yes I *was*, Sharon.

SHARON. Oh!

> (*A beat.*)

What was it?

ROBYN. If you ask me that
and I tell you
it makes you an accomplice
so.

> (*Beat.*)

SHARON. (*Trying the word out.*) An accomplice.

> (*Beat.*)

What did you do?

ROBYN. Sharon.

SHARON. Yeah?

ROBYN. I'm going to go outside and have a cigarette.
And you think about whether or not you want me to answer that.
And when I come back, you can ask it again.
Or
we can finish dinner
and make an online dating profile for you,
and go to bed
and tomorrow will be a whole new day
in which this question does not exist.

> (*She gets up and starts to leave to the porch.*)

SHARON. Are you really gonna quit smoking, or is that like
part of this whole
multiple personality thing?

ROBYN. I, as me, as myself, am *going* to quit
as soon as I have this next, last,
cigarette.

> (ROBYN *goes outside.*
> *A beat.*
> SHARON *wants to do so many things!*
> *She gets up*
> *she sits down*
> *she gets up*
> *she opens her mouth*
> *she sits down*
> *she goes to the phone*
> *checking nervously over her shoulder.*
> ROBYN *isn't looking.*

She calls her son.

Voicemail!

She has no idea what she's going to say.
She sort of listens to herself stumble through the usual set of communications,
while wondering if she's going to tell him what's happening.)

SHARON. Hi
it's me
your mother
um
I just wanted to see how you're doing!
I just
am thinking about you and
I think you should visit.
I think we should visit each other.
When I told you I smoked marijuana?
I was kidding.
…
I went on a date.
Actually, I wasn't kidding.
I did smoke marijuana.
But I'm not smoking it right now.
…
I didn't go on a date.
I *did* go on a date.
…
My roommate is very
she's very
there's something very
about her
the thing is
…
she's an interesting person.

> (SHARON *is so surprised!*
> *She didn't expect to say this!*
> *But it's true.*)

She knows things.
She does things.
Everybody always told me not to do things.
Your father never   [understood me]
And my mother! She always said *Don't.*

Is that how you feel about me?
Am I a person who says to you: *Don't*?
> *(Beat – maybe she doesn't want that answered.)*
Robyn just says: Do. And then she *does*.
> *(The voicemail cuts her off.)*
Are you there?
Are you…?
Oh.
> *(She calls back, voicemail.)*
Your machine cut me off.
I won't keep you too long.
I just wanted to say that
I'm very
happy
and
that's all.
Goodbye.
> *(She hangs up.*
> ROBYN *is standing in the doorway.*
> *A beat between them.)*

ROBYN. I finished my cigarette.

SHARON. *(With real resolve.)* What do you do, Robyn?

ROBYN. Did.

SHARON. What *did* you do?

> *(A beat. Okay.)*

ROBYN. I took people's money.

SHARON. Like. You robbed them?

ROBYN. Yes.

SHARON. You mugged them?

ROBYN. No. I convinced them to give me their money.

SHARON. That doesn't sound illegal.

ROBYN. Under false pretenses.
I called them up. Old people. Mostly.
They could donate to save the whales or the orphans or the ozone layer.
Whatever.
And they did.
And it all went to me.

SHARON. *(Horrified… but also impressed.)* You did that?

ROBYN. Yeah.

But that wasn't enough money.

So then I started telling people they'd won things.

People are a lot more willing to risk when there's tangible reward.

And to collect the prize, they'd have to provide information.

SHARON. Are you the Nigerians?

ROBYN. Sorry?

SHARON. All those emails from Princess whatsit

trying to store her millions in my whatever—

were those actually from *you?*

ROBYN. Oh! No. I'm much more detail-oriented. Precise. Grammatic.

SHARON. But that's the general idea.

ROBYN. That's the general idea, yes.

> (*A beat as* SHARON *takes this all in.*)

Do you want me to stop telling you?

SHARON. No,

go on.

ROBYN. …So that happened for a while.

And it was actually substantially lucrative.

SHARON. What about your daughter??

Did she know?

ROBYN. We teach our children whatever skill sets we have, Sharon. Didn't you?

SHARON. You *taught* your *daughter* how to *scam* people?

ROBYN. She's the one who came up with the driver's license thing.

We started manufacturing fake IDs, and then she'd sell them at school.

But that wasn't until college.

SHARON. Your *daughter* is a *con artist?*

ROBYN. My daughter is an intelligent and resourceful young woman.

> (*A beat.*)

SHARON. I don't know.

ROBYN. What.

SHARON. What you said… before.

I don't know if I gave my son any kind of…

Skill set.

ROBYN. He sounds successful.

SHARON. I think he might have done that on his own.

Or, worse, in spite of me.

We're not close.

Why aren't we close?

ROBYN. Well. Amanda and I aren't close either.

SHARON. You *scammed* people together.

You were *con artists* together.

You were like Bonnie and Clyde, but mother and daughter.

That's so… I don't know! Close!

ROBYN. We have to give our kids things, and they have to reject those things.

At some point.

Amanda temps at a law firm now and she wears these little power suits

and she tells everybody that her mother lives in another country

so all of her boyfriends bring her home for the holidays

and their mothers are extra sympathetic because her own is

so far away.

So.

> (*A beat.*)

SHARON. I'm sorry.

ROBYN. It's fine.

SHARON. It's not fine.

> (*Beat.*)

ROBYN. She doesn't think I can give it up. The lifestyle.

She doesn't want to talk to me anymore, but if she talked to me, she'd see that

I can give it up. I mean, I'm in *Iowa.* Talk about giving up.

SHARON. Hey.

ROBYN. Also, I sold pot. But you probably figured that out already.

SHARON. (*Wide-eyed.*) No, I didn't.

ROBYN. You didn't?

SHARON. No! How would I figure that out??

ROBYN. (*Genuinely impressed.*) Wow. What planet are you from?

SHARON. Iowa?

ROBYN. Wow. Iowa.

SHARON. Actually Illinois, though.

ROBYN. Right. I remember.

SHARON. Not quite the Land of Giving Up.

ROBYN. I was

talking about me, not you

maybe also you, but mostly me.

SHARON. You sell pot?

ROBYN. Not too often. Just because I don't really have a grow-house or anything.
And growing pot for real, that's a commitment, it requires a lot of specifics. But I have definitely sold it. And that has also, sporadically, definitely been lucrative.

SHARON. Did Amanda sell pot?

ROBYN. (*With some pride.*) She paid her way through college.

SHARON. Wow.

ROBYN. She went to college in a warm state though, so she definitely had a little grow-house going on.

SHARON. Seriously?

ROBYN. (*Really proud.*) And she has a green thumb, I mean I'm not bad with plants but she's got a real talent.
Yeah.

SHARON. (*Impressed.*) That's great.

ROBYN. It is.

> (*Beat.*)

She refuses to talk about any of that now.
When we talk, which is not often, she wants to keep things "present-tense."
She says her therapist told her to do that.
And I'm like, what kind of a therapist refuses to speak in the past tense?
Things *happened*. They *accumulated*. We *became*.
Or the future, for that matter. *We will become.*
But no. Amanda says, "Today I am eating a sandwich. I am grocery shopping."
She says, "We are avoiding conflict."

> (*Half-beat.*)

I don't think conflict is a bad thing.

SHARON. You know my son does that too
the present-tense thing
I don't know if anybody told him to do it
But I'll be like, "Remember when I visited you and we had fun?"
And he'll be like, "It's sunny today. It's cloudy today."

> (*A contemplative beat, then:*)

What else did you do?

ROBYN. I mean, I did just a little bit of auto theft, but

SHARON. YOU WHAT.

ROBYN. (*With growing pride.*) But it's a lot of work
high risk
you have to be really really good at it

and that takes time
like a real commitment to craft

SHARON. Okay yeah I mean yeah I imagine

ROBYN. And you have to spend real time building the right networks
and people have to trust you
if you're going to buy stolen property you have to trust the seller

SHARON. Sure OK

ROBYN. And I was *good*
buyers trusted me
and you might not know this from looking at me but
I'm very very good with cars
both jacking them and stripping them down
some people don't do well under pressure and
I don't want to brag, but I would say that I sort of
thrive
in those contexts
but
finally in the end
auto theft just ended up not being time-cost effective. You know?

SHARON. Right!
…Why not?

ROBYN. …Well
because we moved a lot, we had to move a lot
so you build a network of buyers and then you abandon it,
sort of before you've closed the deal.
It becomes wasteful. And ultimately too risky.

SHARON. Are people chasing you?

ROBYN. Right now?

SHARON. Yes, right now!!

ROBYN. I don't think they are *right now*, no.

SHARON. You don't *think?*

ROBYN. I'm fairly certain that *right now* nobody is chasing me.

SHARON. *How* certain?

ROBYN. Fairly.

(*A beat.*)

SHARON. Are you doing something right now? Here?

ROBYN. I just got here.

SHARON. (*A real question.*) Are you scamming me?

ROBYN. You?

SHARON. Me.

ROBYN. You haven't given me any money! How am I scamming you?

SHARON. I don't know, I don't know if you are
I'm just asking.

ROBYN. Do you feel like I'm scamming you?

SHARON. I mean I don't know
Maybe my jewelry is missing or
maybe you've photocopied my credit cards or something
Have you?
I don't know
Have you?

ROBYN. No.

SHARON. No?

ROBYN. No. I have not.

SHARON. Promise?

ROBYN. I mean, I promise but
do you believe me?

>   (*Beat.* SHARON *looks at her. Then:*)

SHARON. Yeah.

ROBYN. Yeah?

SHARON. I do believe you. Yes.

>   (*Beat between them.*)

ROBYN. So that's me.

>   (*Beat.*)

Are you having a nervous breakdown?

>   (*Beat.*)

SHARON. Show me how to do it.

ROBYN. *What?*

SHARON. I want to do it.
What you did.

ROBYN. No!

SHARON. Why not?

ROBYN. Because…!

SHARON. Because what?

ROBYN. Because I'm done with all that.

SHARON. I'm not asking you to do it, just to show me how.

>   (*A real beat.*
>   ROBYN *takes her in. Then:*)

ROBYN. Show you how what, exactly?

SHARON. The phone thing.

ROBYN. I don't do the phone thing anymore.

SHARON. I bet I'd be good, talking to somebody on the phone.

ROBYN. I don't do any of this anymore.

SHARON. Like you don't smoke anymore?

(*Beat.*)

ROBYN. That's not fair.

SHARON. I'm sorry.

ROBYN. Those are entirely different things.

SHARON. I know.
You're right, I know.
Look. All I'm saying is
how
exactly
did you do it—
when you did it
(which you no longer do)?

(*Beat.*)

ROBYN. Well.
There's a few ways.
Either you're asking them for something
or you're telling them something.

SHARON. Okay…

ROBYN. Like, maybe you're telling them that something they value is about to expire.
Auto insurance. Home insurance. Their cable. Whatever.
And you have a deal, and it's kind of an amazing one-time deal, but it's ending in 24 hours. You just caught them at the tail end of this deal.

SHARON. Right.

ROBYN. So they better decide fast if they want to save 60% on their phone bill.
Or upgrade to a new twice-as-fast high-speed internet connection.

SHARON. That sounds easy. I could do that.

ROBYN. But you also have to be personable, keep them on the line until you get their credit card.
It's easy to hang up a phone.

SHARON. I'm personable.

ROBYN. It's harder than you think.

SHARON. It doesn't sound that hard.

ROBYN. Oh really!

Ring ring. I'm gonna pick up.

> (*She "picks up."*)

Hello?

SHARON. Wait, are we pretending?

ROBYN. (We're seeing how good you are)

Hello, who is this?

SHARON. This is Sharon.

ROBYN. I don't know any Sharons.

SHARON. My name is Sharon, and I'm calling about your…

uh

your

life insurance.

Which is about to expire.

ROBYN. It is?

SHARON. (*Helpfully.*) *You* are about to expire.

ROBYN. Let's start with something easier.

You're calling me about my cable bill. Isn't it high? Wouldn't I like it to be lower?

SHARON. Isn't it high?

ROBYN. I guess it is a little…

SHARON. Wouldn't you like it to be lower?

ROBYN. Are you trying to sell me something?

(They get suspicious)

Are you trying to sell me something I don't want, Sharon?

SHARON. I'm calling because

there's a deal and it's about to end

and you're lucky, you are a lucky person

because first of all, there aren't that many deals in life

life is mostly about being charged the full amount

and second of all, timing is everything.

A bullet is a bullet and your head is your head and

if two seconds separate those things

well

those two seconds saved your life.

So.

How would you like to pay less for your cable?

> (*A beat.* ROBYN *is actually impressed.*)

ROBYN. I'd like that a lot.

SHARON. Okay!
Well that's good.
I'd like that too.
Give me your credit card.

ROBYN. (*Make that sound more official. Anything about money has to sound official, so they feel safe.*)

SHARON. Please give me your credit card.

ROBYN. (*Breaks the "call."*) "The next step requires your date of birth and your credit card information."
You don't need it, it *is required.*

SHARON. You *are* good at this.

ROBYN. Yeah, I am, I'm very good at it.

SHARON. How did I do?

ROBYN. Generally? You did OK generally

SHARON. *Okay?*

ROBYN. You did pretty OK.

SHARON. I was good.
You know I was good.

ROBYN. You were pretty good.

SHARON. I was personable. And you liked me.

> (*Half-beat.*)

ROBYN. Yeah.
Yes. You were.

SHARON. You did, didn't you.

ROBYN. Yeah, I liked you.

> (*A moment between them.*
> *The air has shifted suddenly, and they both suddenly feel it, and neither is sure what the shift is. They're both suddenly uneasy.*)

ROBYN. So. That was that.

SHARON. I want to do it for real.

ROBYN. Sharon…

SHARON. I could do it for real, couldn't I.

> (*A beat.*)

ROBYN. I… can't.
Not anymore.

SHARON. You can't? Or you don't want to?
Or you want to, but you think you shouldn't?

(A beat.)

ROBYN. I'm going to bed.

So.

SHARON. Look.

Tomorrow I make one phone call.

OK? Just one. With you.

And if it doesn't go well, then forget it!

I wasn't cut out for it! We'll forget it!

It'll be like it never happened.

But if it goes well

then

you see how you feel about that.

(A beat.)

ROBYN. Sharon…

SHARON. One foot in the grave, who would I even tell.

ROBYN. Sharon, I told you, you are *not old.*

SHARON. I didn't feel old. Just now.

I felt like

I was *thriving*

and I bet you did too.

(A beat.)

ROBYN. Good night.

(She leaves.)

7.

Morning. The kitchen.

Coffee. Light. Rosetta Stone.

Rosetta Stone??

Yes, SHARON *is learning French as she makes coffee.*

SHARON. Je m'appelle Sharon.

Comment allez-vous?

J'aime Paris.

(ROBYN in the doorway.)

ROBYN. *What* are you doing.

SHARON. Parlez-vous Français?

ROBYN. Not to any functional degree, non.

Why are you parlez-ing Français?

SHARON. I always wanted to learn.

ROBYN. You did?

SHARON. In college I was a member of the French club.

ROBYN. I didn't know that.

SHARON. I was going to be a spy. *La Femme Sharon.*
Or a baker.
...Coffee?

ROBYN. Yes please.

(SHARON *gets her coffee.*)

SHARON. So...

ROBYN. Yeah?

SHARON. Have you
you know.
thought about it?

ROBYN. "It"...

SHARON. You know...

ROBYN. I *just* woke up.

SHARON. I know, I made you coffee.

ROBYN. So give it a minute, okay?

SHARON. Okay.

(*She sits and watches* ROBYN *drink her coffee.*
With baleful focus.
Like an iguana.)

ROBYN. Do you mind.

SHARON. What.

ROBYN. You're *watching* me.

SHARON. I'm drinking my coffee.

ROBYN. You are *not* drinking your coffee
you are *watching* me.

(SHARON *lifts her coffee cup to her mouth.*
She gives ROBYN *an iguana-stare over the lip of the mug.*)

ROBYN. Did you sleep?

SHARON. Yeah I slept

ROBYN. Because I heard
French
around five a.m....?

SHARON. Is there like a... list, or...
Did you just dial random numbers, or...

ROBYN. Did you really sleep?

SHARON. I wasn't that sleepy.
How did you know who to target?

ROBYN. "Target" I don't use that word "target"

SHARON. OK...

ROBYN. "Identify," I took some time to identify my client base

SHARON. OK...

> (*Now* ROBYN*'s getting more into it.*
> *She can't help it:* SHARON*'s undivided attention makes her perform.*)

ROBYN. Senior citizens, they were often senior citizens.

SHARON. Right

ROBYN. So for example, assisted living facilities, like cul-de-sacs of elderly people

SHARON. OK!

ROBYN. Or sometimes you can make an educated guess about a whole neighborhood, often in Florida

SHARON. Florida, right

ROBYN. Also Midwesterners

SHARON. Midwesterners?

ROBYN. Specifically yes
Northerners are mean and paranoid
Southerners are nice but suspicious
The West Coast is in a state of anarchy
but the Midwest...

SHARON. Like Iowa?

ROBYN. Like Iowa.

> (*Beat.*)

SHARON. We could call Tanya.

ROBYN. Tanya.

SHARON. She's from Idaho.

ROBYN. Your friend Tanya?

SHARON. She's an acquaintance.

ROBYN. You want to target Tanya.

SHARON. I am identifying our best client base.

> (ROBYN *really takes* SHARON *in. Really in.*)

ROBYN. You're a quick study.

SHARON. (*This compliment means a lot to her.*) My mother always said I was slow.

ROBYN. (*Not meanly.*) Your mother was a bitch, I think.

SHARON. (*Startled, not upset.*) Excuse me?

ROBYN. (*Still not mean.*) I mean it's hard to tell, it was an earlier time, sometimes you think: *that's just how women were taught to be* but it sounds like your mother was kind of a bitch.

SHARON. I don't feel comfortable saying that myself but I really appreciate that you said it.

(*A beat.*)

ROBYN. You'd have to disguise your voice. An accent of some kind.

SHARON. An accent...?

ROBYN. Norwegian? Chinese? Indian!

SHARON. I think I could do French.

ROBYN. Convincingly?

SHARON. Tanya is from *Idaho.*

ROBYN. If this goes badly, I never agreed to it.

SHARON. Understood.

> (*She goes to the phone. She dials Tanya.*
> ROBYN *sits, arms folded, a commanding general surveying the troops.*
> SHARON *blossoms under her undivided attention. In the following sequence,*
> *we see* SHARON *come fully alive. In a French accent.*)

SHARON. Hello?
Yes, is this Tanya?
Tanya, hello, this is
Juliette
DuBois
from The Franco-Global Association for International Orphans
based in Normandy, France
Yes
Normandy is a lovely city
there are stone walls and it is right next to the ocean
and long ago people stormed the beaches with great passion

> (ROBYN *clears her throat.*)

which is all to say
I wonder if you are interested in saving the lives of starving children
orphans, *oui,* orphans
in Senegal
in many places, but specifically Senegal

have you been?
it's lovely
the bright colors, the drums, the hats
yes, Senegal is a place of music and motion and hats
and children without parents
—What?
well
what we do is, we provide orphans with things they generally lack
like *pain au chocolat*
and bicycles
and vegetables
and small hats
and the right kinds of love.
And love requires money.
All kinds of love, but especially the right kinds.
There can be no love of any kinds
without money.

> (*Beat* – *this comes from a personal place.*
> SHARON *thinks about her life as she speaks, and she gets emotional, and it's actually weirdly honest and raw.*)

Think about what it is to be alone.
It is a late night somewhere
wherever you are
and you are alone.
Think about the objects you arrange around you.
But everything is cold under your hand.
And then someone comes into your life.
And you become different.
You find yourself to be… truly… alive.
Think about how one person can change an entire lifetime
of accumulated coldness and objects and silence.

> (*Beat* – *Tanya is affected by this and wants to help.* SHARON *makes direct eye contact with* ROBYN, *speaking with a quiet and inarguable victory:*)

Thank you Tanya.
It's people like you who make the difference.
The next step requires your date of birth
and your credit card information.

8.

The kitchen, two weeks later.

The table is cluttered, piled high with French guidebooks, a stack of new clothes with labels still on, scattered cash, cigarettes. AND… a record player. Stacks of credit card applications litter the table. It looks like the kitchen of high-rolling and sophisticated college kids with money to burn.

ROBYN, *at the table, bagging weed.*

SHARON *is on the cordless phone with a book club lady. She looks younger, somehow, more buoyant.*

SHARON. (*To the phone.*) Yes, how much would you like?
Now, was that the herbal mix or the baked goods?
Bills, yes. Small bills.
    (*Making a joke.*)
Unmarked bills.
    (*The book club lady doesn't get the joke.*)
OK dear, I'll bring it to book club tomorrow.
Bye bye now.
    (*She hangs up.*)
That's another order.
ROBYN. Boom!
Of the brownies, or…?
SHARON. The herbal mix.
ROBYN. (*Makes a note in a notebook.*) Got it.
They're being discreet?
SHARON. Like little mice
little Iowan churchmice
but I must say, it livens up reading group discussion.
Everybody's got opinions now,
they all interrupt each other.
These days Tanya giggles a lot
we read that book about child soldiers and she just
giggled her way through that.
ROBYN. (*Laughing.*) Was that one your pick?
SHARON. I told you—
ROBYN. You're not from here.
SHARON. *I* played the clarinet as a child.
Tanya refers to her book club as a—

SHARON and ROBYN. —reading group.

SHARON. I *look* Iowan, but I'm *not* Iowan, it's my secret weapon.

ROBYN. Yeah I'm learning that about you.

SHARON. What?

ROBYN. Your secret weapons.

>   (*A beat between them.*)

SHARON. (*Pleased.*) You're the one who came home yesterday with a record player.

ROBYN. You're the one who never listens to music
It was an act of mercy on my part

SHARON. I do so listen to music!

ROBYN. You listen to *one* CD, occasionally,
that your son sent you
when he blew off Christmas
which is not the same as Listening To Music
regularly
in a healthy way
on a record player.

>   (*Beat.*)

SHARON. I like it.
The record player.

ROBYN. (*Shy.*) Yeah?

SHARON. Yeah.

ROBYN. Cool.

>   (*Beat.*)

SHARON. Robyn?

ROBYN. Yeah?

SHARON. I was gonna ask you…

ROBYN. What's up?

SHARON. Well
I had this idea
this thought
that I wanted to sort of
run by you

ROBYN. Yes…?

SHARON. I just have been thinking
that
the book club ladies have been really really
receptive

to medicinal herbs

ROBYN. Sure seems like it.

SHARON. I was talking to Betty—

ROBYN. The one with the hair net?

SHARON. Yes, and she mentioned that her goddaughter had one of our brownies

ROBYN. Oh wait a minute

SHARON. Sort of by accident but
she really enjoyed it

ROBYN. How old is she?

SHARON. Twelve?

ROBYN. OH my god

SHARON. (It's fine!) and it occurred to me
you know
those kids have a whole demographic available to them that we don't
and I thought
what if we gave Betty's goddaughter some
supplies
to off-load

ROBYN. Hold up.
Hold up.
You want Betty's twelve-year-old goddaughter
to sell pot brownies for us
to her friends.

SHARON. Or regular pot.

ROBYN. Sharon!

SHARON. To her classmates.

ROBYN. Her classmates?

SHARON. (*Helpfully.*) She might not have many actual *friends*
she's a little strange-looking
(her teeth, and…)
but uh, classmates and
you know, kids she knows from places.

ROBYN. Okay
Sharon?
Okay
listen

SHARON. And I *know* you might have concerns

ROBYN. "concerns"

yes, yes I do
concerns

SHARON. But I just think,
let's think about this.
Expansion is progress.
So. Let's consider.

 (*A beat.*)

ROBYN. "Expansion is progress"
Where did you even...?

SHARON. I read that.

ROBYN. You read it.

SHARON. I was reading this article in Harvard Business Review
yesterday
about women entrepreneurs
and they all said *Expansion is progress.*
Because women settle for things,
we nurture, nurturing requires settlement
to some degree
but
we deserve progress too.
Don't you think?

 (*A beat.*)

ROBYN. Since when do you read Harvard Business Review?

SHARON. I want to know what's going on.

ROBYN. ...by reading *Harvard Business Review*?

SHARON. What!

 (*Pause – refocusing:*)

ROBYN. Sharon... I don't think off-loading pot brownies to Betty's adolescent buck-toothed goddaughter is going to provide *progress*, entrepreneurial or otherwise. And you know, *low profile*, Sharon
we are keeping a *low profile*
we are not *expanding* a *business.*
Sustaining and expanding are two different activities
and it's great that now you read Harvard Business Review
but expanding is no longer an interest of mine.

 (*Beat.*)

SHARON. And then there's this other thing.

ROBYN. What other thing...

SHARON. Well.
I got us something.

ROBYN. What?

SHARON. And it's sort of just in case.

We don't need it *now*

so I don't think we should think that we need it *now*

but I just thought, it's good to be prepared.

ROBYN. What did you buy.

> (SHARON *goes to a large shopping bag.*
> *She takes out a large gun.*)

ROBYN. SHARON.

SHARON. I went to the Walmart in Cedar Rapids

ROBYN. WHAT THE FUCK!

SHARON. and there was a nice young man who   [sold me this]

ROBYN. Do you even know how to use a gun??

SHARON. I've been watching videos on YouTube

it doesn't look hard.

ROBYN. Sharon!

We cannot own a gun.

SHARON. This is Iowa, *everybody* owns a gun.

ROBYN. Okay

a hunting rifle

if you hunted

okay

but *this*

sort of phallic

semi-automatic…

what *is* this?

SHARON. Do you wanna hold it?

It's got a weight to it

it feels warm

like you're holding a sort of pet or

somebody's limb

or your own extra limb

ROBYN. Sharon!

SHARON. What?

ROBYN. Take it back.

SHARON. What??

ROBYN. Do you have the receipt?

Take it back.

SHARON. I got it for us!

ROBYN. We don't need a   [gun]
Jesus

SHARON. Hold it.

ROBYN. I don't want to hold it!!

SHARON. Hold it and I'll look for the receipt.

> (*A beat.*
> ROBYN *holds the gun.*
> SHARON *takes her time looking for the receipt. She watches* ROBYN *hold it.*)

SHARON. What's it feel like?

ROBYN. Heavy.

SHARON. Powerful?

ROBYN. Dangerous.

SHARON. But doesn't it feel good?

> (*Pause.*)

I walked out of that Walmart
and I knew that everybody who looked at me
was looking through me
but I knew what they weren't seeing.
I knew what I had.

> (*Beat.*)

ROBYN. Find your receipt?

SHARON. Still looking.

ROBYN. We're not gonna shoot anybody.
Who did you wanna shoot?

SHARON. I don't want to shoot anybody
I just want to be prepared.

ROBYN. Prepared to shoot?

SHARON. Just prepared.

ROBYN. Take it back. Okay? Sharon?

SHARON. Okay.

ROBYN. Promise?

SHARON. I said okay.
I will.
Robyn, I will.

ROBYN. OK and just
in general, Sharon,
this is not…
expansion… is not…
OK?

SHARON. Okay.

ROBYN. This is just
as this is.
No bigger.

SHARON. No smaller?

ROBYN. Just as we are.

SHARON. I like how we are.

(*Beat.*)

Found it.

ROBYN. Yeah?

SHARON. Right here.

ROBYN. Okay.

SHARON. Are we good?

ROBYN. We're good.

9.

Evening, one week later.
The kitchen.
Music on the record player.

ROBYN *stands, with the box of dolls. She has a large garbage bag. She seems
to be about to throw them out, and then...*
The sound of SHARON, *approaching.*
ROBYN *hides the box quickly.*

SHARON *comes into the kitchen from the outside.*
She is Dressed. Up.
And a teeny little bit drunk.
And it's pretty hot.

ROBYN. Oh hey look who's home!

SHARON. There you are!

ROBYN. (*Taking in the outfit.*) Whoa. Whoa mama.
Look at you.

SHARON. Right? Whaddayou think?

ROBYN. Bold. Bold choice.

SHARON. Right?!

(*Beat.*)

Bold good or bold bad?

(She grabs a joint off the table, lights it.)

ROBYN. Bold is… bold. It exists above the dictates of good and evil.

 (Beat.)

That's for your book club, you *know* we don't smoke that.

SHARON. It's just a little bit.

Do you want me to put this out?

ROBYN. No, just—next time—

 (Beat.)

SO.

SHARON. *(Can't wait to be asked.)* Yeeeees?

ROBYN. How was your date?

SHARON. WELL.

 (This is a good thing!)

He's an ophthalmologist!

ROBYN. Okay…

SHARON. Eyes, that's eyes.

He knows about eyes.

ROBYN. Yeah okay, eyes.

SHARON. *(This is not a good thing…)* He's going bald…

ROBYN. Bald, okay.

SHARON. *(Not sure how she feels about this.)* He was a child star?

ROBYN. What kind?

SHARON. Gerber food commercial.

ROBYN. Hmm.

SHARON. His experiences with fame haunted him. To this day.

ROBYN. Fame! Okay!

Overall verdict?

 (Beat.)

SHARON. And he kissed me.

ROBYN. You mean like an end-of-night kiss

or like a Kiss?

SHARON. Well we kissed on the cheek when I first arrived at the restaurant

but those don't count

(I mean in Paris everybody kisses each other on the cheek *all the time*)

but *after* dinner he drove me home

and then we made out.

In the car.

And he was very passionate
he kept bumping me into things
like the gear shift because he drives stick.

ROBYN. Well done!

SHARON. I don't think I ever really did that as a teenager.
Like, forty years late, I made out in a car.

(*Beat.*)

And he put his
hand
on my

(*Breasts.*)

you know

ROBYN. *Oh*-kay, I don't think we need to

SHARON. And he squeezed

ROBYN. *Oh*-kay

SHARON. And I just thought
is *this* what all the fuss is about?

ROBYN. …What?

SHARON. I just. I don't know. I was bored.

ROBYN. You were making out in a car!
You were banging into the gear shift!
He was squeezing various parts of you!
How were you bored?

SHARON. It just felt like
I don't know
he was so… normal.
He told me I was pretty.
It was very unambiguous.
He had kids, he showed me pictures of them.
They looked like kids.

ROBYN. Sharon! You went on a nice date
with a man who was NOT a serial killer—

SHARON. I sort of just started entertaining myself
after a time.

ROBYN. What does that mean?

(SHARON *takes a series of objects out of her pocket: cigarettes, a fancy lighter.*)

SHARON. I took these out of his pocket while we were kissing.

ROBYN. You—!

SHARON. (*With pride.*) He didn't even notice.

ROBYN. You *robbed* him
while he was *kissing* you.

SHARON. He won't miss them
It's just cigarettes

ROBYN. And a nice lighter!

SHARON. A lighter is a lighter.

ROBYN. That's not the point and you know it.

SHARON. When I was a girl I stole a penny candy from the store
and my mother slapped me across the face.
She said, "Little girls don't take what isn't theirs."
And you know what?
She was right.
Little girls *don't* take what's not theirs.
It takes a grown lady to do that.

> (*Despite herself,* ROBYN *is laughing.*)

ROBYN. Sharon!!

SHARON. (*Takes out a watch, sets it on the table.*) Right off his wrist, and he
didn't notice.
Turns out, I'm good. Who knew!

ROBYN. *Sharon!*

SHARON. What!

ROBYN. Sharon you *cannot* just
go on dates with people and
mug them

SHARON. He wasn't complaining.

ROBYN. *I* am complaining! (I think I'm complaining.)
The point is—

SHARON. The point *is*, if you'd been on a date with me
I wouldn't have mugged you.

> (*Beat. The air changes just a little.*)

ROBYN. What does *that* mean.

SHARON. I just mean
you're more exciting
than the rest of them.
I wouldn't have had to.

> (*Beat.*)

Are you *mad* at me?

> (*Beat.*)

He's just a guy
you don't even know him.

(*Beat.* ROBYN *is sober now.*)

ROBYN. Careful. With that.

SHARON. What!

ROBYN. "Just a guy"

SHARON. I mean I didn't *kill* him.
I didn't like, *poison* him.
You know?
Everything's fine.

ROBYN. And the next time you go on a date?
And you get bored?
And it's just a guy?

SHARON. Don't you think you're overreacting?

(*Beat.*)

ROBYN. I meant to give this up.
I really did.
Until you, I did.

SHARON. Oh…

ROBYN. Until you
and how it was so
fun
and how you
surprised me
(you always surprise me)
until *that*
I really
really
did.

SHARON. …Thank you.

ROBYN. It's hard to go back to the normal world.
To getting what you want so slowly, over so much time,
or sometimes to never getting it at all.
You start to need this.

SHARON. I'm doing this for fun.

ROBYN. Or you want it so bad it feels like you need it.

SHARON. I don't *need* it, Robyn.

ROBYN. Are you sure?

(*Beat.* SHARON *is NOT sure.*)

SHARON. (*Quiet.*) I'm not a kid who doesn't know right from wrong.
You aren't raising me. Somebody already raised me, and they did a shitty job
and then I raised somebody and *I* did a shitty job
and you, generally, all you've done is be a really
really
great
roommate.

> (*Beat.*
> ROBYN *almost laughs, but also she's too sad to laugh. She takes* SHARON'*s
> joint. She smokes and* SHARON *tries to make out her expression.*)

SHARON. Robyn.

ROBYN. What.

SHARON. Don't be sad.
Are you sad?
Don't be sad.

ROBYN. (*Means it.*) I'm glad you had a good date.

SHARON. Fuck that.
I don't care about that.

ROBYN. Sharon…

SHARON. I've had a good month. With you.
I've had good coffee
good conversations
and now we're making good money and that's good
but actually, it's not the money, it's the *making*.
Making something with you.

ROBYN. Sharon…

SHARON. I look forward to waking up in the morning.
Everything is a Yes.
I'm smarter and faster and
younger
than I knew I could be.
Don't be sad. I can't remember ever having been this happy.

> (*A beat and then* SHARON *gets up decisively.*)

We are gonna dance.

ROBYN. Oh come on.

SHARON. No
No
We are gonna dance.
You can't go to bed sad.

> (*She puts on a record.*

Something you can dance to. From the 20s.)

ROBYN. What *is* that.

SHARON. It's World War Two London.
The whole world has been bombed.

ROBYN. *London?*

SHARON. We're the only two people left, in the ruins of a building
that has *also* been bombed but still, oddly, is standing.
You're a pickpocket. And I'm a soldier.
Or maybe I'm a pickpocket and you're a sailor.
I don't know.

ROBYN. (*But laughing.*) You're crazy.

SHARON. We're sheltering. From the cold cold English wind.
And then suddenly
from somewhere far away
a lone apartment somewhere high off the street
we hear music.
It drifts.
It comes to us.
It catches us.

ROBYN. And then what?

(SHARON *takes* ROBYN's *hand. They dance.*
Old School WW2 Bombed-Out London Dance. It's playful and funny at first,
and then it's quieter, and then it's tender and sweet and kind of shy, and then it
heats up. And then SHARON *kisses* ROBYN.

A beat. ROBYN *pulls away. Wide-eyed.*
A moment between them.)

SHARON. I'm sorry.

(*Silence.*)

I'm so sorry.

(*Silence.*)

Should I be sorry?

ROBYN. I have to go to bed.

SHARON. Are you mad at me?

ROBYN. I have to go to bed.

(*Beat.*)

I'm not mad at you.

SHARON. Robyn…

ROBYN. Good night.

10.

Late morning. Sunlight slants in.
The kitchen, as they left it: a mess.
SHARON *comes downstairs in her bathrobe, groggy, a little hungover.*

She starts to clean up a little.
Puts the coffee on.
She's waiting for ROBYN.
She goes to the stairs a few times, listens to see if ROBYN *is awake yet.*

She starts making a little extra noise to see if ROBYN *will wake up.*
Dropping things, "accidentally."
She puts a record on.
Louder.
A little louder.
Too loud.
Turns it off.
Goes to the bottom of the stairs again.
Still nothing.

Back to the kitchen, resigned.

And then sees a note.
She picks it up.
Reads it.
Can't quite wrap her mind around it.
She rushes to the door, opens it onto the driveway. ROBYN's *car is gone. She comes back inside. She opens the cabinets.* ROBYN's *things are gone. Out to the porch—most of* ROBYN's *boxes are gone.*

A beat.
She sits down heavily at the kitchen table.

A beat.
She picks the note back up.
Reads it.
Crumples it.
She makes a phone call. It goes to voicemail.

SHARON. Robyn, hi.
This is Sharon.
Obviously.
I just woke up and I saw your things are all gone and
did we get robbed in the night? I just got worried
so

call me.
>   (*Beat.*)

Actually I got your note, so
>   (*Beat.*)

call me anyway.
>   (*Beat.*)

You didn't have to…   [leave]
>   (*Beat.*)

I mean if it was—you know—
I was drunk and I *barely* remember what I was even   [doing]
and it's not like I'm *even*   [gay]
but even if I *was*   [gay]
it's not like I want to date you
so
you don't have to worry about that!
There's lots of other women I'd date
if I was going to date a woman
so…
>   (*Beat, disentangling herself.*)

Call me.
OK?

>   (*She hangs up.*
>
>   *Time passes.*
>   *She might go through the space again, looking for items of* ROBYN'*s. There*
>   *are very few.*
>
>   *It becomes afternoon.*
>   *She calls* ROBYN *again. Voicemail.*)

SHARON. Hi Robyn it's me again
clearly
you probably aren't checking your phone
and you're probably going to check it sometime soon
sometime later
but soon
and then you'll see I've been trying to reach you
and I'm sorry if I'm being alarmist
but
I went into your bedroom
(I'm sorry I probably shouldn't have done that but)
it's pretty

empty.
Your bedroom.
Is empty.
And I just.
I think you should call me?
So.

> (*Beat – this is raw.*)

I miss you.

> (*Beat – attempting to recover.*)

OK.
Bye.

> (*She hangs up.*
>
> *Time passes.*
> *She finds a small box under things.*
> ROBYN's *ceramic dolls.*
> *She takes one out, sits and holds it.*
>
> *It becomes evening.*
> *It becomes dark.*
>
> *She calls* ROBYN *again. Voicemail.*)

SHARON. If you're going to leave because I kissed you?
That's bullshit.
And if you're leaving for some other reason?
That's also bullshit.
I am a grown-ass adult.
Okay.
If you just don't want to be *responsible* for me,
then don't worry!
You're not responsible!
I absolve you!
And if you don't want to do the things we were doing
the phone calls and the book club weed-ring and whatever
that's fine!
Don't do it!
I won't do it!
I don't care, I'm done anyway.
Or if I did it, I'd do it without you!
And where are you going to go, anyway?
Nobody wants you.
Amanda doesn't want you!
So come back!

(She hangs up.
She smashes the doll.
That felt good.
Another one.
Another one.
Then freezes.
Inside the third doll, is a small plastic bag.
She lifts it out.
The ceramic doll was stuffed with coke.
Another one of ROBYN's *businesses.*

She smashes more dolls. More bags of coke.

She sits with the bags and the pieces of doll.
Time passes.

It becomes night.
It becomes late.

She plays the WW2 London record.
She falls asleep at the kitchen table.)

11.

The kitchen.
Morning.

SHARON *sleeps at the kitchen table. She looks terrible. Not entirely sober.*

Days have passed. Maybe a week.
We see this by the accumulated filth. Dishes unwashed, food left out, clothes strewn. The same WW2 London record has been playing on loop but now the record spins and the needle scratches.

The phone rings.
SHARON *jolts awake.*
It goes to the answering machine.

SHARON'S SON. Mom. Hey. It's me.
You home?

     (SHARON sits up and listens but makes no move to answer it.)
Haven't heard from you in a while.
I mean that's cool, you must be
Doing Things so
that's awesome!

But
Your roommate called me.

> (*Now* SHARON *is alert in a way she hasn't been in a week. But she still doesn't pick up.*)

She said she had to leave for business
and she wanted me to check in on you
and I realized, we hadn't talked in a bit
like a little bit
and uh
you left me some messages?
That, frankly, were kind of
crazy messages?
so I thought…
I'd call you
but
I guess I'll try you later.

> (SHARON *lunges up off the couch and toward the phone with a sudden burst of purpose.*
> *Just as she gets there:*)

Bye Mom.

> (*He hangs up.*
> *A beat.*
> SHARON *picks up the phone.*
> *She listens to the dial tone.*
> *She looks around her kitchen.*
> *She starts to wake up in a way.*
>
> *A breath. Still holding the dial-tone phone.*)

SHARON. Hi, God.
It's Sharon.
I'm standing in my kitchen.
My husband is not   [here]
and my son is not   [here]
and
my roommate is not   [here]
and You are possibly also
not…   [here]

> (*Beat.*)

My roommate told me that
people find words for themselves but
those words are not always right

and I think I don't have the right words, right now.
Sharon doesn't feel   [right]
Mother isn't quite   [right]
and Wife hasn't been right for some time now.
"Roommate" was good.
That was a good word.
But now it's not quite   [right.]
      (*Beat.*)
God, I just think
that there is a better way to do things
than the one where we live a certain life
and then we lose it completely.
      (*Beat – a moment of revelation and a genuine question to herself.*)
Is this a poem??
      (*Beat.*)
I don't think so.
      (*Beat.*)
I slept in the kitchen for a week, God.
I didn't have the right words to answer the phone
or go to my book club
or go get the mail
so
I didn't do any of those things.
But now I'm awake.
And I don't know where to start. Exactly.
Except: over.
Again.

      (*She hangs up.*
      And then, in her hand,
      the phone rings.

      Beat.
      She answers it.)

SHARON. …Hello…?

      (*Perhaps we see* ROBYN. *Somewhere shadowy. Perhaps we just hear her voice,*
      soft and filling the entire space.)

ROBYN. Hello. This is Victoria Jones from the Franco-Global Society of
International Orphans. Is this Sharon?

      (*A beat.*)

SHARON. This is Sharon.

ROBYN. Hi Sharon.

I'm calling you because we want to thank you.

For your hard work.

Your... donations. Your... support.

SHARON. My...?

ROBYN. We recognize that it is hard to... care for strangers.

People who maybe

their lives have taken place on the other side of the world from you

and their lives will continue to take place on the other side of the world

and someone with a less... developed... heart

might think: *what does that have to do with me.*

But you cared.

You are a caring person.

And the Franco-Global Society of International Orphans just wants to thank you for that.

> (*A beat.*)

SHARON. (*Soft.*) Are you coming back?

ROBYN. Orphans, once they have left their homes for new placements rarely return.

SHARON. Victoria Jones.

ROBYN. Yes?

SHARON. Why is that.

ROBYN. Because sometimes their pasts are

contentious

and they recognize that they could cause great harm

to those they have come to care for

by returning.

SHARON. Or maybe sometimes they forget and move on and don't care anymore.

ROBYN. No. That's not it.

I've done this job for a hundred years.

And that's not it.

SHARON. Are you with Amanda?

> (*A beat.*)

ROBYN. I have to go now, Sharon, but

on behalf of all of us

here at FGSIO

please take care of yourself.

SHARON. Wait!

ROBYN. What is it?

SHARON. Will I ever hear from you again?

    (A beat.)

ROBYN. We might occasionally make a courtesy call, to check in on some of our most helpful donors.

    (A beat.)

SHARON. Bye Victoria Jones.

ROBYN. Goodbye.

    (She hangs up.
    A beat.
    SHARON stands in her kitchen.)

SHARON. Well.

Well then.

    (She gets a giant garbage bag.
    Begins to throw out the doll-shards and coke baggies.

    A beat.

    She pulls the bags of coke back out.
    Sets them all on the table in a long row.
    Ideas dawn.)

SHARON. *(Soft.)* All first poems are bad poems.

But there's a great liberty in being bad.

    (As she considers her loot, and a glorious future of illegal activity…

    Blackout.)

End of Play

SO UNNATURAL A LEVEL
by Gary Winter

BIOGRAPHY

Gary Winter was a member of Obie Award-winner 13P—thirteen playwrights who produced their own work. His plays have been produced at Actors Theatre of Louisville (2015 Heideman Award), PS122, The Flea Theater, The Chocolate Factory, Defunkt Theatre, HERE, The Brick, and The Cherry Lane Alternative. Winter has received support from The New Group, Playwrights Horizons, The Jewish Play Project, Ensemble Studio Theatre, The Goldberg Award, Lark Theater Fellowship, SEG Voices, The Puffin Foundation, Dramatists Guild Fellowship, The MacDowell Colony, and Yaddo. He was awarded a Spielberg Foundation Righteous Persons Fellowship to study Eastern European Jewry in Krakow. From 1998 to 2008, Winter volunteered as Literary Manager of The Flea Theater, where he currently helps organize Pataphysics, workshops for playwrights. He holds an M.F.A. from New York University.

ACKNOWLEDGMENTS

So Unnatural a Level premiered at the Humana Festival of New American Plays in April 2015. It was directed by Les Waters with the following cast:

SUSAN	Lexi Lapp
GAIL	Birgit Huppuch
LARRY	José Leon
MOHAMMED	Ramiz Monsef
THOMAS	Bruce McKenzie
EDDIE (Sea Monster)	Aaron Lynn
ABIGAIL	Kayla Jackmon

and the following production staff:

Scenic Designer	Dane Laffrey
Costume Designer	Beatrice Vena
Lighting Designer	Mike Inwood
Sound Designer	Christian Frederickson
Stage Manager	Stephen Horton
Assistant Stage Manager	Jason Pacella
Dramaturg	Jessica Reese
Properties Master	Mark Walston

CHARACTERS

THOMAS, Supervisor
GAIL, Insurance Salesman
LARRY, Insurance Salesman
MOHAMMED, Insurance Salesman
SUSAN, Intern
ABIGAIL, Typing Woman, African-American
SEA MONSTER, Puppet

SUSAN *should be in her late teens or early 20s. The ages of the other characters are flexible.*

SETTING

An insurance office. The time is the very near future.

But power of blood itself releases blood.
It goes by might of being such a flood
Held high at so unnatural a level.

—From "The Flood" by Robert Frost

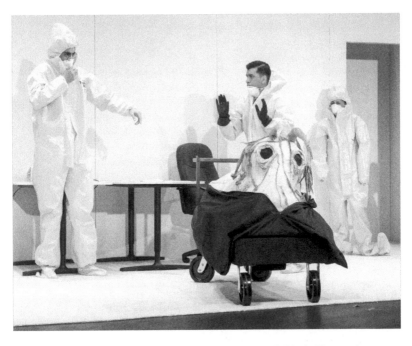

Ramiz Monsef, Aaron Lynn, José Leon, and Birgit Huppuch
in *So Unnatural a Level*

39th Humana Festival of New American Plays
Actors Theatre of Louisville, 2015
Photo by Bill Brymer

SO UNNATURAL A LEVEL

THOMAS, GAIL, MOHAMMED, SUSAN *and* LARRY *are in the space.* ABIGAIL *sits in a corner typing on a laptop. For the most part, she ignores the action in the room. Those in the room don't notice her.*

SUSAN. Coffee?

GAIL. Yes.

LARRY. Yes no sugar.

MOHAMMED. No.

SUSAN. Is that no coffee or no sugar?

MOHAMMED. I don't drink coffee.

THOMAS. Sweet.

SUSAN. Okay. One sweet, one without sugar, one regular, one not.

GAIL. Black. With sugar.

LARRY. Black too.

THOMAS. Milk.

SUSAN. Okay. Um… One sugar black. One no sugar black. One sweet with milk. One…nothing.

> *(BLACKOUT.*
> *LIGHTS UP.*
> THOMAS *is alone.*
> SUSAN *wheels in a state-of-the-art coffee machine. She reads the instruction manual.)*

THOMAS. *(On the phone.)* Yes, I told you we're on it! Oh give me a break, it's ten times worse than Sandy!

> *(GAIL and MOHAMMED enter in hazmat suits. THOMAS hangs up.)*

MOHAMMED. We saw this in Bhopal, Indian Point, Katrina, Chernobyl, Fukushima. Damage control?
Anyone?

THOMAS. *(Meaning insurance claims.)* It'll slam us like a tidal wave if we're not prepared.

GAIL. Well it's certainly understandable considering the levels of radiation…

THOMAS. Radiation is a non-insurable anomaly. A few years ago there was a movement to slot it under Force Majeure. That died in committee.
Susan? Do you have a thought?

SUSAN. Um, well… It's really awful.

MOHAMMED. Thank you for that insight Susan.

THOMAS. Where is Larry? Larry?!

SUSAN. Do you have a body count?

THOMAS. Is that our coffee machine?

LARRY. (*Offstage.*) You want to talk about work-life balance? Right now? Suck on this!

SUSAN. I think so. I found it in the break room. I don't think anyone's ever used it.
It's quite sophisticated.

MOHAMMED. Susan, did someone ask you for a body count?

SUSAN. No, I just thought it might be…it would be good to know…

GAIL. It's not what we do here Susan.

SUSAN. But I assumed…we're a life insurance company…so I thought… on-the-ground statistics…would help us facilitate…claims…

THOMAS. FEMA will take care of the dead. We take care of the living.

MOHAMMED. *Life* insurance Susan, not *after life* insurance.

GAIL. We couldn't possibly insure the living after life.
Wait, could we?

MOHAMMED. We've been talking about diversifying…

LARRY. (*From offstage.*) What the fuck is that? What are you bringing in here? Don't leave your shit in the lobby! Hey!

THOMAS. Nice thinking outside the box Gail. Would you bring that up at the next director's meeting?

> (GAIL *makes a note to bring up after-life insurance at the next director's meeting.*)

SUSAN. Hey I think I'm getting the hang of this.

MOHAMMED. These suits are hot.

GAIL. I tried to order the ventilated ones but budget says they're too expensive.

THOMAS. Susan will drive you to the site when she's done with the coffee.

SUSAN. Oh? Um…should I wear a hazmat suit?

MOHAMMED. Stay 16 feet away from the sludge and hold your breath and you'll be fine.

SUSAN. Oh…okay.

LARRY. (*Offstage.*) I can't feel my dick in this thing!

GAIL. Tom, do we even have any lime left over from Poseidon?

THOMAS. 'Fraid all our lime went like hotcakes on that one.

GAIL. Damn. Okay…

SUSAN. Guatemalan Roast or Ecuador?

GAIL. Compost! We can use compost. Guatemalan.

MOHAMMED. Compost? You think?
I said I don't drink coffee.

GAIL. Sure compost breaks down organic matter… No—Ecuador.

THOMAS. Brilliant Gail, let's go with compost. Ecuador.

SUSAN. Looks like Ecuador wins.

> (LARRY *enters, pushing a rolling cart with a large duffel bag on it.*
> LARRY *wears a hazmat suit.*)

THOMAS. How did these people get into the building? Does security have its head up its ass?

SUSAN. Coffee Larry?

MOHAMMED. What is that?

LARRY. Hell do I know. Yes, light with sugar.

GAIL. It's toxic sludge. They pulled this stunt last time.

THOMAS. Fucking eco-terrorists!

LARRY. The guy who dropped it off said the weirdest thing.

MOHAMMED. What's that?

LARRY. He said it ate three children and two cats.

> (*Silence.*
> MOHAMMED *goes over to the bag and opens it.*
> *Inside is a terribly deformed and awful-smelling* SEA MONSTER.)

MOHAMMED. Holy mother of the prophet!

LARRY. Jesus!

GAIL. What is that?!

THOMAS. That my friends is a byproduct of globalization.

SUSAN. It smells like my grandmother's attic after they found her collection of…um…never mind.

GAIL. What are we going to do with it?

LARRY. I'll toss it in the dumpster.

SUSAN. Oh no! It's a living thing!

THOMAS. I'll consult the manual.

LARRY. Yeah do that Thomas.

> (THOMAS *consults the insurance manual.*
> *All stare at the* SEA MONSTER. *It stares at them.*
> *Suddenly they all turn to* ABIGAIL, *who has been typing all this time.*)

GAIL. Who is that?

MOHAMMED. I dunno.

LARRY. I've never seen her before.

THOMAS. Here's a section entitled "Care and maintenance of rare or exotic wildlife."

MOHAMMED. Hi.

(ABIGAIL *looks up.*)

ABIGAIL. Hello.

GAIL. What department do you work in?

ABIGAIL. Billing.

LARRY. This isn't Billing. This is Processing.

ABIGAIL. Okay.

SUSAN. What's your name?

ABIGAIL. Abigail.

GAIL. What are you doing?

ABIGAIL. Writing my novel.

THOMAS. The manual only covers rare and exotic species. Nothing on *new* species.
Hello? Who is this?

GAIL. It's Abigail.

THOMAS. Oh? Hi Abigail.

ABIGAIL. Hello.

MOHAMMED. Your novel?

ABIGAIL. Yes. My third.

LARRY. How long have you worked here?

ABIGAIL. Eight years.

SUSAN. And this is your third novel?

ABIGAIL. Yes.

MOHAMMED. Wow.

SUSAN. Wow.

LARRY. Wow.

THOMAS. Nuts. There's nothing in the manual about sea creatures.

LARRY. I always wanted to write a novel.

GAIL. Right now I'm making notes on yellow sticky pads for a play about the history of margarine.

MOHAMMED. I've been thinking about a cookbook using only enzyme-free food sources.

SUSAN. Would you like some coffee Abigail?

ABIGAIL. I'm okay, thank you.

(*Silence. No one is really sure what to do now.*

The SEA MONSTER *emits a mournful and frightening wail.*)

THOMAS. I'll drive you guys to the site.

GAIL. K.

MOHAMMED. K.

LARRY. K.

SUSAN. Oh, but I thought…

THOMAS. Susan, expedite that thing will you?

SUSAN. Expedite? I've never…

THOMAS. You're doing a good job Susan. I like your initiative. That's the first thing an employer looks for.
Hard work, initiative and the ability to bend time.

(*They all exit. Silence.*)

ABIGAIL. So. How do you like being an intern here, Susan?

SUSAN. It's been…dynamic. Educational. I'm learning so much. How's your novel coming along?

ABIGAIL. Very well.

SUSAN. Eight years. Wow. That must be a record. You like working here?

ABIGAIL. It has its moments, but for the most part I can't complain.

(*Both turn their attention to the* SEA MONSTER.)

SUSAN. Look what the storm washed up.

ABIGAIL. The ocean is a vast and unexplored territory, isn't it?

SUSAN. Maybe the storm wrecked its home too? You think?

ABIGAIL. That's possible.

SUSAN. Maybe it's here to breed and take over the planet. I mean, why not? We fucked it up so maybe it's time for a new species to give it a shot.

ABIGAIL. That's an interesting theory.

SUSAN. What should I do with it?

ABIGAIL. I don't know.

SUSAN. I think it might like the swimming pool in Red Hook.

ABIGAIL. Oh I love that pool.

(*Pause.*)

SUSAN. When I was growing up I did everything I could to be hidden. I would hide in the washing machine, my sister's toy chest, my father's golf bag, the dishwasher, the attic, the spare tire, the kitchen cabinets, the doghouse, the rug, piles of leaves. It's one of the few powers you have as a child; the power to be invisible. But wherever I was they found me and plopped me back into the human orbit. For some reason adults are hell-bent on taking this power away from you.

This poor creature. I bet you were nice and cozy in your little cave beneath the sea until the storm swept you from your hiding place and into the decadent company of mankind.

    (Pause.)

Can I ask you something Abigail?

ABIGAIL. What's that Susan?

SUSAN. How did you get away with being invisible for so long?

    (Lights fade.)

End of Play

JOSHUA CONSUMED AN UNFORTUNATE PEAR

by Steve Yockey

BIOGRAPHY

Steve Yockey is a Los Angeles-based writer with work produced throughout the country, Europe, and Asia. His plays *Afterlife*, *Octopus*, *Large Animal Games*, *CARTOON*, *Subculture*, *Very Still & Hard to See*, *The Fisherman's Wife*, *Wolves*, *Disassembly*, and *Niagara Falls & Other Plays* are published and available from Samuel French. He was one of two writers selected for the U.S./Australia playwright exchange in February 2013, sponsored by the National New Play Network and Playwriting Australia. Yockey holds an M.F.A. in Dramatic Writing from NYU's Tisch School of the Arts. He currently contributes issues to the Zenescope comic book series *Grimm Tales of Terror* and writes for MTV's *Scream*.

ACKNOWLEDGMENTS

Joshua Consumed an Unfortunate Pear was produced at the Humana Festival of New American Plays in April 2015. It was directed by Meredith McDonough with the following cast:

JOSHUA	Andrew Garman
AMELIA	Megan Byrne
DEATH	Rachel Leslie
CHORUS	Seth Clayton, Kevin R. Free, Tasha Lawrence, Mallory Moser, David Ryan Smith

and the following production staff:

Scenic Designer	Dane Laffrey
Costume Designer	Beatrice Vena
Lighting Designer	Mike Inwood
Sound Designer	Christian Frederickson
Stage Manager	Stephen Horton
Assistant Stage Manager	Jason Pacella
Dramaturg	Jessica Reese
Properties Master	Mark Walston

CHARACTERS

JOSHUA: a man, sort of an everyman, a little too obsessed with the big things and definitely not the best at being attentive

AMELIA: a woman, Joshua's wife, frustrated by all of the little things, way past grand gestures, and filled with a rage she doesn't like

DEATH: a woman, busy, fond of making an entrance, annoyed when her precious time is wasted

CHORUS: a group of people with a lot of inside information, a knack for moving and speaking in unison, and a penchant for honesty regardless of the circumstances

NOTES

When things get bloody, they should really get bloody. You could probably just put a bucket of the stuff under the small table.

Megan Byrne, Seth Clayton, Mallory Moser, Kevin R. Free,
Tasha Lawrence, David Ryan Smith, and Andrew Garman
in *Joshua Consumed an Unfortunate Pear*

39th Humana Festival of New American Plays
Actors Theatre of Louisville, 2015
Photo by Bill Brymer

JOSHUA CONSUMED AN UNFORTUNATE PEAR

JOSHUA, *a bit of an everyman but beat up, bruised, probably with a bloody gauze bandage on his forehead and a black eye, sits in one of two chairs at a small table. It has a floor-length tablecloth. The other chair is empty. He is eating a green pear. It's juicy. A wooden bowl on the table holds more pears.*
As he eats, a group of people enters. They move as a group. They speak as a group. They speak to the audience. They are a CHORUS.

CHORUS. This is Joshua eating a pear
Happy with his delicious choice
Trust us; it tastes like no other
This bite you see extends his life
Not just a bit but forever

This is Joshua eating a pear
And now he can't die, not ever
Trust us, even if you stabbed him
Over and over and over and over
And over again with a knife

JOSHUA. This pear is fantastic!

CHORUS. He really enjoys the pear.

JOSHUA. Ugh, you have no idea.

(AMELIA *enters in a form-fitting cardigan, a pencil skirt and heels. She carries a lightweight jacket and wears a fashionable hat. She is beautiful. She also carries on a small suitcase. She sets it down.*)

AMELIA. Well, you look like you got your ass kicked. But I see your big quest to find those "magical immortality pears" was successful.

JOSHUA. They're so delicious.

AMELIA. They just look like pears. I'm unimpressed.

JOSHUA. You have to have one, Amelia.

CHORUS. This is Amelia.
She doesn't want a pear.

AMELIA. No, thank you.

JOSHUA. Why are you wearing a hat?

CHORUS. This is Amelia.
She enjoys a jaunty hat.

AMELIA. It's a bit windy outside.

JOSHUA. Are you going out?

AMELIA. I have a suitcase and I'm wearing a hat, Joshua. What do you think?

JOSHUA. I think that I fought many ferocious beasts to win these pears so we could live forever together in love and happiness. So you should cancel your plans, sit down, and eat some of this eternal life I won for us.

AMELIA. And who asked you to do that?

JOSHUA. Who asked me to get us eternal life?

AMELIA. I asked you to stop by the store and get some fresh milk. Did you do that? No, of course not. I asked you to do one little thing and instead you went on some big adventure, risked your life, and got us magical immortality pears, but look in the fridge and there's still no milk.

JOSHUA. I didn't realize getting the milk was such a big deal.

AMELIA. I know!

(*She grabs one of the pears and smashes it on the ground. She steps on the pear a few times, smashing it to further make her point.*)

JOSHUA. Now you're just being wasteful.

AMELIA. Ha!

JOSHUA. So to be clear, you don't want to be immortal?

CHORUS. This is Amelia.
She doesn't want to be immortal.

AMELIA. Be quiet.

JOSHUA. I kind of wish you'd told me you didn't want to be immortal before I went and risked my life so we could be together forever.

AMELIA. I kind of wish you were a more attentive partner, more engaged in our home life, and better in bed so I'd want to be together forever.

JOSHUA. Whoa.

AMELIA. Yep.

CHORUS. This is Amelia.
She's less than satisfied.

JOSHUA. Shut-up!

AMELIA. No, they're right. That is accurate. I am less than satisfied.

JOSHUA. This is sort of coming out of nowhere.

AMELIA. Oh my God, that's because you don't pay attention. Ever! Did I ever once express any interest in magical immortality pears? Did I? When you said you were going to find them, what did I say?

JOSHUA. You said, "It's too dangerous, don't go."

AMELIA. I said, "It's too dangerous, don't go."

JOSHUA. I thought you were expressing concern, heartfelt concern?!

AMELIA. I was expressing, "I'm not ready to break up yet so I'll feign concern in an effort to keep you from doing something crazy."

JOSHUA. Well, that's some bullshit.

AMELIA. It's called "communication."

CHORUS. Joshua is correct to call Amelia on her bullshit.

AMELIA. Huh. Okay, fine. Maybe it was less than honest, but it doesn't change the fact you're inattentive and a terrible lover.

JOSHUA. Fucking stop saying that; I always get you off.

CHORUS. Joshua is incorrect in stating that he always gets her off.

JOSHUA. Wait, what?

AMELIA. I hate our sex life.

JOSHUA. Our sex life is great!

AMELIA. Really?!

JOSHUA. I don't know, yes? But look, okay, I'm getting older and sometimes it's not as easy to perform. And sometimes I'm just tired. And, okay, sometimes maybe I rush it now; I'm willing to own that.

AMELIA. Do you know how I would describe our sex life? To other people? If other people asked? I'd say, "Oh, I suppose our sex life is like one of those old black and white movies where Godzilla destroys Tokyo."

JOSHUA. Oh, come on!

AMELIA. And I'm Tokyo!!

(*She makes small Godzilla noises. And mimes tiny claws.*)

JOSHUA. Amelia.

(*She makes larger Godzilla noises, scoops up some of the smashed pear from the floor, and throws it at him.*)

Calm down!

AMELIA. I'm calm!

CHORUS. This is Amelia.

She's not really calm

AMELIA. No, no, I'm totally calm. I'm breathing. I'm breathing. I just get so mad. The sex thing is bad, but I don't want you to think that's why I'm leaving you. Sex goes downhill, that's a reality of long-term relationships that I'm fully prepared to accept. I suppose, if I have to. More importantly, you don't treat me well. I can't literally spend forever with a guy who's too self-involved to take care of me.

JOSHUA. Okay, here we go.

AMELIA. Not in a needy way. You just make me so angry. I'm filled with this rage!

JOSHUA. Look, every relationship has problems. That's why they're called relationships. People have to "relate" to one another. It's an ongoing process. I'm sorry that you hate our sex life and I'm sorry you are feeling neglected. I am. But I just killed a bunch of monsters to get us immortality, so clearly I'm looking out for the relationship. Maybe, and I'm saying maybe, maybe you need to work on communicating your feelings and desires in a less passive aggressive way?

(*It's clear he thinks he's being really understanding.* AMELIA*'s eyes go wide and the clenches her fists with rage.*)

CHORUS. This is Joshua.
He started out on the right track
But then the train really derailed

JOSHUA. Wait, what did I say wrong?

AMELIA. Oh my God.

JOSHUA. No, I was just trying to explain things from my perspective.

AMELIA. Oh my God!!!

JOSHUA. I'm sorry!

AMELIA. Sorry for what?!

JOSHUA. I don't know!!

AMELIA. It's not your fault. Ugh. It is, but you can't help it. And I'm miserable!!

JOSHUA. Please, Amelia, I don't want you to be unhappy. I can make it better, I can change; I know I can change.

AMELIA. No, you can't!

JOSHUA. Yes, I can! Not by myself, but with your help. Tell me what to do.

(*She picks up her suitcase and begins to leave.*)

AMELIA. Goodbye.

JOSHUA. There has to be something I can do. I'm going to live forever now and I can't live forever without you. Yell at me if you're angry. Hit me. Beat me. Just don't leave. I'll do anything. Anything!

(*She stops at the door.*)

AMELIA. Anything?

JOSHUA. Yes! Yes.

CHORUS. This is Amelia.
She has a flicker of an idea

AMELIA. You just make me irate. And I don't have anywhere to put that anger.

JOSHUA. I'm terrible. I'm the worst. Please forgive me. What can I do?

(*She sets down her suitcase, opens it, and takes out a hammer.*)

AMELIA. You ate one of those stupid magical immortality pears, right?

JOSHUA. Yes. Why? What are you gonna do with that hammer?

AMELIA. Nothing.

(She rushes towards him with a scream and hits him in the head, maybe more than once, sending him crashing behind the table. There's probably some blood spray. Breathing heavy, she waits. DEATH *enters in a red suit, red heels, and a red scarf. She's ringing a hand bell. It should probably be a large hand bell. She stops when she sees* AMELIA. *She glances behind the table and makes a face.)*

DEATH. Did you strike him with that hammer?

*(*AMELIA *quickly hides the hammer behind her back and plays it cool.)*

AMELIA. I beg your pardon?

CHORUS. This is Amelia.
She struck him with a hammer.

*(*AMELIA *laughs nervously.)*

AMELIA. Just ignore them.

DEATH. What a mess. And I just had this pantsuit dry cleaned. It's dry clean only. Fancy, right? More like inconvenient. Well, I suppose I've seen worse messes. Oh, I'm Death. The Death. And I'm here to collect him. I ring the bell so people know I'm coming. Do you like it? It's so brassy. Makes for quite an entrance. Unfortunately, the sound can be confusing. Sometimes dead people think they're going to get ice cream, but they're not. Oh God damn it, are those magical immortality pears?

CHORUS. This is Death.
She hates those fucking pears.

DEATH. I do! I do hate those fucking pears. You know, you don't have to waste my time like this. He's not going to die and I'm a busy woman.

*(*DEATH *exits in a huff, carrying the bell to her side.* AMELIA *looks confused. The* CHORUS *exhales sharply and snaps in unison.)*

CHORUS. Live again.

(Slowly, JOSHUA *gets up, profusely bleeding from his head. She laughs.)*

JOSHUA. Are you fucking kidding me, Amelia?! That hammer hurts so much!!

*(*AMELIA *brings the hammer down with a scream, sending him crashing down behind the table. She hits him several times as blood sprays and splashes into view. Breathing heavy, she waits again.*
The bell sound again and DEATH *enters. When she sees* AMELIA *she stops. She looks behind the table again and makes a sour face.)*

DEATH. Again? Please stop doing that. You're really screwing with my schedule and this bell is heavy. Look, you're just making the mess worse. Like I said, he's not going to die. And I'm getting really annoyed. You got me?

(*She exits again. The* CHORUS *exhales sharply and snaps in unison.*)

CHORUS. Live again

(*Slowly* JOSHUA *gets up from behind the table, now covered in blood. There's probably a pool of blood forming at the base of the table.*)

AMELIA. Okay. Okay, okay. Okay, maybe this relationship can work. I'll stay.

JOSHUA. And you're just gonna bludgeon me with a hammer any time you get frustrated with our relationship?

AMELIA. Don't be silly. It doesn't have to be a hammer.

(*He drags himself into the chair and eats as she sits down, drops the bloody hammer on the table, picks up a pear, and also takes a bite.*)

CHORUS. This is Joshua eating a pear
Happy with his delicious choice
Trust us; his head really hurts

JOSHUA. I love you.

AMELIA. I love you, too.

(*They kiss. It's messy.*)

End of Play

I PROMISED MYSELF
TO LIVE FASTER

A QUEER SPACE OPERA IN THE DECADENT STYLE

directed by Dan Rothenberg
text by Gregory S Moss and Pig Iron Theatre Company
conceived and created by Pig Iron Theatre Company

ABOUT *I PROMISED MYSELF TO LIVE FASTER*

This article first ran in the Limelight Guide to the 39th Humana Festival of New American Plays, *published by Actors Theatre of Louisville, and is based on conversations with the creative team before rehearsals for the Humana Festival production began.*

When Tim, restless with routine and the slow-moving rhythms of stable adulthood, steps out into the night in search of a little "action," the last thing he expects is that he'll find it. But the next thing Tim knows, he's thrust into a whirlwind escape from down-to-earth reality beyond his wildest dreams: an intergalactic quest of epic proportions. In Pig Iron Theatre Company's delightfully decadent *I Promised Myself to Live Faster*, an ensemble creation with text by playwright Gregory S Moss, an unlikely hero must fight to save the futures of Homosexuals everywhere—taking us on a fabulously gay adventure that's full of enjoyably familiar sci-fi and pop culture conceits, hilarious humor, and stunning spectacle.

I Promised Myself to Live Faster launches Tim almost immediately into a sizzling space battle with life-or-death consequences. He's beset by a comic trio of Space Nuns, who inform him that he's "the Chosen One." A priceless treasure, the Holy Gay Flame, has been stolen from them—and according to prophecy, only Tim can recover it, thereby saving the Flame from destruction by the evil emperor Moody Garland. The stakes are high: if Tim fails, the race of Homosexuals is doomed. But no sooner has Tim arrived in space than he falls captive into the glittering clutches of Bishop Ahni. Ahni will stop at nothing to use Tim to snatch the Flame for his own nefarious purposes. Will Tim succeed in his mission, despite Anhi's dark temptations? And will he find the action he was looking for all along?

In crafting the imaginative, whimsical, and irreverent world of *I Promised Myself to Live Faster*, Pig Iron and Moss weave in a wealth of recognizable references. The plot and aesthetic of this "queer space opera" is a pastiche of popular cinematic influences, ranging from 1970s sci-fi flicks like *Star Wars* to 1950s melodramas and such classics as *The Wizard of Oz*. As in any good sci-fi space odyssey, our heroes whiz through the stars on a variety of vessels, visiting many planets and encountering aliens and mythical space beasts. Meanwhile, the characters' dialogue—as well as their several '80s-style dance numbers—freely embraces camp, a highly theatrical acting style, and raunchy, self-referential puns and wisecracks. Indeed, it's with a big wink and a nudge that *Live Faster* paints Tim as a modern-day Dorothy. Blown far from home on the winds of adventure, his journey through a fantastical alternate realm becomes a journey of self-discovery.

In addition to its bevy of screen sources, *I Promised Myself to Live Faster* was inspired by 20th-century gay playwright/actor Charles Ludlam. In his work with his Ridiculous Theatrical Company, Ludlam also played with comedic pop culture pastiche, genre conventions, pun-filled humor, and bending the traditional boundaries of gender and sexuality onstage. For example, he's best known for his 1984 gothic horror satire *The Mystery of Irma Vep*, in which he dressed in drag to perform a variety of both male and female characters. In Ludlam-esque fashion, Pig Iron conceived *Live Faster* with its Founding Artistic Director, Dito van Reigersberg—a.k.a. drag queen Martha Graham Cracker—in mind. "Pig Iron was originally inspired by several ensembles from the '60s and '70s, Ludlam's Ridiculous Theatrical Company among them," Dan Rothenberg, Pig Iron's Co-Artistic Director and the director of *Live Faster*, explains. "Now it's been 20 years since we started our company, and Dito's alter-ego, Martha Graham Cracker, has become Philadelphia's biggest drag queen. She stands at 6'7" in heels, with a proudly hairy chest—not unlike Ludlam, another hairy-chested female impersonator who, like Dito, loved poetry."

Throughout every stage of the play's ongoing development, Pig Iron's process in putting together *I Promised Myself to Live Faster* has been as fascinating and varied as the material itself. "We get on our feet surprisingly early," says Rothenberg. "We start with provocations—in this case about cross-dressing, how dressing up can permit the forbidden, and about the powers that come from impersonating the glamorous *femme fatales* of the 1950s. That allows us to get things cooking in the space right away, to find out if there's a world there, something we can elaborate on and embroider." Pig Iron then recruited playwright Gregory S Moss to help them shape their improvisations into a script. Moss is known for work that experiments with form in unexpected ways—his 2009 tribute to '80s music subculture, *punkplay*, is laid out on the page like a graphic novel and performed entirely on roller skates; 2014's *Reunion* turns a seemingly familiar tale of old high school buddies meeting up for a class reunion suddenly on its head. Of this collaboration with Pig Iron, Moss enthuses: "I've been a fan of Pig Iron for years, so working with them is really a dream come true. Connecting with them, and with Ludlam, is a real gift—it turns out we actually have a lot in common aesthetically."

For Pig Iron, an ensemble whose mission hinges on making work that resists easy classification, *Live Faster* fits perfectly within the group's aesthetic. Since the company's founding in 1995, they've brought their avant-garde theatrical sensibilities to a diverse array of subject matter. Productions include an absurdist adaptation of a Polish novel in 2005's Obie Award-winning *Hell*

Meets Henry Halfway; *Chekhov Lizardbrain*, a 2008 Obie Award-winner that interweaves the signature themes of Russian dramatist Anton Chekhov's plays with neurological research and dreamlike explorations of the nature of memory; and a 2011 rendition of Shakespeare's *Twelfth Night* accompanied live by a Balkan band, which received four Barrymore Awards for Excellence in Theatre. As with *Live Faster*, Pig Iron's shows are typically ensemble-generated, experiment with a variety of influences and styles, and include many highly physical moments.

They're known also for their use of mask and puppetry (which *Live Faster*'s costumes reflect), and for design elements that are incredibly well-crafted but can appear homemade—as if to emphasize theatre's transformative power over the trappings of our everyday world. While this stage design is often relatively minimalist, *Live Faster* is more lavish in its look. "Recent plays like *Twelfth Night*—and now *Live Faster*—show us flexing our 'maximalist' muscles," Rothenberg comments. "We want to make a world that's falling apart from abundance and energy. We're working with this remarkable costume designer named Machine Dazzle, a fixture of queer New York nightlife and Pride parades. His costumes are like floats, like cheap fireworks, in all the best ways."

You don't need to be a sci-fi fan or drag show aficionado to tumble head over heels into the glitz and glamor of *I Promised Myself to Live Faster*. With its lively combination of song and dance, lots of laughs, and adventure aplenty, *Live Faster* reminds us that growing up doesn't have to mean slowing down. And amidst its zany space antics, the play takes us on one of the most universal quests of all: the search for who we truly are. In Pig Iron Theatre Company and Gregory S Moss's allegory of identity, Tim and his companions learn that just as there's no place like home, there's no place like being at home with yourself.

—Hannah Rae Montgomery

BIOGRAPHIES

Gregory S Moss is a writer, performer and educator from Newburyport, Massachusetts. His work has been seen at La Comédie Française, Clubbed Thumb, the Guthrie Theater, Playwrights Horizons, PlayPenn, Soho Rep, the Steppenwolf Garage, and New York Theatre Workshop. Moss is a 2012 MacDowell Fellow, a Playwrights' Center Core Writer, and the recipient of a 2010–2011 Jerome Fellowship and a 2011–2012 McKnight Fellowship. His work has been published by *Play: A Journal of Plays*, *n+1*, and Playscripts. He is currently working on commissions from Woolly Mammoth Theatre Company and Broadway Across America. In collaboration with composer/lyricist Joe Iconis, he's creating a new musical based on the life and work of Hunter S. Thompson, which will premiere at La Jolla Playhouse in the summer of 2017. Recent and upcoming productions include *I Promised Myself to Live Faster* in collaboration with Pig Iron Theatre Company, at the 2015 Humana Festival of New American Plays at Actors Theatre of Louisville; *Reunion* at South Coast Repertory ("Best New Play of 2014," *OC Weekly*); *Billy Witch* at Studio 42 and Astoria Performing Arts Center (New York); *House of Gold* at La Comédie Française (Winner, Prix du Public) and at Ensemble Studio Theatre/LA (*Los Angeles Times* and *LA Weekly* Critics' Pick); and *sixsixsix* with AntiMatter Collective, New York (Editor's Pick, *Flavorpill*). His latest play, *Indian Summer*, will premiere at Playwrights Horizons in May 2016. Writing and news are updated regularly at www.gregorysmoss.com.

Pig Iron Theatre Company has been creating original performance works in Philadelphia since 1995, making plays about live music, dead people, neuroscience and thwarted love affairs. A unique method of performance research and collaborative creation, plus a signature physical approach to character, has led to 29 plays, cabaret-ballets, hoaxes, and installations over two decades. Past collaborations include work with the legendary director Joseph Chaikin, playwright Toshiki Okada, choreographer David Brick, composer Cynthia Hopkins, and the rock band Dr. Dog. Pig Iron's work has been presented by FringeArts in Philadelphia and by theatres and festivals around the world. The company has won two Obie Awards, a Total Theatre Award, and eight Barrymore Awards. Other scripts by Pig Iron are anthologized in *Pig Iron: Three Plays*, published by 53rd State Press. For more information, visit pigiron.org.

ACKNOWLEDGMENTS

I Promised Myself to Live Faster premiered at the Humana Festival of New American Plays in March 2015. It was directed by Dan Rothenberg with the following cast:

> Mikéah Ernest Jennings
> Jennifer Kidwell
> Mary McCool
> Dito van Reigersberg
> Michele Tauber

and the following production staff:

Creative Producer	Alex Torra
Scenic Designer	William Boles
Costume Designer	Machine Dazzle
Lighting Designer	Jiyoun Chang
Sound Designer and Additional Music	Robert Kaplowitz
Choreographer	Sam Pinkleton
Stage Manager	E Sara Barnes
Dramaturg	Eric Hoff
Casting	Judy Henderson CSA and Pig Iron Theatre Company
Assistant Sound Designer	Corbin Wescott
Costume Supervisor	Jill Keys
Pig Iron Theatre Company Properties Master	Emily Schuman
Properties Master	Joseph Cunningham
Directing Assistant	Sophie Blumberg
Production Assistant	Leah Pye
Assistant Dramaturg	Robyn Carroll

Major support for *I Promised Myself to Live Faster* has been provided by The Pew Center for Arts & Heritage.

CHARACTERS

DRAG QUEEN
TIM
MYSTERIOUS GRINDR DUDE
MADAME GEORGE
MOTHER SUPERIOR
SPACE NUN
SPACE NUN 2
MRITHRA
ARGOSHAUN GUARD
ARGOSHAUN GUARD 2
BISHOP AHNI
EXOTIC EXTRATERRESTRIAL DANCER
KING TROUT
ALIENS
CHINESE FOOD CARTON / THEO / LOTUSIAN
MOVIE STAR BOY
MOVIE STAR 1
MOVIE STAR 2
MOVIE STAR 3
IMPERIAL GUARDS
EMPEROR MOODY GARLAND (Voice)

Jennifer Kidwell, Dito van Reigersberg, and Mary McCool
in *I Promised Myself to Live Faster*

39th Humana Festival of New American Plays
Actors Theatre of Louisville, 2015
Photo by Bill Brymer

I PROMISED MYSELF
TO LIVE FASTER
A QUEER SPACE OPERA IN THE DECADENT STYLE

OPENING SONG

> *Bare stage*
> *Piano chords*
> DRAG QUEEN *enters, transcendent janky glamour with body hair and a*
> *cheap wig*

DRAG QUEEN. (*spoken.*) No One is Promised Tomorrow

> (*sung in a slow torch song style.*)

I promised myself so many things
Promised with ribbons
Promised with rings
But the only promise that matters
is to live faster

> (*spoken.*)

I have some bad news: I am not the Protagonist of this show. That is. Tim.

> (*revealed:* TIM, *melancholy, in a bed two sizes too large for him, lays amidst the*
> *debris of a depression—half-empty Chinese takeout containers and unwashed*
> *sheets.*)

DRAG QUEEN. (*gestures to* TIM.) This broken-hearted homo you see before
you is stuck in a rut
Bound to his Bed
Like some latter day Prometheus
He's watching his Life Pass Him By
But even the bird that eats his liver
Don't come around much anymore

> (*sung.*)

Run run run run
Don't hesitate
Cause soon all will be lost or broken
If I'm courting you
and the world is courting disaster
And the doomsday clock is ticking away
If the seas are slowly rising and the universe is ending anyway

Make this oath with me:

    (*spoken.*)

I promise myself to live faster

    (PHONE RINGS

    DRAG QUEEN *scowls*

    TIM *answers*

    DRAG QUEEN *speaks as* TIM *lip synchs.*)

DRAG QUEEN. (*spoken, as* TIM.) Oh

Hey

Wait—was that tonight?

What time?

10:30? Uh…

I'm pretty tired, guys.

I think I'm just gonna stay in.

Yeah I'm

I'm just, really busy these days, so—

K.

K.

Yeah next weekend maybe.

K.

Bye.

    (TIM *hangs up and eats noodles in bed.*)

DRAG QUEEN. (*sung.*)

This is Tim

Look at him

It's this time of night

When this feeling creeps in

It's been two years

Since the break-up

it's time to wake up

But he's thinking of Him again

Back, back, back, back, back, back in the past

We were all in one place,

Face to face

    (*DING! A grotesque GRINDR pic appears beside the bed*

    TIM *looks at his phone*

    Ding! *and picture are repeated several times under the following.*)

DRAG QUEEN. (*sung.*)

If you need a reminder

There's always GRINDR
When the night is too sad and cold
If there's no face to face
And we're all just castaways

> (TIM *swipes—wooosh!—and the GRINDR pics vanish.*)

DRAG QUEEN. (*sung.*)
Make this oath with me:
I promise myself to Live Faster

> (*spoken, ad lib.*)

Ok, ladies and gentlemen. I hope you're comfortable…
because this show is Four, Hours, Long.
But don't worry. It'll feel like a brisk 90 minutes.
Enjoy.
Goodbye.
Good luck.
You'll never… see me… aGAYN…

> (DRAG QUEEN *exits, dragging mic stand.*)

GRINDR

> *Phone DINGs!*
> TIM *looks, ignores it*
> *DING!*
> TIM *looks again*
> *DING!*
> TIM *grabs the phone, exasperated*
> MYSTERIOUS GRINDR DUDE *appears.*

MYSTERIOUS GRINDR MESSAGE. (*voiceover.*) Hi
TIM. (*typing, talking.*) uhm
"hi"?
MYSTERIOUS GRINDR MESSAGE. stormy night out there
TIM. Yeah, stormy, night.
MYSTERIOUS GRINDR MESSAGE. What are you doing?
TIM. nothing
MYSTERIOUS GRINDR MESSAGE. lonely?
TIM. (*"yes."*) naw
MYSTERIOUS GRINDR MESSAGE. I've been watching you

TIM. "ha ha"

MYSTERIOUS GRINDR MESSAGE. I think you're beautiful

>   (*beat.*)

TIM. shut up

MYSTERIOUS GRINDR MESSAGE. come meet me

TIM. just chatting
not looking to hook up
plus: no pic, question mark?

MYSTERIOUS GRINDR MESSAGE. I need your help

TIM. Help? this a scam?

MYSTERIOUS GRINDR MESSAGE. No. I just need a friend tonight.

TIM. I don't think I can—
I have a lot of things I'm //

MYSTERIOUS GRINDR MESSAGE. put down the noodles and come
meet me at the bar on the corner
fifteen minutes

>   (TIM *looks around—is this a prank?*)

TIM. how did you know I // was

MYSTERIOUS GRINDR MESSAGE. don't be late
hurry please I need you
you're my only hope

>   (*whoosh*
>   MYSTERIOUS GRINDR DUDE *disappears*
>   *a deliberation—*
>   then TIM *dons his shitty bathrobe and slippers and heads out.*)

DOWN THE STREET

>   *Out walking, a deserted city street*

TIM. (*tracking* GRINDR DUDE *on his phone.*) 500 feet
this is stupid this is stupid what am I doing? I should just go back home

…

300 feet

>   (*a* DOG *trots by*
>   *led by a veiled woman*
>   TIM *greets* DOG
>   DOG *growls!*
>   TIM *shoos* DOG *away.*)

TIM. stupid dog
> (*back to phone.*)

50 feet…
> (*looking up.*)

I'm here it says I'm here
but—where?, there's nothing…
> (*a sign flickers to life*
> *letters lighting up out of order*
> *twitching and dissolving*
> M
> G
> E
> O
> *as if the sign, the bar, the building*
> *were forming out of the shadows, coalescing before him:*
> *"MADAME GEORGE"*
> *in green and pink neon.*)

TIM. "Madame George's"
huh
> (*with a shrug.*)

well

MADAME GEORGE

> TIM *enters Madame George's*
> INSIDE:
> *a dreary, empty gay bar, fallen out of favor*
> *a few rotating lights some limp tinsel from the ceiling*
> *behind the counter stands* MADAME GEORGE
> *an old queen washing glasses and wiping them behind the bar*

> MADAME GEORGE *looks at* TIM, *raises eyebrows, turns back to wiping*
> *glasses*

TIM. you open?
MADAME GEORGE. for the right customer
TIM. quiet in here tonight
MADAME GEORGE. what can I getcha
TIM. uh
I'll have a diet ginger ale

MADAME GEORGE. (*stops, stares:*)

…

…don't fuck with me

TIM. sorry?

MADAME GEORGE. (*pouring something from an elaborate tacky bottle.*) Here:
drink this

TIM. what's this

MADAME GEORGE. Riunite *White*

it's a classic

        (TIM *drinks, coughs, chokes.*)

TIM. (*through tears.*) that's disgusting

        (MADAME GEORGE *takes the glass back and finishes it.*)

MADAME GEORGE. eh

it's better cold

you develop a taste for it

plus we got a hundred cases left over in the back so

I gotta push it

TIM. maybe a beer

        (*the* DOG *blows by in a very strong wind*
        neither of them notice.)

MADAME GEORGE. *rough* out there

TIM. a little windy

strange night

MADAME GEORGE. big *storm* blowing through

TIM. yeah

yeah

        (*chuckling, trying to be liked.*)

like Dorothy

MADAME GEORGE. like

TIM. you know

"Wizard of Oz"

        (*beat.*)

MADAME GEORGE. (*nope.*) uh-uh

TIM. what

MADAME GEORGE. listen baby:

just cause we're *queer*?

doesn't give us the right to be *Hack.* Y'see what I'm sayin'?

It's a Storm.

And We're Gay.

Dig deeper.

so what, couldn't sleep?

TIM. how'd you know

MADAME GEORGE. you're in your pajamas

TIM. ooh
so I am
"whoops"
heh

MADAME GEORGE. You cruisin'?

TIM. "Cruising?"
No, no I live around the corner

MADAME GEORGE. But are you meeting someone?

TIM. oh No
No I mean Yes but
just a friend

MADAME GEORGE. what's your friend's name

TIM. I
actually
he didn't say

MADAME GEORGE. what does he look like

TIM. I don't know

MADAME GEORGE. You don't know.
so lemmee get this straight:
you come into my bar,
alone,
on a Friday night,
in your pajamas,
to meet a friend whose name you don't know—
and you're tellin' me you're not *cruisin'*?

TIM. Um—

MADAME GEORGE. I think you're looking for something... *dirty*

TIM. oh, I

MADAME GEORGE. something... *nasty*

TIM. I mean, I'm not like

MADAME GEORGE. some deep down OLD FASHIONED bad-ass meat-slappin' '70s vintage FUCKIN'!
is what you need!

TIM. (*unravelling.*) that's a
it's

I'm
this was a mistake I shouldn't have come here I shouldn't have//

MADAME GEORGE. easy kid
don't have a stroke
I just wanna tell you that we *got* that here

TIM. you—do?

MADAME GEORGE. oh sure
we don't have "Wi Fi" or Satellite TEE vee, but vintage orgasms we can provide
Here

TIM. what's this

MADAME GEORGE. key

TIM. I can see that

MADAME GEORGE. to the *Men's* Room

TIM. oh but I don't need to

MADAME GEORGE. Oh Baby but you DO need to
lookit you
skanky-ass unwashed bathrobe
floppy slippers
sad sack boxer shorts with the Soy Sauce stains on 'em
living in the past but you don't know what the past IS
you're a walkin' shame
take the key
get in there
gonna plug you back in
lil broken toy
gonna reconnect you to the SOURCE
Take you back to the MOTHERSHIP

TIM. do you
but—do you think it'll help me?
cause
I've been feeling
kinda sad
lately

MADAME GEORGE. mmm
get down there
follow directions
you're gonna feel better
trust ol' Madame George one time

TIM. I don't know

MADAME GEORGE. GO!

TIM. Ok—fuck it

MADAME GEORGE. good boy

have fun

   (TIM *exits.*)

huh

thought he'd be taller

THE HOLE OF GLORY

   The Men's Room:
   sleazy
   dirty tile
   late twentieth century homo-pornographic hieroglyphics on the walls (looks like
   the cover for <u>Beggars Banquet</u>*)*
   three stalls
   filthy yellow light
   seedy and stanky
   and yet inexplicably redolent
   of a covert, furtive sex appeal
   lost to time

TIM. (*unlocking door.*) The "Men's Room"…

Oh god

this place is disgusting

   (*looks around.*)

I don't see how this //

MADAME GEORGE. (*firmly, from off.*) Follow Directions!

TIM. (*obedient.*) Ok

   (TIM *goes to stall*
   a HOLE is revealed in the wall of the stall.)

Oh!

oh now wait a minute

you know I've never seen one of these in real life

I'll just take a peek

just

don't touch anything

   (TIM *leans down to look through Glory Hole…*
   —*a ROLLING EYE appears in the Hole, PEERING back out at him!*)

oh! sorry!

I didn't know anyone was in there

I was just
just looking
sorry

>*(indistinct grumbling in the stall*
>*a mouth appears in hole, blowing outward.)*

sounds like you're
busy in there
like you got plenty going on so
I'm gonna (go)

>*(something Pink and Phallic*
>*EMERGES from the Glory Hole.)*

oh
OH!
"Hello there!" ha

>*(the pink protrusion extends further, swaying gently.)*

That's
I mean I'm flattered
but

>*(more whispering*
>*the protrusion extends even further*
>*long, pink, sticky and writhing around sensuously.)*

OH!
oh
euh
I gotta go actually I think I gotta go and WOAH

>*(protrusion extends further, unsettlingly long now.)*

Ok now wait a minute now like I mean, like, what!—what!—what—even IS
that?!

>*(BOOM!*
>*an explosion of music and light*
>*as the bathroom stalls fly apart*
>*three EXOTIC SPACE NUNS are revealed!)*

MOTHER SUPERIOR. HEY BRO!

SISTERS. *(chanting.)* Hey Bro! Hey Bro!

TIM. Ahhh!

NUN. the Galactic Key WORKED Mother!

NUN 2. I knew it would!

MOTHER. yes Sisters, just needed to spit on it
gets a bit *sticky* in these old Earth holes

TIM. (*calling off.*) Hey uh Madame George!
I think your bathroom's out of order!

NUN. we're not here for terrestrial wees and poos, Earth Man

NUN 2. no way!

MOTHER. are you the one who attempted to penetrate the antimatter space portal

TIM. you mean the Glory Hole?

NUN. yes Earth Male, the HOLE of Glory!

NUN 2. The HOLE OF GLORY

MOTHER. Are you He?

TIM. Well yeah I was looking but I hadn't actually stuck my //

NUN. (*vicious.*) Shut Up Earthoid!

> (*180 emotional turn, Polyanna.*)

But Mother! how can HE be the Chosen One? He's an *EARTH* MAN!

NUN 2. (*touching* TIM*'s sleeve appreciatively.*) don't listen to her—

NUN. Watch yourself Sister—

NUN 2. —she just had a bad experience with earthlings a few Cronospecks back—

NUN. —filthy short-sighted carbon-based BARBARIANS—

NUN 2. —her whole family was killed in a freak accident by a bunch of earthlings who—

NUN. Can it, Sister!

> (*Jan Brady tantrum.*)

Oh he just CAN'T be the Chosen One, Mother! We aren't even supposed to have CONTACT with these EARTH CREATURES for another 700 years...

> (*to* TIM.)

The Human Race has a LOT of growing up to do!

TIM. well Ok fine but—I'm doing my part—I recycle and I'm starting a little compost in the // back yard

NUN. Oh FUCK you!

MOTHER. Enough, Sister! Whatever happenstance led to The Hole of Glory landing in THIS bathroom is all interstellar water under the transgalactic bridge! Earth Man, did you answer the Call?

TIM. What, on Grindr?

NUNS. (*ecstatic.*) Grindr!

TIM. (*of phone.*) You mean, this thing?

> (*gasps!*)

NUN. Grindr is not a THING Earth Man!

NUN 2. it's a WHO!

MOTHER. Grindr is an ancient celestial intelligence, a demigod embedded in a microchip, searching the universe for the Chosen One.

TIM. the "chosen one"?

NUN. The Homosexual Savior! Grindr calls to him—whoever he is—across the vast reaches of space!

NUN 2. And you answered the Call!

TIM. what? no!

NUN. (*innocently, politely.*) May I see that please?

TIM. I actually uninstalled it and only just re-installed it because I—look I practically never use this

> (NUN *grabs his phone—she fake looks at it, then drops it on the floor and STOMPS it.*)

Hey! That is a Very Expensive Phone!

NUN. Your primitive technology is useless where WE'RE going Earth Man!

MOTHER. Come! We must return home immediately—before it's Too Late! Here! Quickly! Take my HAND!

> (TIM *examines his phone sadly.*)

MOTHER. (*exceedingly melodramatic.*) My Hand! Take it! Take my HAND!

TIM. Oh good the screen is just cracked a little

MOTHER. (*huger.*) TAKE IT! MY HAND! TAKE IT!

NUN 2. You really oughta take her hand, Tim!

TIM. ah—Ok
I'll

> (TIM *takes* MOTHER SUPERIOR's *hand.*
> HUM PEAKING into EXPLOSION SOUND.*)

NUNS ONE: MRITHRA RIDE

> TIM *and* NUNS *aboard the* MRITHRA (*a spangled alien dog/dragon*).

TIM. AHHHH!

NUN 2. That's right Tim! That's right, you just let it all out!

TIM. What
what IS all this

MOTHER. Why this—this is our Mrithra!

MRITHRA. Rrrrrr!

NUN. It's the way we travel about space

MOTHER. Hoy Mrithra!

MRITHRA. Rrrrr!

NUN 2. Hold on tight, Tim!

TIM. Is—is—is this outer SPACE? and and
is that the EARTH down there?

NUN. yes Eurrth Man
there's your puny undeveloped backwater of a planet

TIM. Oh
I'm
I think I'm going to be sick

NUN 2. quick! inhale this!

      (NUN 2 *opens a small glass jar under* TIM's *nose.*)

TIM. but I

NUN 2. breathe it in! it'll help!

TIM. Ok I

      (*he inhales deeply—beat.*)
ahhh yeah that IS better

NUN 2. I told ya Tim!

TIM. what is it?

MOTHER. antigravity acclimation spores

NUN 2. It'll loosen ya right up!

TIM. (*immediately intoxicated.*) yeah
Yeah
I feel good

NUN 2. we're ridin' high now!

MOTHER. now hear my tale Eurrth Man…
these sisters and I are beholden to a sacred order

NUN. We are the nuns of Virgynia

MOTHER. our charge is to bring forth and protect the gentle race of
Homosexuals

TIM. "homosexuals"?

MOTHER. yes
you have a strain of them on your planet as well
I believe you call them
"homosexuals"

TIM. (*saying it exactly the same.*) "homosexuals"

NUN. He's saying it wrong!

TIM. and you all "bring them forth"

NUN 2. sure do!

TIM. so what you're taking me to your planet to

NUN. to—

TIM. you know—"procure my seed"

MOTHER. your SEED?

NUN. You mean MATE with you?

NUN 2. HOO hoo oh man

MOTHER. Oh no

NUN 2. nonononono

MOTHER. ha HA ha
Heavens no!

> (*the* NUNS *all laugh*
> TIM *laughs too.*)

TIM. "phew" heh heh

MOTHER. no Tim no
I don't know what Nuns are like on eurrrth
but we on Virgynia are entirely celibate

NUN. completely

NUN 2. we gotta stay pure!

TIM. then how do you uh make them?

NUN. with our WOMBS Earth Man!

NUN 2. she's got one growing inside her right now!

MOTHER. when the Virgynia moon grows fat and blue
we take seed from the Holy Gay Flame into our sacred personal area

NUN 2. really get it in there!

MOTHER. and in approximately nine solar cycles

NUN 2. A whole LITTER of Homos is born!

TIM. wow

MOTHER. but the Flame was STOLEN

NUN. Stolen!

MOTHER. Pilfered!

TIM. Pilfered?

NUN 2. It means "Stolen"!

TIM. I know what it means!

MOTHER. If the Flame isn't retrieved it will mean the end of all the Homosexuals on Virgynia!

NUN 2. we can't make new Homos without the Flame!

MOTHER. you MUST find the Flame and return it to us Tim
the universe has spoken

TIM. this sounds made up

NUN. well it isn't!

TIM. Look I'm sorry but
I don't think I can help you
I think you have the wrong "homosexual"

NUN. Ugh! You see Mother? I told you this repulsive eurrth man was a coward!
He doesn't give a Damn about my Gay Baby!

TIM. it's not that
I LOVE Gay Babies but
look I can barely get out of bed most days
I was just trying to help someone out
I wasn't looking for—for *Space* Nuns and *Gay* Flames and //

MOTHER. Argoshauns!

TIM. Right
"ARGO SHAUNS"
whatever that is

MOTHER. no!
Look!
THERE

      (NUNS *GASP!*)

NUN. it's an Argoshaun Predator Vessel!

NUN 2. they must have picked up our heat signature!

MOTHER. it's heading straight for us!

TIM. who

MOTHER. our sworn enemy!

NUN. Hideous to look upon!

NUN 2. A stone cold bummer

NUN. they're killers and colonists

MOTHER. the most oppressive force in the known galaxy

NUN 2. WHOA MRITHRA

TIM. Ok I'm out
take me home
Take Me Home
TAKE ME HOME

MOTHER. it's too late! it's sucking us into its Tractorum!

(*the* MRITHRA *HOWLS in pain*
spiraling out of control
being drawn against its will toward the Argoshaun Predator Vessel...)

NUN. Whatever shall we DO, Mother?

NUN 2. If they capture us, we're gonna get MURDERED!

MOTHER. There's only ONE solution!

TIM. yeah?

(MOTHER *grabs the hand of* NUN *and* NUN 2 *and leaps off the back of*
the MRITHRA
leaving TIM *alone, clinging to the animal's back*
spiraling closer and closer to the Argoshaun ship

NUNS *open umbrellas and float away.*)

TIM. Wait! Where are you GOING? I don't know what I'm DOING! I don't know how to fly this thing!

MOTHER. I'm sorry Tim! But we cannot let ourselves get caught! It's up to you now!

NUN. Retrieve the Holy Gay Flame!

MOTHER. and bring it back to us on the Planet Virgynia!

NUN. otherwise all will be lost

MOTHER. save our Homosexuals Tim

NUN 2. You can DO it!

TIM. (*falling away toward Argoshaun Predator Ship.*) Whyyyyyyyyy mmmmmmm-meeeeeeeeee...???

(*pause.*)

MOTHER. (*tiny voice, very distant.*) Because you are the Chosen One, Tim.
...because you...
...are the Chosen One...

(*the* NUNS *drift off, back to Virgynia.*)

ABOARD THE ARGOSHAUN PREDATOR VESSEL

TIM *is flanked by two* ARGOSHAUN GUARDS
Sexy gender-fucked Space Nazis by way of The Village People
TIM*'s now dressed in a* GLITTERY LOINCLOTH *and a* THIN MESH
SHIRT, *lookin like some kinda Star Trek-style sexy space captive*

GUARD. let's go

TIM. what the hell am I wearing?

GUARD 2. keep moving

TIM. I am entirely willing to cooperate or like
I mean
whatever you want guys!

GUARD. we're not buying what you're selling, Tim

GUARD 2. no thank you ha ha

> (GUARDS *drag* TIM *into an elaborately appointed personal chamber, draped silks and phallic obsidian sculptures all around.*)

GUARD 2. Kneel down.

GUARD. Give me your hand

GUARD 2. Give me your other hand

TIM. (*lust and fear.*) what are you going to do to me?

> (GUARD *ZAPS* TIM *with a weird crystal penis wand.*)

AHHHH!

GUARD. No TALKING!

> (TIM *loses all control of his body temporarily and the* GUARDS *bind him to a tall black elaborately carved pillar
> a* VOICE *emerges from the shadows
> a previously unnoticed* FIGURE *now seen in silhouette in the darkness.*)

VOICE. is this the Infiltrator?

TIM. Infiltrator?

> (*ZZZAP!
> falling down again, weakly:*)

but…
why?

GUARDS. it is your worship

VOICE. that will be all

GUARD. but your worship shouldn't we—

VOICE. (*histrionic.*) I said THAT WILL BE ALL!

> (VOICE *turns and reveals himself:
> the* BISHOP AHNI*! Magnificent and bizarre
> glittering, caped, with elaborate headpiece.*)

AHNI. so
you're a Virgynian?

TIM. …no…

AHNI. no?

TIM. no
I'm from Earth

AHNI. ah
"eurrth"
well
Eurrth creature
tell me...
—are you a little boy? or a girl?

TIM. me?

AHNI. (*grabbing* TIM*'s crotch.*) do you have a little Ronald?
or a Nancy?

TIM. (*terrified.*) a...
a Ronald?

AHNI. (*appraising him.*) hm
        (*beat—then releasing* TIM*'s crotch.*)
good
we may be able to USE you
what do they call you, Earth Man?

TIM. uh
Tim

AHNI. "a 'Tim"
stupid name
I am the Bishop Ahni
Imperial Legislator of the Argoshaun Empire
Second only to His Lordship, the Emperor Moody Garland.

TIM. Moody Garland?

AHNI. Moody Garland.

TIM. Moody Garland.

AHNI. Moody Garland.
        (*pause
        a volley of looks.*)
you puzzle me, Earth Man
you're like a tiny book of childish riddles
one with a silly baby bunny on the cover
I like that
a little of that
just be sure you stay on the right side of my curiosity

TIM. or else

AHNI. or else
        (*THWAK!*
        AHNI *ZAPS* TIM.)

TIM. ah!

AHNI. or else you'll taste the sting of my little Plasma-Prod here!

TIM. ow

AHNI. tell me "a 'Tim"
are you a Homosexual?

TIM. well honestly I don't see what that has to do with
> (*ZAP!*)

ah!

AHNI. just ANSWER my QUESTIONS!

TIM. yes! if it matters
yes
I'm a "homosexual"!

AHNI. oh good
You see we need a Homosexual

TIM. (*snorts.*) seems like you have your "fair share" up here already

AHNI. I don't know what you mean

TIM. I mean
This all seems pretty "homosexual"

AHNI. What? No it's not.

TIM. really? because your *guards* seem—

AHNI. We have no Homosexuals on our planet.
> (*pause.*)

What? There are no Homosexuals on this planet. Only Married Men. Men
With Wives. And Children. Like me. I have two.
> (*pause.*)

TIM. (*"if you say so."*) Ok.

AHNI. I don't like the way you're smiling at me.

TIM. I'm sorry I—

AHNI. I don't like the way you're looking at me, and I have to tell you, I am
sorely tempted to smack that smirk right off your face.

TIM. No no. Please. Carry on.

AHNI. Yes. We need a Homosexual.

TIM. So you said.

AHNI. Because we're looking—for the Holy Gay Flame.

TIM. Well I don't know where it is!

AHNI. Your *MIND* doesn't... but your *BODY* does.

TIM. My... body?

AHNI. Yes. When a true Homosexual comes into the presence of the Holy Gay Flame? They begin to shake.

TIM. To shake?

AHNI. To quiver like a dollop of tapioca pudding quaking at the bottom of a fat kid's bowl. A true Homosexual cannot help but twitch and jerk when he draws near to the Holy Flame.

TIM. Great, so—what do you want from me?

AHNI. You are going to be my personal queer dowsing rod, and lead me to the hiding place of the Holy Gay Flame.

TIM. And if I refuse?

AHNI. (*indignant.*) "If You Refuse?"

(BISHOP *swats* TIM, *has a little star fit tantrum.*)

No one!

(*swat!*)

EVAH!

(*swat!*)

REFUSES!

(*swat!*)

ME!

(*swat!*
swat!
beat
a spectrum of emotion passes rapidly over the BISHOP's *face as he recovers from this vaguely erotic exertion.*)

AHNI. (*turning away, pulling himself together.*) You made me lose my temper! I don't like to lose my temper.
My wife says I'm ugly when I get angry like that.

TIM. (*through pain.*) Your *wife*—?

AHNI. Never mind! Just you remember the taste of that cold electro-magneton against your hot Eaurrth flesh. There's plenty more where that came from!

TIM. why should I help you?

AHNI. what would you say if I told you that
as we speak
a fleet of Argoshaun Murder Vessels are heading to your precious Eurrth
and if you don't help me
they will atomize your home planet
and every living thing on it

TIM. fine

do it

blow it all up

there's nothing there for me any more anyway

AHNI. (*reaching dramatically for a LARGE RED BUTTON on the tip of his wand.*) oh really? well alright then, I'll just *press* this little DOOMSDAY BUTTON here… Ok here I go—

TIM. (*reaching out abruptly.*) Wait!

> (*beat.*)

look:

if I help you

will you spare the Earth?

AHNI. I will

> (*pause.*)

TIM. alright then

what choice do I have

AHNI. good boy a 'Tim

Guards! Prepare the captive for travel. But WAIT!

First… would you like to see how we dance on Argoshaun? It is said we are the most elegant and graceful dancers in all of the Flossy Penobscot Nebulae.

TIM. Ah—

AHNI. Guards! Music! Let us DANCE!

> (*The* GUARDS *and* BISHOP *perform an angular Futurist ballet— half cuckoo clock, half '80's vogueing. The* BISHOP *takes a solo. At the* GUARDS' *urging,* TIM *busts some vintage moves, a bit of breakin', a bit of disco. The* GUARDS *and* BISHOP *watch, stunned. Music ends. Abruptly:*)

AHNI. (*clap clap.*) Take him away.

> (*the* GUARDS *start dragging* TIM *off.*)

Oh and… a 'Tim?

> (GUARDS *halt.*)

TIM. …yes?

AHNI. You're a *terrible* dancer.

GUARD 1. hah hah it's really true you know!

> (GUARDS *exit with* TIM.)

NUNS TWO: BACK ON VIRGYNIA

The Planet Virgynia. The Nuns' Cloister—a windswept promontory over a raging orange ammonia sea. The skies are stormy and swirling. A Maddening Wind blows outside. MOTHER *and* NUN *convene. Solemn music.*

MOTHER. Close the door tight, Sister, the storm outside is raging.

NUN. The Gods are angered, Mother. This unnatural storm is proof of it.

MOTHER. They rage at the loss of the Holy Gay Flame.

NUN. The sound is enough to drive one MAD!

> (*sound of storm SWELLS*
> *the door SWINGS open!*
> *Music STOPS!*
> NUN 2 *enters drinking Grape Soda from a can with a straw.*)

NUN 2. (*entering, slurping the last of her drink.*) Man! Sure is WINDY out there!

> (*she is ignored*
> *solemn music resumes.*)

MOTHER. (*touching* NUN*'s belly.*) How is the child, Sister?

NUN. Resting now. The wee Homosexual was kicking up a storm himself earlier!

MOTHER. They are rambunctious in the womb. Why, I remember my first litter...

NUN. But Mother—
do you really think this earth man will retrieve the Flame in time?

MOTHER. all the prophecies say so

NUN. of course they do, Mother...
and far be it for me to gainsay the ancient writs—
and yet—
something about that earth man leaves me unsettled

NUN 2. that's probably cause your whole family was accidentally killed by earthlings! you just HATE 'em!

> (*pause.*)

right?

> (*pause*
> *she is ignored.*)

MOTHER. do not fret, Sister
the Gods work wonders through humble means
and use humble tools to achieve lofty aims

NUN. I know Mother but
if the Flame is not retrieved within these three days—

NUN 2. (*without a shred of darkness.*) then the whole damn planet's gonna go up in flames and all the Homosexuals with it!

> (*pause*
> *picking up on the solemnity and displeasure of the others.*)

…and that'd be a shame.

MOTHER. I know you fear for your child
and for all the Homosexual children Sister
but all we can do is maintain our faith
come: let us peer through the mists of space
Perhaps we can contact Tim and aid his progress

There! I see him! He is in a dark place, but he is facing the right direction.

NUN 2. That sounds like a start!

NUN. Look up here dummy!

NUN 2. (I don't think he can hear you)

> (NUNS *SING the following, in the manner of a classic church choir.*)

NUNS and MOTHER. (*a beautiful harmony.*) HMMMMMMMMMMM

MOTHER. Take courage Timmmmmm

NUN. We need you Tim.

NUN 2. What's up Tim!

MOTHER. Be strong of heart!

NUN. Don't fuck this uhhhhhhhhhhp

NUN 2. (*pulling Cheez-Its out of her hat.*) Oh Man! I totally forgot I had these!

> (NUN 2 *crunches away, very very happy.*)

MOUNTING THE MRITHRA

> TIM *and the* BISHOP.

AHNI. So. This is the Mrithra.

TIM. I guess.

AHNI. I thought they were mythological creatures. Like unicorns. Or New Zealanders.

TIM. what

AHNI. I never thought I'd have the chance to see one up close. It's horrible. Yet strangely beautiful. I respect you, Mrithra. So—how does it work?

TIM. you're asking ME?

AHNI. you rode IN on it

TIM. yeah but I was like ABDUCTED

AHNI. but you have SOME experience

TIM. I wasn't DRIVING it

AHNI. why are you being so STUBBORN

TIM. I'm not being STUBBORN I just don't know how it works!

AHNI. (*brandishing a Laser Crystal Penis Weapon.*) just TEACH ME TO RIDE Earth Man!

TIM. Ok!

lemme see

with horses, they say

don't ever show the animal your FEAR

You gotta let it know who's Boss.

AHNI. me

TIM. Right.

So…

> (TIM *approaches*
> the MRITHRA *snorts and rears up.*)

TIM. whoa

AHNI. you're showing your fear you're too afraid

TIM. you're not helping!

lemme try again…

Hi there Mrithra.

How are you?

My name is Tim.

I'm from Earth. That's a long way away from here.

I'm just gonna hop on your back now. Are you ready? Here we go…

> (TIM *mounts the* MRITHRA
> MRITHRA *rears up, shudders and bucks.*)

whoa!

> (TIM *holds tight, stays on the creature's back.*)

whoa

easy there

steady now

good boy

> (MRITHRA *settles.*)

Ok

now you

> (AHNI *approaches*
> MRITHRA *shrugs.*)

MRITHRA. GrawAARRRWARrrrrRRR!

AHNI. (*pointing weapon at* MRITHRA.) Arrrgh! Why does it always SNORT at me like that? It's mocking me!

I'll soon TEACH you to SNORT, you unruly—

TIM. Jeez don't THREATEN IT!

you have to MAKE FRIENDS with it

AHNI. how am I supposed to BEFRIEND this—this—this aubergine monstrosity

TIM. do something nice

soothe it

> (AHNI *touches the snout gingerly*
> MRITHRA *purrs.*)

TIM. there you go

see?

he likes you

AHNI. I'm flattered

and now what?

TIM. And now:

you mount him.

AHNI. Do what now

TIM. Mount him.

> (*beat.*)

Mount him.

> (*beat.*)

Mount him //

AHNI. Stop saying that!

Ok

ah

so

TIM. what

AHNI. so

do you want me

"in the rear"

as they say

TIM. What? Oh

I

AHNI. or

I could "take the front" // you know

TIM. it's
really,
you could go...

AHNI. which... behind is...//

TIM. I think um
maybe

AHNI. Probably
I think
I think I'd prefer behind
if that's alright with you

TIM. no that's probably, I mean, I can go either—

AHNI. I mean you're

TIM. I can

AHNI. you can
kind of
GUIDE it to the right place
that way

TIM. right

> (AHNI *crouches near the beast. He slings one leg over.* TIM *pulls him up behind. A moment of awkward adjustment.* AHNI *and* TIM *trying very hard not to touch.*)

there you go
not so bad right

AHNI. no
not so bad
Earth Man

TIM. alright then
HOY Mrithra!

> (*the* MRITHRA *LIFTS OFF*
> *they're flying*
> *the space erupts in stars and swirls of nebulae*
> *galaxies and constellations*
> *planets and moons and comets race by*
> *it should have the effect of a run-down but still somehow magical '70s planetarium.*)

AHNI. Oh, slow, easy! Hahahaha.

TIM. Hahahahaha.

AHNI. I'm falling! I'm going to fall off!

TIM. You're not gonna fall!
Just hold on to me.

AHNI. like
this?

TIM. yeah
hold on tight

AHNI. yes…
that's better

TIM. now let's see what this thing can do
> (*spurring it on.*)

HOY Mrithra!

AHNI. (*gleeful.*) Hoy Mrithra!
> (*pause.*)

Ah! The galaxy looks so beautiful tonight.
It's as if…
…as if I've never really seen the stars before…

A DISREPUTABLE PLACE

> TIM *and* AHNI *enter a dank dirty dive bar somewhere on the edge of the Red Light Sector of Tiajuarez 9*
>
> *An* EXOTIC EXTRATERRESTRIAL DANCER *dances in a cage to exotic music center, her fur swirling about her in soft ripples*
>
> *a lot of really creepy nasty fucked up looking xenomorphic life forms are giving our heroes the stink eye*

AHNI. (*loud, over music.*) Now Tim: listen to me: this is a Very Dangerous Place
we don't want to draw any unwanted attention our way
just try to *blend in*—can you do that?

TIM. yeah sure of course
I'm cool

> (AHNI *leads,* TIM *follows*
> TIM *is blocked by* ET DANCER, AHNI *pulls* TIM *away before anything terrible can happen to him*
> KING TROUT, *a low-down cool-ass Han Solo type, occupies a corner table*
> TIM *and* AHNI *slip in opposite.*)

KING TROUT. Ahni
never thought I'd see *you* walk in here again

AHNI. King Trout
been a long time

(*beat*
AHNI *and* TROUT *complete a complicated* THREE CARD MONTE
CHEERS *with the cups assembled on the table, half-toast half-secret handshake
when the ritual is complete all three have cups in front of them.*)

AHNI and TROUT. (*skol!*) Keeantcha!

(TROUT *and* AHNI *drink*
TIM *follows behind.*)

TIM. Sri Ratcha

(TIM *drinks*
TIM *swallows*
immediately, AHNI *and* TROUT *spit the liquid back in their cups.*)

AHNI and TROUT. Ptui!

(TROUT *and* AHNI *look at* TIM.)

AHNI. Tim—you didn't *swallow* that did you?

TIM. (*so what?*) yeah

AHNI. That's Ithorian Moonshine! You're only supposed to *swish* it around
in your mouth! Not SWALLOW it!

TIM. But I—

TROUT. (*very amused.*) Better fasten your seat belt, Kid
you're about to get cosmically FUCKED UP heh heh

TIM. Naw, I'm cool I can hold my liquor

(*beat*
TIM *collapses, immediately* WASTED.)

TROUT. Hm
well it's good to see you again Ahni

AHNI. Can't say the same of you Trout
the years haven't been kind

TIM. you two know each other

KING TROUT. oh sure kid
me n "The Bishop" go WAY back

AHNI. we grew up together

KING TROUT. if you call that growing up
living offa scraps in a satellite orphanage orbiting the moons of Zarkoff Five

TIM. wait wait wait wait wait so hold up so:
you're an orphan?

KING TROUT. yes

TIM. and *you're* an orphan

AHNI. we both are, yes

TIM. Orphan… Ahni?

AHNI. what of it

TIM. Little... Orphan... Ahni

TROUT. you let him talk to you like that?

AHNI. ignore him he's drunk

TIM. I'm not druck!

AHNI. (*hissed.*) (Hold It Together!)

TIM. (*wandering away.*) Pfft! Ok MOM!

KING TROUT. (*sarcastic.*) and what does the Empire need from me today, your worship?

AHNI. this earthoid and I seek the Holy Gay Flame

      (TIM *is getting felt up and patted down by* ET DANCER.)

KING TROUT. (*serious.*) The Holy Gay Flame

AHNI. it's been stolen

KING TROUT. stolen?

AHNI. Pilfered.

KING TROUT. Pilfered?

TIM. (*drunk know-it-all.*) It means "Stolen" dummy!

TROUT. What was that?

TIM. (*hollering, gesturing to no one in particular.*) Hey can I get some more of a 'nother one of these up in here? Barkeep. BARKEEP!

AHNI. (What did I say? Cut it out!)

TIM. Right Shhhhh!
oh shit I feel floaty

AHNI. The Emperor is seizing this opportunity to claim the Flame for his own

      (TIM *crosses the room.*)

TIM. Wooooooo!

KING TROUT. awright well
let me check my connections
see what I can stir up
and Hey:

AHNI. yes?

KING TROUT. Better keep an eye on your little friend there...
...the clientele here aren't known for their tolerance...

AHNI. Well neither is he.

      (*they both laugh, menacingly.*)

TIM. This place is AWESOME!
I'm having a wonderful time are you having a wonderful time

AHNI. Tim, You Are A DISGRACE to the human race, Tim! Parading around like a drunk Saloozhian at a Bachelorette Party! Do you want to get us both KILLED?!

TIM. Look BISSHSOP or whatever your dumb name is
I haven't GONE OUT and HAD FUN in like TWO WHOLE YEARS
I've been a very depressed gen'lman
and so I want you
I WANT EVERYBODY HERE TO KNOW
That If Tim wants to party
TIM IS…
GONNA PARTY!!!

AHNI. SIT DOWN! People are staring!

TIM. and ANYONE WHO DOESN'T LIKE IT CAN KISS MY BLACK ASS! //

        (TIM *dances briefly then collapses again.*)

KING TROUT. (*interrupting.*) Ok gentlemen I—
am I interrupting something here?

TIM. (*simultaneously.*) yes

AHNI. (*simultaneously.*) no

KING TROUT. I have some news
        (*briskly:*)

AHNI. Spill it

KING TROUT. gonna cost you

AHNI. how much

KING TROUT. forty thousand kaltrons

AHNI. ridiculous

TIM. (*to himself.*) Kaltrons—pfft—*dumb*

KING TROUT. you gonna haggle when the fate of the entire UNIVERSE rests in the balance

AHNI. fine

KING TROUT. (*leaning in, holding out hand.*) Orphan's Honor?

AHNI. (*beat, then taking hand.*) Orphan's Honor.

TIM. (*to no one.*) I'm gonna have sex tonight!

        (TIM *bursts into tears*
        an ALIEN *comforts him.*)

KING TROUT. Ok: seems the HGF was last seen at the edge of the Yars Cluster

AHNI. but the Yars Cluster is a wasteland
the mercury vapors and sub atomic temperatures make life there unsustainable

KING TROUT. nothing but hobos and hermits in those parts, it's true but whatta ya want: I'm just the messenger

AHNI. excellent

our work is done here

> (AHNI *pulls* TIM *from another* ALIEN.)

let's go

TIM. hey!

KING TROUT. what no time for a drink? don't you wanna catch up old friend?

AHNI. we were never *friends*, Trout

KING TROUT. seem to recall a time back in the Orphanage, we had a Holy Gay Flame of our own//

> (AHNI *cuts* KING TROUT *off with a BLAST from the crystal penis weapon thing*
> KING TROUT *falls in a seizure, electrocuted and stunned.*)

AHNI. I don't remember that, King. But take this as a warning: I will not tolerate lies and slander. I have a reputation to uphold. And a wife.

KING TROUT. (*incredulity through the pain.*) …a… wife?

> (*general laughter and contempt for* AHNI. AHNI *in response SHOOTS HIS GUN IN THE AIR and COMMANDS RESPECT—ALIENS go SILENT.*)

AHNI. (*with great dignity, confidence and authority.*) That's right!: A Wife. In fact, I should probably call her. Right now. She's probably worried sick about me. Her and our three children //

TIM. —you said two children //

AHNI. —two children! Two or three, I can't recall. A number of children, in any case. That we had through making marital love. In a bed. Like *civilized* people. Now, if you'll excuse me—

> (*with an unmistakable swish,* AHNI *turns to go, followed by* TIM.)

KING TROUT. (*still huddled on the floor in pain.*) wait! what about my money…?

AHNI. Oh, King. Surely you remember?

> (*beat.*)

You can never trust an Orphan's Promise.

> (*middle finger to* TROUT.)

let's go

> (*they exit.*)

KING TROUT. Ahni! Come back here! If I ever see you again, I'll kill you, you sonovabitch! Ahhhh!

> (*music swells.*)

IN THE YARS CLUSTER

TIM. (*hungover.*) ooooh gawwdd

AHNI. oooh are we feeling BAD now?

TIM. Yeszzzz

AHNI. Good! Suffer! you really embarrassed me back there!

TIM. You could have warned me about the booze!

AHNI. Well I didn't expect you'd go and swallow every strange thing that comes into your mouth!

TIM. I'm sorry Ok! it's been a long time since I've been able to "cut loose" and—

I've got a lot of pent up feelings

AHNI. "Feelings"—pfft

You need to *behave* yourself! Be strong, hard, firm—like an Argoshaun man! we're on a mission

TIM. Ugh god I feel like Death

…my head…

Ooh… "I think this is the big one"

AHNI. Are you alright?

TIM. "You hear that lizabeth? I'm comin to join you honey!" (heh heh)

AHNI. what, what was that

TIM. oh it's just

it's from this show I used to watch as a kid

it was like this old man running like a junk shop—you know a junk shop? and like every time he's

SHOCKED or

DISMAYED

he like throws his HAND over his HEART

looks up to heaven and shouts

"YOU HEAR THAT, LIZBETH?

I'M COMIN TO JOIN YA HONEY!" Ha!

        (*pause for reaction, none comes.*)

Elizabeth is his dead wife I think?

and whatever just happened makes him think, like,

Ah! This is TOO MUCH! I'm gonna have a heart attack and DIE already!

AHNI. and this is *comical?*

TIM. Well, yeah. I mean he's not REALLY having a heart attack he's just play acting.

For comedic effect.

AHNI. (*very prim.*) "Did you hear that Elizabeth? I'm coming to join you honey"
like that?

TIM. kind of
it's like a fake heart attack
so he's a little more emphatic

AHNI. Argoshaunians have three hearts

TIM. no

AHNI. one in the sole of the foot
one in the back of the neck

TIM. weird

AHNI. and one in a jar on the top shelf of the medicine chest

TIM. what?

AHNI. it's a baby heart

TIM. EW, God!

AHNI. No not torn from a baby! We're not BARBARIANS

TIM. well

AHNI. no it's
like the way your people shed teeth as babies? it's like that
as we grow older we shed our baby hearts and store them in a jar of mineral oil

TIM. why do you keep them though?

AHNI. superstition I guess
or as some kind of reminder

TIM. do you have yours

AHNI. well
no
I think I told you
I am an orphan so

TIM. oh right so
you don't really know where your heart is

AHNI. or if I have one...
I mean
I am ARGOSHAUN by heritage but

TIM. but like, in terms of species

AHNI. I actually don't know. What I am.

(*pause.*)

are you feeling bad for me? don't feel bad for me! I'll Blast you if you start feeling bad for me!

TIM. I wasn't feeling BAD for you!
I was just expressing some normal
interplanetary empathy
but it wasn't PITY—
where ARE we now anyway?

LOTUSIAN HAZE

      TIM *and* AHNI *fly into clouds of lavender and silver…*

AHNI. I'm not quite sure
it's a strange part of the galaxy out here, Tim
far afield of the rules and laws that bind the Argoshaun Empire…
…much further out than I've ever been before…

TIM. (*sniffing.*) what is this? some kind of—smoke? it smells like lilacs…

AHNI. I'm not sure, but it seems… familiar…
Oh no
OH NO
Pull Up Mrithra!
PULL UP!

MRITHRA. RRRrrrr!

TIM. what is it!

AHNI. We've passed into a Lotusian Haze! You musn't breathe it in!

TIM. (*cough.*) too late!

AHNI. It's a trap devised by the Lotusians—a race of 5th dimensional Man
Hunters!

TIM. what do they want from us?

AHNI. they want to bewilder us with visions of our innermost desires…

TIM. and then?

AHNI. and then?
they'll eat us alive!

TIM. no! Turn around, Mrithra!

AHNI. too late to turn back now
the only way… is *through!*

MOTHER. you are passing through a VEIL of ILLUSIONS Tim
stay your course and don't be swayed
trust the one you have least cause to trust
and deny those that appear most familiar to you

(*the stage is filled with smoke and psychedelic lights
a buzzing*

TIM *and* AHNI *leave the* MRITHRA [*in their minds*] *and wander separately.*)

TIM. Bishop?

AHNI. (*off, very distant.*) Tim? (Tim? tim? tim?)

TIM. where are you? I—I can't see you—

(AHNI *disappears*
TIM *is left alone in the fog*

an enormous CHINESE FOOD CARTON *approaches* VERY SLOWLY.)

THEO. (*voice over, sexy, male.*) Hey Tim.

TIM. Theo?

THEO. (*coming closer.*) Yeah Tim. It's me. Theo. I really miss you.

TIM. But Theo—we broke up two years ago—

THEO. (*coming closer.*) I know. And it was the biggest mistake I ever made. Come back to me Tim. Come back.

TIM. you totally broke my heart Theo—I've been a mess since you left—how can I trust you again?

THEO. I'll make it up to you Tim
just come back to me
we can stay in tonight
and watch TV
and order Chinese Food
and eat it in bed

TIM. I want to Theo—but—

THEO. Give me one more chance, Tim
Please

MOTHER. (*reappearing suddenly.*) Don't DO IT Tim!

(TIM *stops.*)

TIM. but it's my ex!
and he wants me back!

MOTHER. Don't be deceived!
He is but a figment of your imagination
you must shed that part of yourself in order to survive!

THEO. Come to me Tim.

TIM. but—but—

THEO. COME TO ME TIM.

(THEO *grabs* TIM—TIM *opens the carton to reveal a* MONSTROUS FACE: *the* CHINESE FOOD CONTAINER *spills out* VILE OILY LO MEIN NOODLES WITH HORRIBLE BLOODSHOT EYES *in IT!* THEO's *hands and noodles ensnare* TIM!)

THEO. come stay with me EARTH MAN... FOREVER!

TIM. no!

(TIM *struggles.*)

THEO. arggg

TIM. I don't need you anymore, Theo! I'm in outer space now! and you're not even REAL!

THEO / LOTUSIAN. I will DESTROY YOU Earth Man!

TIM. Bishop? Bishop?

AHNI. (*delighted laughter.*) ha ha
hahaha
ha HA

(AHNI *is ensnared in an enormous* WEB
TIM *reaches for him.*)

TIM. hang on—I'm coming—

AHNI. Tim? Is that you?

TIM. here—take my hand

AHNI. but I don't want to leave... I love it here...

TIM. reach for me

AHNI. ah!

TIM. almost there...

(TIM *reaches for* AHNI.
AHNI *reaches*
REACH, REACH.)

Got you!

(TIM *grabs* AHNI *and the* WEBS FALL AWAY *from both.*)

AHNI. Ahh!

LOTUSIANS. ahhhhhhhhh! nooo!

(MOTHER *exits*
TIM *and* AHNI *appear back on the* MRITHRA
[*miniature*].)

AHNI. but Tim: you are my prisoner...
and yet you saved me

TIM. yeah I guess

AHNI. But why? An Argoshaun would have left me there to die

TIM. yeah well great
"hurray" I saved the day
now can we go find the Flame and get this over with please?

AHNI. (*pulling himself together.*) of course
Hoy Mrithra!
Heh heh—I have to say, that was a *pretty* close call…
But it looks like Smooth Sailing from here on out…
Yes sir—things are really looking UP for the two of us AHHHHHHHH

> (*abruptly a CATASTROPHE FROM OUTER SPACE [ASTEROIDS] attacks AHNI and TIM.*)

TIM and AHNI. ahhhhhH!

MRITHRA. AHGGGGRRRR!

> (TIM *and* AHNI *go flying off into the nether reaches of space.*)

TIM and AHNI. AHHHHHHHHhhhhhhh!

NUNS THREE: IT'S GETTING WORSE!

> *Howling winds and rain*
> NUN *is sprawled out on a fainting couch*
> *sweating, feverish*
> MOTHER *and* NUN 2 *stand beside her, tending to her*

NUN. ooooh!

MOTHER. easy now, Sister, easy

NUN. oh Mother
the pain is very great!
I fear my Homosexual baby has been deprived of the nourishment of the Holy Gay Flame for too long…

NUN 2. well, this is a real bump in the road

NUN. Mother
Please
please tell me
is my gay baby going to //

MOTHER. not yet, Sister
there's still time

NUN 2. looks like about 12 hours by that Doomsday Clock over there!

NUN. Ironic, isn't it?
My life
and that of my future gay unborn son

in the hands of that
that

NUN 2. earth man!

NUN. he of the same race that
so many years ago
mowed down my parents in a freak accident

MOTHER. the god and goddesses crave balance, Sister
perhaps Tim's mission is their way of repaying you for taking your family
while you were yet so young

NUN. perhaps Mother
I hope for our sakes
and the sakes of all Homosexuals everywhere
that you're right
for if the Flame is not returned in time, it won't just be my gay baby that
comes out dead

NUN 2. No sirree Bob that'll mean the end of EVERY gay baby EVERY-
WHERE!

       (MOTHER *and* NUN *look at each other, then daggers at* NUN 2.
       NUN 2 *smiles, oblivious.*)

but I'll tell ya guys
I think
even with time running down the way it is?
I tell ya, I just have a good feeling about that Tim.
I just think—gosh! I just think everything's gonna turn out GREAT in the end!

       (MOTHER *pushes* NUN 2 *offstage.*)

MOTHER. Come Sister, let's let our other Sister rest in SILENCE

NUN. Yes please, the DIN in here is UNBEARABLE to my sensitive, pain-
wracked ears!

NUN 2. Ok—but I'll be just offstage if you guys need anything!

       (*clock strikes eleven.*)

NUN. Oh Mother, harken thine ears to the grim ringing of that bell!

MOTHER. Time grows short

NUN. Oh Tim

MOTHER. Come back to us

NUN. Come back to us soon

MOTHER. Come back to us…

MOTHER and NUN. VICTORIOUS!

       (NUN 2 *re-enters.*)

NUN 2. There's no DOOR over there!

THE MOVIE STAR PLANET

Elsewhere
on a tiny grey planet

TIM. No YOU'RE a piece of shit cause look I SAID Hey:
that METEOR STORM looks like TROUBLE:
why don't we TURN LEFT and avoid it:
and you //

AHNI. I could have negotiated it if you weren't PULING and WHINING
in my ear
"watch out for that fire ball"
"you're flying too close to that black hole"
you're like a Megamite you know that? Like a nine year old Megamite in a pink
frilly dress!

TIM. ALL I WAS DOING was looking out for YOUR well-being and safety

AHNI. Well DON'T! I'm the ARCHBISHOP of an INTERGALACTIC
EMPIRE I think I can TAKE CARE OF MYSELF!

TIM. Oh yeah, big shot, big man, walking around in an evening gown with
CHICKEN WINGS sewn on the back!

AHNI. These are not CHICKEN WINGS! They are the Ritual Garb of the
CAPTAIN of the IMPERIAL ARMY! And they're supposed to look like
BAT WINGS not CHICKEN

TIM. Oh yeah, I see it now: you're exactly like a bat: except for one thing—

AHNI. —oh don't you dare, don't you—

TIM. BATS! KNOW HOW! TO FLY!

AHNI. oh that is it that is it I'm gonna Blast you so hard

TIM. Go ahead! Blast me! Do your worst! What is there left to lose! The
Mrithra's Dead—

AHNI. —actually I think it was still breathing—

TIM. —we're stranded on some UNINHABITABLE PLANET light years
away from Earth—

AHNI. —yes well count your blessings—

TIM. —and we have exactly 11 hours to find the HOLY GAY FLAME or
else every homosexual in the known universe is going to—

MOVIE STAR BOY. excuse me

(*pause.*)

TIM. um
yes?

MOVIE STAR BOY. excuse me and pardon me for interrupting, but are you two talking about the "Holy Gay Flame"?

> (*beat.*)

TIM. uh
yeah, we—

> (AHNI *pushes forward, grabs the* BOY *by his collar.*)

AHNI. (*threatening.*) if you know where the Flame is, Boy, then you had best render it up to us posthaste or I shall—

> (TIM *intercedes.*)

TIM. Come on Man, look at yourself
what're you doing? This is just a kid, just a little—

MOVIE STAR BOY. I know where the Flame is.

TIM. you do?

MOVIE STAR BOY. Yep.

TIM. Ok well
how do you know that?

MOVIE STAR BOY. Because it's mine.
I took it.

> (*beat*
> AHNI *goes for the* BOY, *Blaster raised high*
> *again* TIM *runs interference.*)

AHNI. Ok well NOW you have to let me zap him, the little fucker took the Flame

TIM. no no NO we're not BLASTING or ZAPPING anyone with that weird penis-shaped weapon you keep swinging around. I mean, Paging Doctor Freud already...

> (*turning to* BOY.)

listen, um
I don't want to freak you out but
this missing Flame has been causing a LOT of trouble in the universe and
if there's any way you can lead us to it, that would be //

MOVIE STAR BOY. Yeah, sure, no problem. I'm done with it anyway. Here, follow me back to my house. Come on. This way.

> (*The* BOY *trots off.* TIM *looks at* AHNI. TIM *shrugs.* TIM *follows* BOY. *Beat.* AHNI *follows behind, looking at his Blaster.*)

AHNI. ..."penis-shaped"...?

> (*it really is though.*)

THE MOVIE STARS

Several MOVIE STARS—*much larger and brighter than they could ever be in real life—more the size they must have been when projected on a movie screen—in black and white with some touches of color—move in slow beautiful arcs around* BOY, AHNI *and* TIM.

Moved about on rolling platforms, they perform bits and fragments from their films—the most dramatic moments from their most dramatic roles...

MOVIE STAR 1. (*arcing past.*) You don't have to tell me, Clarence. You don't have to say anything at all. Your eyes have given you away. You don't love me anymore. The silly thing is—I already knew. I've known for so long... No, please. No more words. Just *kiss* me one more time...

MOVIE STAR 2. (*different scene, different movie.*) Aw but Ma! You gotta believe me! I would never do anything to hurt you! I'd nevah do anything to hurt our family! I'm just tryin to be free! You understand? To be FREE!

MOVIE STAR BOY. I used to be a full-grown man like you guys.
I was a normal human baby. And I grew into a child.
My mother used to take me to the movies all the time.
We lived across the street from a cinema.
I saw the same movie over and over.
I practically memorized them.
Because even then I knew—
I think I knew—
that this was information I would need some day.

Then I died.

MOVIE STAR 1. (*again different scene.*) My baby! My baby! My BABY!
MOVIE STAR BOY. (*directing.*) turn to me
hold it there
now raise your head—very slowly... very slowly...

> (*back to* AHNI *and* TIM.)

When I died, I went to space.
I found an asteroid.
I thought,
this is a perfect place for me to make my movies.

MOVIE STAR 3. (*again different film.*) No, Marjorie. It wasn't haughtiness in me. It wasn't pride, or putting on airs, or any of those other things you accuse me of. No. What it was... it was Shame.

MOVIE STAR BOY. I take them and cut them up.

The bits of them I can remember.
I rearrange them.
So they look more like me.
So they resemble me.
They were so good, so beautiful, when I was little.
I just always wanted to be a part of them.
Now I am.
I am a Leading Lady. Watch me walk:

> (*he walks.*)

Hear my laugh, like a little bell

> (*laughs like a star.*)

Check me out when I get into a RAGE

> (*star tantrum.*)

"Roses? I said I wanted LILIES for my dressing room!"

> (*change.*)

now see me die:

> (*a long, drawn out, balletic death—then he bounces back up.*)

It's good.
it's taken years
and a lot of sacrifice
I work all the time on it
but now it's almost ready
it's almost perfect
so I needed that fire
and I took it
I used as much as I needed
I made it actually a little brighter, I think
you can have it back now though
be careful with it
there might be other kids like me
try n like
share it
Ok?
try n like
spread it around.

TIM. so
where is it

MOVIE STAR BOY. I left it just over there
on the other side of the planet
you can walk to it

it's not very far
you'll find it pretty quick I think
good luck

> (*turning back to* MOVIE STARS.)

Ok: CUT

FINDING THE FLAME

> *Walking*

TIM. so

AHNI. what

TIM. you said you would tell me

AHNI. tell you—

TIM. what the Emperor—

AHNI. Moody Garland

TIM. —what he is planning to do with the Holy Gay Flame once we bring
it back

AHNI. oh
well, yes
I suppose this would be the right time to tell you

TIM. we're getting close

AHNI. oh
well
yes, I suppose I have
grown fond of you
Over the course of our—

TIM. No I meant we're close to the FLAME
like we're near to it
see?
I'm starting to shake

AHNI. right
I knew that
I was just
making small talk

> (AHNI *hides his hands.*)

TIM. but yeah but so—
—man I'm really starting to vibrate here—

AHNI. (*covering his own quivering.*) Of course you are
your Homosexual Body is
responding to the Flame
that's why I took you prisoner and brought you along on this—mission

TIM. but what's the Emperor going to do with it then?

AHNI. He's going to eat it.

    (TIM *stops. Beat.*)

TIM. he's what

AHNI. he's going to eat it
The Emperor Moody Garland is going to devour the Holy Gay Flame.

    (*beat.*)

TIM. But

AHNI. What, are you surprised?

TIM. well yes
YES I'm fucking SURPRISED
if he eats that Flame that means that no more homosexuals can be born!

AHNI. right

TIM. and there will be no more homosexuals in the universe

AHNI. so?

TIM. So?! Those are my PEOPLE, motherfucker!

AHNI. I don't understand how this can be a surprise to you

TIM. well it is!

AHNI. I mean the Emperor's full title is Emperor Moody Garland, Imperial
Ruler of the Known Universe, and Conqueror and DEVOURER OF WORLDS

TIM. you didn't tell me that

AHNI. didn't I

TIM. you should have told me that

AHNI. Oh why should I! What are you to me?
You're my PRISONER! DO you understand that?
Sure, we've been palling around the universe for a couple days,
off the leash in parts unknown,
But make no mistake:
when we return to Argoshaunia,
to my WIFE and CHILDREN—

TIM. your wife

AHNI. —you will go back to being just another what's that now?

TIM. your wife
I said

AHNI. Yes
MY WIFE

TIM. that's all

AHNI. No No that's NOT all What did that MEAN

TIM. nothing

AHNI. no
no
your tone was definitely IMPLYING something

TIM. what tone

AHNI. oh my god I'm going to

TIM. going to what? "Blast" me with that like
surrogate destructive cock thing you carry around?
pssh

AHNI. this does NOT look like

TIM. show it to your "wife"—ask *her* what she thinks it looks like

AHNI. my wife wouldn't be able to identify a penis

TIM. exactly
cause she's never seen one

AHNI. Of course She's seen a PENIS my wife has seen TONS of PENISES

TIM. "Tons"?

AHNI. Not "tons" I don't mean TONS but—SOME

TIM. yours?

AHNI. No! Yes!
YES of course mine I mean
we have three children
two children
we have
we have some we

TIM. you're shaking

> (*he is*
> *they both are*
> *shaking and stammering with increasing intensity.*)

AHNI. No I'm not

TIM. look at your hands
"Like a pudding in a fat kid's bowl"

AHNI. it's
I
I must be developing some kind of

Palsy
from
from
From being around YOU!
probably some kind of EARTH BACTERIA that's causing this

TIM. no!

AHNI. and plus also it's a very Brisk Night!

TIM. No!

AHNI. and anyways I'm not shaking I'm just
I'm
I'm nervous
I'm

TIM. no

AHNI. stop it stop it I'm NOT a Homosexual!
I'm an Argoshaunian—
I'm an Argoshaunian—
I'm an Argoshaunian—

> (AHNI *kisses* TIM
> *Shaking STOPS*
> BOTH *pull back shocked*
> AHNI *slaps* TIM *across the face*
> *then plunges back into a*
> *DEEP HOT PASSIONATE KISS*
>
> *THE HOLY GAY FLAME floats in*
> *all the strange animals and aliens come out of their various holes and nests*
> *sweet sexy French music plays*
> *soon the whole ALIEN WORLD is moving in a rhythm of seduction and*
> *arousal*
>
> *catching the scent of libidinous pleasure*
> *they begin to couple [and treble and quadruple]*
> *mounting each other in strange novel ways*
>
> *The group rearranges into one pulsating sex machine, expanding and contracting*
>
> *Orgasm.*
>
> *Sexy classy saxophone jazz as the creatures depart.)*

POST COITAL

> *A bit later*
> *dawn*
> AHNI *awakens*
> *He looks at the stars, then back at* TIM *sleeping*
> AHNI *draws a knife…*

AHNI. Now might I do it
Now he is sleeping
and now I'll do it—
I promised the Emperor
he said:
"once the Flame is found" he said
"you must cut eliminate the Earthman"
atomize him or cut his throat
burn the body and leave no trace…
and I will, I said
I will.
so do it now
and do it quick, Ahni
and with him let the secrets of this night die too…
I mean… what would happen to me if this got out?
…what would my wife say?
Ah—who'm I kidding? She knows, she knows…

look there how he sleeps
his lips moving silently like a child's
mouthing secret words in his dreams

I can't kill him like this.
I can't kill him at all.
I—.
What do I do? I something him. Some feeling I can't yet describe, a feeling for
which no word has yet been coined. Some combination of GIDDY and FREE and
FALLING APART in the best, the sweetest, the most PLEASURABLE way…
Some feeling I cannot name that says:
"Let him live."
oh and worse:
"let him live with me."

> (TIM *wakes*
> AHNI *hides knife*
> TIM *stretches*
> *smiles.*)

TIM. morning

AHNI. "morning"
sleep well?

TIM. ahhhh
yes
so well

> (*shy looks.*)

AHNI. ...I am not so
experienced in the ways of—
"Carnal Love"
but I do hope I was able to
provide you with some—
pleasure

TIM. heh heh
yeah
you did
you did good

AHNI. I seem to have stopped shaking

TIM. Yeah me too—I guess there was some sort of release? Like our energy
went into the Flame? or the Flame went into us? I feel so much better! This
was exactly what I needed.

AHNI. (*"me"? "love"?*) What you—needed?

TIM. To—to get my life back on track. I needed to—"plug back in"
"reconnect to the source"

AHNI. (*"me"? "love"?*) to the—source?

TIM. Come on! Let's get this Flame back to the Nuns!

AHNI. oh! yes of course
to the Nuns

TIM. I mean, after all that, you can't let the Emperor devour it can you?

AHNI. no no of course
and then I suppose—
you'll be going back to EARTH, will you?

TIM. well yeah
of course
that's what this is all about, right?
I needed to rescue the Flame so I can get back home
I mean this was Great this was like SO FUN
but //

AHNI. I understand

TIM. No, Ahni, it's // not

AHNI. I UNDERSTAND.

> (*a loud SWOOSH overhead.*)

our escort has arrived

come

gather the Flame and let's be off

> (TIM *goes to gather Flame*
> AHNI *exits*
> TIM *turns to address* AHNI.)

TIM. Ahni, I, wait I want to tell you

> (*he's gone.*)

oh

> (TIM *follows.*)

NUNS FOUR: WE CAN'T WAIT ANYMORE!

NUN 2. Sisters! Sisters! The Mrithra's come back to us!

MOTHER. The Mrithra returnéd?

NUN 2. yes, Mother

and it was burnt and beat up and cut up and exhausted

NUN. poor beast!

MOTHER. yes but

what of the earth man and the Flame, little Sister?

NUN 2. that's the worst part, Mother!

there's no sign of Tim or the Flame! Just the Mrithra all by itself!

NUN. No!

NUN 2. I know!

MOTHER. this bodes not well

come, Sisters

we have no more time to wait

we must ride to Argoshaunia and throw ourselves upon the Emperor Moody Garland's mercy

NUN. but Mother!

that villain has never shown mercy to anyone!

NUN 2. he's a rascal! I mean a real... a real fink

MOTHER. What choice have we Sisters? The clock is run down

and already the Homosexuals of Virgynia weaken and wither, their frolicsome games reduced to mere simpering and mincing in the fallow valleys of our world...

MOTHER. Let us hope the Argoshauns have located the Flame
and the Emperor will see the necessity of sustaining the Homosexual race...

NUN 2. or else?

MOTHER. or else all balance shall be lost throughout the universe... forever...

NUN. ...forever...

NUN 2. let's ride!

> (*they board the* MRITHRA *and ride off.*)

MOODY GARLAND

TIM. why are we back on Argoshaunia?!

AHNI. Imperial protocol: We would never have made it past the Empire's legions. The only recourse is to report back to the Emperor and persuade him to SPARE the Homosexuals

TIM. will he listen

AHNI. I've been like a son to him
I think he'll permit me this one favor

TIM. and then we bring the Flame back to the Nuns right?

AHNI. (*inscrutable.*) of course
right back to the Nuns...
before we go in
I need to warn you about Moody

TIM. Ok

AHNI. when we get in there just
DON'T STARE

TIM. what like Tom Cruise
like
"don't look him directly in the eyes"

AHNI. no
no
he's
you see Moody is
SEVERAL MILLENNIA OLD

TIM. so what

AHNI. you'll see

> (*they begin to enter, then* AHNI *stops them again.*)

there may also be a SMELL

TIM. a smell?

AHNI. he's

certain um FLUIDS need to be pumped into him and also DRAINED out of him on a pretty regular basis so

> (*an ENORMOUS DOOR opens*
> *an* IMPERIAL GUARD *emerges.*)

GUARD. the Emperor will see you now

AHNI. very good

> (*they enter an ENORMOUS and ELABORATE CHAMBER of pale brushed steel*
> *interlocking gears in the walls*
> *huge tubes of brightly colored liquids*
> *some clean, some filthy*
> *extending from hidden reservoirs high up in the walls*
> *Two* GUARDS *in black Imperial Armor flank a set of stairs leading up to a platform*
> *upon which sits a STAINLESS STEEL THRONE*
> *—half-medical half-regal—*
> *supporting a LARGE GLASS JAR*
> *filled with a pinkish viscous liquid*
>
> *this JAR is the focal point of all the machinery, lights and medical equipment in the room*
> *all of it extending outwards from the jar like an enormous spider web*
>
> *in the JAR floats*
> *a large ball with frayed edges*
> *part tumor part dust mite*
> *with a vestigial mouth and tiny useless limbs*
>
> *a kind of raw yellow and green malevolent energy PULSES*
> *inside the glass of his bio-supportive hyperbaric chamber*

TIM. that's the Emperor?

AHNI. (*hush up!*) (*yes!*)

HAIL your Majesty

> (*an echoing voice emerges from far above*
> *speaking in an unfathomable burbling language.*)

MOODY. deez trul mug nah nahz pugh Ahni

AHNI. yes I have the Flame

the Earth Man bears it for us as we discussed

MOODY. tush tush nug phenog pumb ya

TIM. (what's he saying)

AHNI. (he wants you to come forward and present him with the Flame)

TIM. (me?)

AHNI. (of course you! You're the only Homosexual in here, remember?)

TIM. (but)

AHNI. (GO!)

> (TIM *takes a step forward*
> *and is hit with an OVERWHELMING STENCH.*)

TIM. ah

oh my GAWD that SMELL

AHNI. hold it together!

MOODY. nuh frenz doo CHANGA?

AHNI. he approaches your majesty

he's merely

OVERWHELMED by the intensity of your presence

MOODY. Voo NUG gah

> (TIM *arrives before the* EMPEROR.)

AHNI. bow

> (TIM *bows with the Flame.*)

TIM. Your Highness

we all appreciate the uh

mercy and

um

WISDOM you have shown here today

MOODY. oog nuh fellooze

AHNI. alright

now

Feed him the Flame

TIM. what

> (AHNI *draws his weapon.*)

AHNI. I said

Feed Him The Flame

TIM. but you

you promised!

AHNI. Oh Tim. Don't you remember?

You should never trust an Orphan's Promise.

Now feed him the Flame. Or your whole precious EARTH and whoever or whatever it is you LOVE on that beastly planet with be atomized.

MOODY. Hng GAR puh MY-toe!

AHNI. Do it!

TIM. NO!

MOODY. Guh Poo Nah FOO-foo

AHNI. DO IT

> (AHNI *uses the Zapper to control* TIM*'s feet. He is forced to bring the Flame to* MOODY. MOODY*'s mouth-whiskers extend and suck the Flame in.*)

TIM. I'm sorry, Homosexuals…

MOODY. (*mouth full.*) Argh Naut Puh Chi Chi!

AHNI. and now Tim
it is the Emperor's wish
that you DIE

TIM. what

MOODY. Chi Chi! Chi Chi!

TIM. after everything I told you? after everything we shared?!

AHNI. I did what I had to do
Ha! and what did you expect, *Earth* Man?
that I'd stay with you forever?

TIM. I thought we had a connection

AHNI. well you thought wrong!

MOODY. (*mouth full.*) Puh Chi Chi NINO

AHNI. Now, close your horrible human eyes, Tim, and mutter your final earthly words, for the time has come for you to die!

TIM. Fine then—shoot me!

> (*grabs pistol.*)

but I want you to look me in the eyes when you pull the trigger

AHNI. Ha! You Fool! You think I'll fall prey to your Homosexual sentimentality? Pss! "Your *eyes*"? Ha! I can do this—I can do this—I—I—I can't DO it!

> (AHNI *is very close to* TIM *now*
> BUT
> *instead of* SHOOTING *him*
> *he grabs him*
> *and pushes* TIM BEHIND HIM
> *Protecting him from the* GUARDS
> AHNI *holds the* GUARDS *at bay with his weapon*
> TIM *faces the* EMPEROR
> AHNI *and* TIM *stand back to back.*)

MOODY. Voo Voo Nug Sta?

AHNI. No Moody
I won't!

MOODY. KAHM NAH PUH CHINO!

AHNI. I don't care anymore! I've learned something from this Earth Man!

And though you've been like a Father to me—

MOODY. Meex Vah POO nah

AHNI. —I cannot let you destroy another World!

TIM. Bishop
I thought you

AHNI. There's no time for that now
grab the Flame, quickly
and I'll keep these guards at bay
quickly now
we're going to have to blast our way out of here, or—

TIM. or?

AHNI. or DIE trying

TIM. here

AHNI. what

　　　　(TIM *kisses* AHNI *full on the mouth in front of everybody.*)

TIM. for luck

　　　　(AHNI *kisses* TIM.)

MOODY. Vah Nah! Vah Nah!

AHNI. On my signal Tim
One… Two…

MOODY. Vah NAH MA GOONIEZ!

AHNI. THREE!

　　　　(ALL *launch into a slow motion beautifully choreographed early John Woo-style*
　　　　ballet of destruction—guns blazing, operatic music, bodies flying through the air,
　　　　smoke and laser blasts ripping the room apart

　　　　TIM, *with great effort and difficulty, approaches* MOODY's JAR—*the JAR*
　　　　pulses with FEAR

　　　　simultaneously, AHNI *trades LASER FIRE with the* GUARDS—AHNI
　　　　gets winged here and there, but seems to be getting the best of them

　　　　TIM *throws off the lid to the* EMPEROR's *glass jar, reaches into the horrible*
　　　　solution…

　　　　…and pulls forth the NOW-EXTINGUISHED HOLY GAY FLAME!

　　　　A HUGE AMPLIFIED METALLIC SHRIEK fills the vast chamber,
　　　　the death cry of the EMPEROR as the bacteria in the room and his own hunger
　　　　consume what remains of his earthly form

　　　　the shriek ends and the lights within the jar go dead
　　　　TIM *holds the dripping Holy Gay Flame in his hand*

GUARDS *have been vanquished*

we are BACK IN REAL TIME.)

PIETÀ

TIM *turns to* AHNI.

TIM. we did it!

AHNI. yes, Tim…

…we did…

TIM. come on—quickly! we have to get back to the Nuns! They can re-kindle the Flame—

AHNI. I think… that's a journey… you'll have to take… on your own…

TIM. but why? I don't understand, we just—

AHNI. (*ironically.*) I seem to have—*stained* my *blouse*—

(AHNI *pulls open his robe to reveal a TERRIBLE WOUND just below HIS HEART—previously hidden, now obviously fatal.*)

TIM. no

(AHNI *collapses into* TIM'*s arms*
they resolve into a PIETÀ.)

Please

let me carry you

if we get to the Nuns they'll be able to—

AHNI. No Tim

No

it's too late for that now

TIM. I—I thought you betrayed me

AHNI. I could never do that

you know I couldn't

not to you

TIM. but

why

AHNI. oh Tim

don't you know

I've spent my life a stranger to my self

No mother or father, no family to speak of

I have never known who I was

I thought these medals and my ambition would fill that void inside me

but it never did

nothing ever did

TIM. Ahni

AHNI. shhh
I look back over the field of my life
and I think:
what did I have?
I thought I had everything
but really
what did I have?
Years and years of nothing.
And then
at the very end
of *course*, at the very end,
I find *you*.

TIM. what can I do
what can I do for you

AHNI. nothing
there's nothing to do
but hold me, won't you?
hold me as I die
come closer to me now
I want to ask you something

TIM. (*leaning in.*) yes

AHNI. Tim
tell me
what am I?

TIM. what are you?

AHNI. yes
tell me
what do you think I am

TIM. I think
You are
a Homosexual

AHNI. me?

TIM. yes
you are

AHNI. What
The Great Bishop Ahni
a Homosexual…?

(*puts his hand to his heart.*)

GASP!

(*hold, then:*)

"you hear that Lizabeth?

I'm comin' to join you honey!"

(*pause.*)

was that good

TIM. that was good

AHNI. was it

TIM. it was very good

AHNI. thanks

(*beat.*)

I love you Tim

I hope you will

remember me

TIM. I will and Bishop

AHNI. shh

no more time

kiss me

(TIM *does, gently.* AHNI *dies.*)

TIM. (*pulling away.*) he's gone

and I didn't tell him—I never got to tell him, I—

(*the* NUNS *enter, in a tizzy.*)

NUN. oh God

NUN 2. this just looks like a catastrophe!

MOTHER. oh God oh GOD

NUN 2. what happened? Are we too late?

TIM. too late to save the Bishop

MOTHER. but the Flame

NUN. Earth Man, tell us

MOTHER. were you able to retrieve the Flame?

TIM. No

(*turning back to* AHNI.)

I think it's gone out…

MOTHER. Look!

NUN. it's so dim Mother

MOTHER. (*Flame flickers back to life, faintly.*) dim but still lit

NUN. so that means

MOTHER. yes
The Homosexuals will live yet another day

NUN. and my baby—
my baby is saved!

MOTHER. yes that's right

NUN 2. Aw yeah
up top Tim
I knew you could do it!

NUN. I misjudged you, Earth Man
I thought your people were all goomBAHS and rapscallIONS
but I guess I was wrong
I guess some earth creatures—
Some Earth Creatures—
are *Heroes*

TIM. I can't take all the credit
in the end
it was the Bishop Ahni who saved the Flame

MOTHER. (*nodding sadly.*) our great enemy, the Bishop Ahni

NUN. but that's impossible—
was he a Homosexual?

NUN 2. are you kidding? I knew it all the time!

MOTHER. of course he was
he was my first

NUN. He was one of YOURS Mother?

MOTHER. from my first litter when I was but a girl
abducted as a baby and raised in the hell of an Argoshaun Orphanage
his natural beauty deformed by the Emperor Moody Garland…
no matter:
we will give this Homosexual—
—my son—
a hero's burial
And Tim:
you—*loved* him?

TIM. Yes. I did.
I loved him.

> (*receiving microphone, spoken, by way of elegy:*)

No One is Promised Tomorrow

> (*sung.*)

I promised myself so many things
Promised with ribbons

Promised with rings
But the only promise that matters
is to live faster

Run run run run
Don't hesitate
Cause soon all will be lost or broken
If I'm courting you
and the world is courting disaster
And the doomsday clock is ticking away
If the seas are slowly rising and the universe is ending anyway
Make this oath with me:
I promise myself to live faster

> (*during the song,*
> *the Altar lights up in flames, like a Viking funeral ship*
> *slowly it rolls off, into the dark, glowing faintly as it goes*
> *music ends*
> *sound of WIND*
> TIM *flies up*
> *disappears into the mists of space.*)

BACK OUT THROUGH THE GLORY HOLE

> TIM *is SPEWED back out*
> *pushed and evacuated through time and space*
> *and finally EXPELLED through the Glory Hole*
> *back into the Men's Room of MADAME GEORGE's bar*
> *It's as sleazy and dirty and conventionally earth-bound as can be*

> TIM *looks around*
> *stunned*
> *still dressed only in his shiny loin cloth*
> *and sacrificial Argoshaun headdress*
> *a little bleary and teary*

TIM. woah

> (*he picks himself up slowly*
> *dusts himself off*
> *a KNOCK at the bathroom door.*)

MADAME GEORGE. (*through the door.*) ya decent?

TIM. I
guess

(MADAME GEORGE *enters with a little package*
sees TIM *and chuckles.*)

MADAME GEORGE. heh
that's cute
here
put these on

TIM. what's this

MADAME GEORGE. spare clothes. I always keep some spare clothes
behind the bar.
never know what kinda mess people are gonna make of themselves back here

TIM. cool
thanks

MADAME GEORGE. might wanna keep that spangly loincloth thing though
make a nice Halloween costume

TIM. oh
right

MADAME GEORGE. some kinda *Star Trek*-style sexy space captive
that's what you look like
kinda hot. kinda flashy

TIM. yeah
yeah
good thinking

      (*pause.*)

MADAME GEORGE. you all right then

TIM. I guess

MADAME GEORGE. you have fun

TIM. sort of
it got kinda
sad
at the end

MADAME GEORGE. sometimes it's like that
you find some action though?

TIM. that I definitely did
I definitely definitely did

MADAME GEORGE. ah
well
mazel tov
I gotta lock up now
you get yourself changed and cleaned up and I'll let you out the back
K?

TIM. K

MADAME GEORGE. and there's a bottle of Riunite over there if you want it

TIM. Ok

MADAME GEORGE. so mucha that crap left over what am I gonna do with it

TIM. right

thanks

MADAME GEORGE. Ok then

> (MADAME GEORGE *exits*
> TIM *changes*
> *brushes himself down*
> *smoothes his hair*
> *gathers up his space clothes*
> *he moves to exit*
> *then pauses*
> *has a thought*
> *turns back to the stall*
> *nothing*
> *examines the Glory Hole*
> *closes his eyes and puts his hand into the hole…*
> *nothing*
> *his hand wiggles through on the other side*
> *a perfectly normal hole in a perfectly normal wall*
> *in a perfectly normal bathroom*
> *in a normal divey gay bar in a normal American city on Earth*
>
> *pause*.)

TIM. huh

all gone

> (*beat*.)

too bad

> (*beat*
>
> TIM *exits*
> *the three stalls*
> *all empty*
> *pause*
> *pause*.)

THE END

THAT HIGH LONESOME SOUND
by Jeff Augustin, Diana Grisanti, Cory Hinkle, and Charise Castro Smith

ABOUT *THAT HIGH LONESOME SOUND*

This article first ran in the Limelight Guide to the 39th Humana Festival of New American Plays*, published by Actors Theatre of Louisville, and is based on conversations with the creative team before rehearsals for the Humana Festival production began.*

From the signature songs of classic artists like Bill Monroe and the Blue Grass Boys to the catchy new takes on traditional tunes on the *O Brother, Where Art Thou?* soundtrack, over the years bluegrass has blossomed from a little-known offshoot of country music to become embedded in the popular consciousness. Characterized by fast-paced fingerpicking on stringed instruments like the fiddle and the banjo, hard-drivin' rhythms, and virtuosic vocal harmonies, this acoustic folk genre has won a place in our hearts. Bluegrass is a quintessentially American art form, born from a melting pot of many musical traditions. We may associate it with the hills and woods of Appalachia, but bluegrass also draws from ancient Scotch-Irish ballads, African-American work songs, protest anthems, and more to arrive at its distinctive sound. It's a musical hybrid of sorts, a collage of diverse cultures and instrumental styles coming together to create something new. So it's fitting that in this year's Humana Festival, bluegrass is the inspiration for a project in which a variety of playwrights combine their unique voices to create a show for our Acting Apprentice Company.

That show is *That High Lonesome Sound*, authored by four writers—Jeff Augustin, Diana Grisanti, Cory Hinkle, and Charise Castro Smith—who were commissioned to craft a theatrical album of short pieces responding to bluegrass music. (The title comes from a phrase commonly used to describe the wistful tenor twang of many bluegrass singers.) The goal wasn't to take a documentary look at the genre, but instead for the writing team to explore the ways in which this music and its rich legacy resonate with them. To help focus their exploration, director Pirronne Yousefzadeh and dramaturg Hannah Rae Montgomery selected several songs representative of the range of influences that have shaped bluegrass over the decades. These songs serve as the playwrights' entry points into the world of bluegrass, so that they can engage with its history and culture in the context of particular selections. Their finished pieces inspired by these songs aren't musicals (though some include moments of singing or instrumentation). Rather, we're interested in how different mediums can talk to one another—how dramatic text can capture the memories, emotions, or other such imaginative associations that music might evoke.

Our hope is that the overall structure of *That High Lonesome Sound* can take a cue from the way a bluegrass band performs. One of the main things that distinguishes bluegrass from other types of country and folk music is that, much like jazz, it features extended moments of improvisation. Each band member usually has a turn to step forward and solo, while the remaining instruments maintain the basic rhythm and melody in the background. In *That High Lonesome Sound*, we're interested in how we might apply that dynamic to an evening of theatre. Just as band members listen carefully to one another and adjust their playing accordingly, the playwrights have read one another's work throughout every step of the writing process and have shaped their own pieces in response to those of their collaborators. A bit like a bluegrass jam, each new scene will be its author's equivalent of a solo, a distinct and memorable showcase of an individual voice that contributes to the creation of a greater, cohesive whole.

As with past incarnations of Humana Festival plays written for the Acting Apprentices, *That High Lonesome Sound* was composed with this specific company of young actors in mind. In the fall of 2014, the playwrights came to Louisville for two fun-filled workshops in which they met the Apprentices and began delving into research and generating material with them. For example, the group listened to and discussed various bluegrass songs together, even playfully creating some of their own. For the Apprentices, this project is the apex of an entire season spent learning about how new work is created; during their time at Actors Theatre, they've also had the opportunity to write their own solo pieces, devise plays as part of an ensemble, and premiere new ten-minute plays. In collaborating with Augustin, Grisanti, Hinkle, and Smith throughout workshops and rehearsals for *That High Lonesome Sound*, they gain a vital understanding of what it's like to be part of a professional play development process.

The Humana Festival project commissioned for the Apprentices has become a tradition at Actors Theatre, and this year's focus on bluegrass music gives us an exciting chance to explore another artistic tradition near and dear to our local community. "Bluegrass" takes its name from the Bluegrass State— musician Bill Monroe, widely credited as the "Father of Bluegrass," hailed from Kentucky. *That High Lonesome Sound* reflects our ongoing interest in bringing stories and culture rooted in this part of the country to our stages. We hope you enjoy it, y'all.

—Hannah Rae Montgomery

BIOGRAPHIES

Jeff Augustin's play *Little Children Dream of God* received its world premiere at the Roundabout Underground, where he was the inaugural Tow Foundation Playwright-in-Residence. His plays have also been produced at Actors Theatre of Louisville (*Cry Old Kingdom*, 2013 Humana Festival; *That High Lonesome Sound*, 2015 Humana Festival), and Western Washington University (*Corktown*). His work has been developed at the Eugene O'Neill Theater Center's National Playwrights Conference, La Jolla Playhouse, The Ground Floor at Berkeley Repertory Theatre, American Conservatory Theater, and Seattle Repertory Theatre. Augustin is the Shank Playwright in Residence at Playwrights Horizons, and a member of The Working Farm at SPACE on Ryder Farm as well as the Rita Goldberg Playwrights Workshop at The Lark. He is the recipient of the Barrie and Bernice Stavis Playwriting Award and Lorraine Hansberry Award, and was a New York Theatre Workshop 2050 Fellow. Augustin is currently under commission from Manhattan Theatre Club and Roundabout Theatre Company. He holds a B.A. from Boston College and an M.F.A. from the University of California, San Diego.

Diana Grisanti is a Playwright in Residence at Theatre [502] in Louisville, Kentucky. Her play *The Patron Saint of Losing Sleep* was produced at Actor's Theatre of Charlotte, and her play *River City* received a Rolling World Premiere through the National New Play Network. Her other plays include *The Class Of '94*, *Abilene*, *Semantics*, *Dorina and The Plague*, and many shorter works. Additionally, Grisanti and her husband, the playwright Steve Moulds, have co-written three plays: *The Stranger and Ludlow Quinn* (a serialized epic in 11 chapters, commissioned and produced by Theatre [502]), *The Baker Goes to War* (commissioned and produced by Walden Theatre), and *The Two Lobbyists of Verona* (the first world premiere in the 55-year history of Kentucky Shakespeare Festival). Grisanti was a Core Apprentice at the Playwrights' Center, the inaugural recipient of the Marsha Norman Spirit of Achievement Lilly Award, a finalist for the Kendeda National Graduate Playwriting Competition, a nominee for the Wasserstein Prize, and a runner-up for the Leah Ryan Prize. She is an Al Smith Fellow through the Kentucky Arts Council. She holds an M.F.A. from the Michener Center for Writers, University of Texas at Austin.

Cory Hinkle is a Los Angeles-based playwright who has received the McKnight Advancement Grant, two Jerome Fellowships, and a Jerome Foundation Travel and Study Grant. His plays include *The Killing of Michael X* (Jackalope Theatre, Bay Area Playwrights Festival, Brown/Trinity Playwrights Rep), *The End of Beauty* (Cape Cod Theatre Project), and *A Disappearance in Two Parts* (HERE Arts Center). His play *Little Eyes* had its world premiere at the Guthrie Theater, where Hinkle has been commissioned twice to write plays for the Guthrie's B.F.A. students. *SadGrrl13* premiered at the Workhaus Collective, a company he co-ran with eight other playwrights from 2007–2012. He has devised a number of shows with other artists, including *Fissures* (*lost and found*) (co-created with writers from Workhaus Collective and artists from Theatre de la Jeune Lune; 2010 Humana Festival); *Clandestino* (co-created with the Wilhelm Brothers and Victoria Stewart; 2015 Sundance Institute Theatre Lab at MASS MoCA, Mixed Blood Theatre, and recipient of a MAP Fund Grant); *Rehearsing Failure* (recipient of a Playwrights' Center/Network of Ensemble Theatres Grant, Southern Theatre); and *All's Fair/The War Within* (co-created with Dominique Serrand and Steven Epp, Southern Theatre). He has received residences from The MacDowell Colony, the Hermitage Artist Retreat, Tofte Lake Center, and SPACE on Ryder Farm. His work is published by Playscripts, Dramatic Publishing, Vintage, and Heinemann. More information is available at www.coryhinkle.com.

Charise Castro Smith is a playwright, television writer, and actor from Miami, currently residing in Los Angeles. Playwriting credits include: *Feathers and Teeth* (Goodman Theatre/developed at Atlantic Theater Company), *Estrella Cruz [The Junkyard Queen]* (Ars Nova/Yale Cabaret/Halcyon Theatre), *The Hunchback of Seville* (Washington Ensemble Theatre/Trinity Repertory Company), *Washeteria* (Soho Rep.), and *Boomcracklefly* (Miracle Theatre). She is currently under commission by South Coast Repertory and Trinity Repertory Company. Select acting credits include *Antony and Cleopatra* (Royal Shakespeare Company/The Public Theater), *An Enemy of the People* (Baltimore Center Stage), and *The Good Wife* (CBS). Smith is the recipient of a Van Lier Fellowship at New Dramatists, and is an alumna of Ars Nova's Play Group and The New Georges Jam. She holds an M.F.A. from Yale School of Drama and a B.A. from Brown University.

ACKNOWLEDGMENTS

That High Lonesome Sound premiered at the Humana Festival of New American Plays in March 2015. It was directed by Pirronne Yousefzadeh and featured the 2014–2015 Acting Apprentice Company as the Ensemble:

Taylor Abels, Cameron Benoit, Josh Bonzie, Ali Burch, Ure Egbuho, John Ford-Dunker, Erika Grob, Kayla Jackmon, Lexi Lapp, José Leon, Joe Lino, Aaron Lynn, Max Monnig, Collin Morris, Mallory Moser, Brian Muldoon, Madalena Provo, Blake Russell, Lorenzo Villanueva, and Casey Wortmann

with casting for specific pieces as follows:

A Buried History by Jeff Augustin
WOMAN .... Kayla Jackmon

Dot and the Guitar by Charise Castro Smith
EMILY .... Erika Grob
JACOB .... Joe Lino
LOGAN .... Lorenzo Villanueva
CAROLINE .... Mallory Moser
DOROTHY .... Lexi Lapp
THE VOICE OF MOM .... Ali Burch
MAIL MAN .... John Ford-Dunker
THE MAN .... Max Monnig

Florence Reece Goes to Camp by Diana Grisanti
NAN .... Madalena Provo
HALEY .... Erika Grob
JENNA .... Kayla Jackmon
CARLY ANN DEWITT .... Taylor Abels

PunkBitch by Jeff Augustin
SHAW .... Blake Russell
JAY .... Josh Bonzie
DEE .... Ure Egbuho
CHARLIE .... John Ford-Dunker
KATHY .... Ali Burch
JAMIE .... Aaron Lynn
GENIE .... Mallory Moser
TOM .... Collin Morris

The Peace of Wild Things by Cory Hinkle

KADEE ....Ali Burch
GIRL ....Casey Wortmann
CHIP ....Cameron Benoit
ADAM .... Aaron Lynn
BRANT ....Collin Morris
ERIC ....Brian Muldoon

Miss Faye and the Banjo by Charise Castro Smith

MISS FAYE ....John Ford-Dunker
SAM ....Brian Muldoon

Spring Break Dos Mil Quince by Diana Grisanti

KARAOKE JOCKEY ....Josh Bonzie
KAPPA GIRLS ....Taylor Abels, Ure Egbuho,
Madalena Provo
ANTONIO .... Lorenzo Villanueva
CARLITOS ....Joe Lino
ALEX ....José Leon
LANEY ....Mallory Moser
SIGMA CHI GUYS ....Cameron Benoit,
John Ford-Dunker, Collin Morris

It Sounds Like This by Cory Hinkle
The Ensemble

and the following production staff:

Scenic Designer ....Andrew Boyce
Costume Designer ....Beatrice Vena
Lighting Designer ....Paul Toben
Sound Designer ....Daniel Kluger
Music Director/Composer .... Ben Sollee
Stage Manager ....Rachel Nin
Dramaturg ....Hannah Rae Montgomery
Properties Master .... Heather Lindert
Directing Assistant ....Rachel Dart
Assistant Dramaturg ....Ariel Sibert

That High Lonesome Sound was commissioned and developed by Actors Theatre of Louisville.

Lexi Lapp, Joe Lino, Erika Grob, and Mallory Moser
in *That High Lonesome Sound*

39th Humana Festival of New American Plays
Actors Theatre of Louisville, 2015
Photo by Bill Brymer

THAT HIGH LONESOME SOUND

A BURIED HISTORY
by Jeff Augustin

WOMAN's humming a sweet melody. She's on the ground, burying seeds, or maybe an instrument, deep in the earth.

WOMAN. Right after each of our births, I mean right after she pushed out the placenta, my mama would go out to the back, just to the edge, the beginning of our farm and she would plant our umbilical cords deep into the earth. And with them a seed, a fruit seed to grow into a big beautiful tree. You see the idea is to give your newborn child health and strength. To give them roots. And the larger that tree grows, the stronger and healthier your child will be, the more connected to the land they'll be. It's an old tradition—not a myth—a tradition. There is a difference. My mama taught me, my sister and brothers that, that and many other histories, even the histories she didn't know who wrote. My mama was a real hill woman. She knew every crease, every concord of this great land. Oh, and she had the most beautiful of voices. Sharp and clear, smooth and deep like. Soaring, daring and heartbreaking all at once. And no one played the fiddle like my mama.

(She laughs, it's sweet and full.)

I'm a true mama's girl, ain't no shame in saying it. I remember every story she ever told me, every tradition she ever taught me. And before I die, I'm going to bury them right underneath this house, with a new seed. Cause there ain't nobody left here, but me. And histories, got to be remembered, passed down, otherwise they become myths.

(A sound breaks through the wind.)

Like that sound you hear on the quietest of nights, the coldest of nights. When the moon is so bright and so blue. It's a sound that shakes you, it's so lonesome. People think it's some coyotes, it ain't no coyotes. If you listen closely you can hear voices. Singing.

(She leans in like she got a secret to tell.)

It's the ghosts of the men who worked in the mines in Harlan County. The women who went traveling with a guitar and never came back. And that deep voice…that smooth voice that leads them all.

(A man's voice breaks, bellows.)

That there is the strongest most badass motherfucka that ever lived in these here parts. Beat the steel drills, died doing it.

(*She smiles proudly.*)

They just don't make 'em like that anymore.

(*She finishes burying.*)

I got stories like that and many more. You see everyone is fleeing, looking for some life they'll never find. Me? Hmmm…I'm going to stay right here. Planting my seeds and watching them grow.

(*She sings along with the voices. Suddenly the world around her explodes, grows. The music swells.*)

DOT AND THE GUITAR
by Charise Castro Smith

A group of serious-looking little kids in overalls are assembled on the shady front porch of a house in the country.

The girls are occupied with some sort of onerous food-prep chore. The boys shoot things with a BB gun.

LOGAN *takes aim at the cat. He grazes its tail, and the cat lets out an angry growl. Notes: Whenever their mother speaks, it's a booming voice from offstage. We never see her, but she's so loud that she seems like God. Also, when there's a / in the middle of a line, it means that the next character starts speaking.*

EMILY. Logan, why you gotta pick on poor Tinkerbell?! / She ain't never harmed you—

JACOB. I want a turn.

LOGAN. I'm a grown man now.

EMILY. You're thirteen.

LOGAN. I'm the grown man of the house.

EMILY. Are not.

JACOB. What about Daddy?

LOGAN. He's gone.

JACOB. He's coming back.

CAROLINE. He's just gone fishing.

EMILY. Gone north to find work.

JACOB. He's coming back.

DOROTHY. I seen him in the creek.

LOGAN. Lies.

DOROTHY, CAROLINE, JACOB and EMILY. TRUTHS!

(LOGAN *fires three quick shots with the BB gun. There's a loud pissed off cat hiss.*)

LOGAN. Gotta hone my hunting skills so I can provide for the family.

EMILY. You gonna provide us with a cat?

LOGAN. Course not.

EMILY. Then leave Tinkerbell alone.

(CAROLINE, *another little girl on the porch, busts a gut laughing.*)

CAROLINE. Cat stew, roasted cat, cat and dumplings—

LOGAN. Caroline, that's nasty.

CAROLINE. What? It's funny.

JACOB. It's my turn now Logan. You give it back to me or I'll tell—

LOGAN. Tell and see if I care. Itty-bitty cwybaby Jacob…

JACOB. What did you just call me?

LOGAN. I ain't said nothin.

JACOB. Yes you did Logan! You did! You are a liar and you better give me back my BB gun because Grandad gave it to me special for my birthday and not to you and you are just jealous and I only let you borrow it because I am a good Christian and a good brother and now you are repaying my charity by not letting me play with my very own gun so give it back!!

LOGAN. Or what?

> (JACOB *pauses, considers his intractable position and then lets out a frustrated wail.*)

JACOB. Momma! Mama! Mommeeee!! Logan took my gun and now he won't give it back to me—

THE VOICE OF MOM. LOGAN!

LOGAN. Yes'm.

THE VOICE OF MOM. Did you take your little baby brother's gun?

LOGAN. …Yes'm…

THE VOICE OF MOM. You want me to come out there and make you give it back to him?

LOGAN. No'm.

> (LOGAN *still won't part with the gun.*)

THE VOICE OF MOM. 10…9…8…7…

LOGAN. Alright! Fine already. Here's your stupid BB gun. Baby.

> (LOGAN *gives* JACOB *back his gun.* JACOB *sniffles and takes aim at an empty coffee can.*
>
> DOROTHY, *the quiet one, steps off the porch and plucks a dandelion. She closes her eyes and makes a silent wish then blows on it. The seeds scatter.*)

CAROLINE. Wha'd you wish for?

DOROTHY. Can't say or it won't come true.

LOGAN. Probably wished for something stupid.

EMILY. That's enough Logan.

LOGAN. Why does everybody think that they can just / tell me what to do all the time?

DOROTHY. You know what, actually it's fine / I'll tell you.

JACOB. What is it?

DOROTHY. I wished…for the mail to get here soon.

LOGAN. See! That's stupid!

CAROLINE. That's a boring wish. I would have wished for a pony / or a pie.

EMILY. Dorothy is allowed to make any wish she wants.

DOROTHY. The sun's almost set. They don't deliver mail in the nighttime do they?

LOGAN. No.

(DOROTHY *paces and scans the horizon.*)

What you waitin on anyways?

DOROTHY. Four to six weeks, that's how long it's supposed to take… today's six weeks on the dot…

JACOB. What is it Dorothy?

DOROTHY. That's for me to know and you not to find out.

CAROLINE. Secrets secrets are no fun / Secrets secrets hurt someone.

DOROTHY. I'm not hurting anybody.

CAROLINE. Momma! Mama! Moommee!! Dorothy's got a secret and she won't tell nobody—

THE VOICE OF MOM. Mind your business Caroline.

CAROLINE. It's my business because she's my sister / and it ain't friendly to not tell your sister your secrets.

THE VOICE OF MOM. Mind your business Caroline.

CAROLINE. But!

THE VOICE OF MOM. Mind your—

CAROLINE. Alright already. Jeez.

(*The kids go back to shooting and chores.*)

EMILY. Well I think it's exciting Dorothy. Might be a letter from a far off pen pal is my guess.

DOROTHY. Wrong guess.

EMILY. Or a letter from your secret boyfriend—

JACOB. Gross.

CAROLINE. I hope it's either a pony or pie.

DOROTHY. It's neither.

(*The sound of a truck pulling up the unpaved driveway.*)

Sweet Jesus it's coming! / I can't hardly believe it!

EMILY. Do not take the Lord's name in vain Dorothy.

DOROTHY. I'm not. I'm just grateful / is all.

EMILY. Well just mind your tongue then.

(*A MAIL MAN walks on with a stack of letters.*)

MAIL MAN. Evenin' children.

LOGAN. Howdy.

EMILY. Evenin'.

CAROLINE. Evenin'.

JACOB. Howdy.

DOROTHY. Mister.

(*The* MAIL MAN *hands* EMILY *the letters.*)

MAIL MAN. Well, looks like that'll do it.

EMILY. Much obliged mister. Evenin'.

JACOB. Good-bye.

LOGAN. Godspeed.

CAROLINE. Toodle-loo.

DOROTHY. Wait!

(DOROTHY *is biting her lip, tears in her eyes.*)

MAIL MAN. What's the matter little girl?

DOROTHY. It's just…weren't there maybe a package in your truck?

MAIL MAN. I ain't seen one.

(DOROTHY *is about to start crying.*)

DOROTHY. Could you…I mean would you maybe…possibly be able to just take another look?

MAIL MAN. Well all right. I suppose I could do.

(*The* MAIL MAN *exits back to his truck.* DOROTHY *crosses her fingers and mutters a prayer.*)

JACOB. So it's a package, huh?

EMILY. Whatever it is, I'm sure it will be here / tomorrow probably.

CAROLINE. I am burning with anticipation! It feels like my pants are actually on fire—

JACOB. That's for if you're a liar.

CAROLINE. I'm just saying how I feel.

(*There is the crunch of the* MAIL MAN *coming back up the driveway. He's carrying an oblong box.*)

MAIL MAN. Miss Dorothy Miles?

DOROTHY. That's me.

MAIL MAN. Good thing I took another look.

DOROTHY. Thank you sir.

MAIL MAN. So long children.

(*The* MAIL MAN *exits. All the children gather around the box.*)

LOGAN. Sears Roebuck—how come you got a present from Sears Roebuck?

DOROTHY. I ordered it.

JACOB. What?!

DOROTHY. I saved up my candy nickels for a year.

EMILY. Well open it already. Let's see what's inside.

(DOROTHY *very carefully opens the box. Inside the box there is a smaller black cardboard box. Inside the smaller black cardboard box is a guitar.*)

CAROLINE. Whoa!

EMILY. It's beautiful.

JACOB. Can I hold it?

DOROTHY. Not now Jacob.

(DOROTHY *starts to strum the guitar and hum. She hums and plays "Blue Moon of Kentucky." Lost in a reverie.*)

CAROLINE. Wow. She sounds like a bluegrass angel from heaven.

EMILY. Dorothy you got a real talent for that / you know?

JACOB. Can I hold it *now?*

EMILY. Let her be Jacob.

CAROLINE. How'd you learn to play so good Dorothy?

DOROTHY. Dunno. Just came to me somehow…

EMILY. Dorothy Miles. I can see your name in lights—

CAROLINE. She could be in the Grand Ole Opry!

JACOB. Louisville!

EMILY. Nashville!

CAROLINE. NEW YORK CITY!!

LOGAN. You pick like a girl.

(DOROTHY *abruptly stops playing. Stares at* LOGAN.)

DOROTHY. I *am* a girl.

LOGAN. I know. / And you pick like one.

DOROTHY. What's so bad about pickin' like a girl?

LOGAN. It ain't right.

THE VOICE OF MOM. Says who?

(LOGAN*'s got no response to this.* THE VOICE OF MOM *starts to sing the first two lines of "Blue Moon of Kentucky."*

DOROTHY *starts to play again. She and* THE VOICE OF MOM *start to harmonize.* EMILY, CAROLINE *and* JACOB *join in and they sing the first verse and chorus of "Blue Moon of Kentucky." It's a moment of unselfconscious family time. Just singing together and enjoying one another's company.* LOGAN *does not join in—he's off on his own.*

In the midst of their song, LOGAN *suddenly rushes* DOROTHY, *grabs the guitar mid-strum and cracks the body in two.* DOROTHY *screams, everybody gasps.* LOGAN *throws* DOROTHY's *broken guitar onto the ground.*)

EMILY. Logan, what have you done?

LOGAN. Shut up Emily. You might not like it or respect it, but I'm the man around here / and I'll be damned if my little sister—

THE VOICE OF MOM. Says who you're the / man?

JACOB. What about Daddy?

LOGAN. Runs off to Nashville or New York City to go write her name on some goddamn lights.

EMILY. Don't see how that's your prerogative Logan.

LOGAN. Well then whose is it?

THE VOICE OF MOM. LOGAN!

LOGAN. All due respect ma'am, I don't answer to you no more.

> (LOGAN *storms off. Everyone is in shock for a moment.*
>
> *Then it fades to nighttime and* DOROTHY *sits alone on the porch. She hasn't moved. She hums.*)

THE VOICE OF MOM. Dorothy, I got some biscuits on the kitchen table for you.

DOROTHY. Thank you ma'am but I'm not hungry at present.

THE VOICE OF MOM. Come on inside now Dorothy.

DOROTHY. If it's all the same to you ma'am I'd like to sit and watch the moon a moment more.

THE VOICE OF MOM. Alright Dorothy, but don't linger too long. The night is damp and full of mysteries that ain't fit for little girls.

DOROTHY. Yes ma'am.

> (DOROTHY *is alone. Crickets.*)

I ain't never seen a blue moon before.
What shade blue is it, I wonder?
Blue like Emily's eyes, or Mama's dress, or like a blue sky?
I'd like to see one.
My heart's a blue moon.
A deep watery satellite.
I love my family. I even love Logan.
But this blue moon in my chest just won't let me be.

> (*A* MAN *appears in shadows. He's soaking wet.*)

THE MAN. Dottie?

DOROTHY. Who's there?

THE MAN. Dottie, it's me.

DOROTHY. Papa?

(THE MAN *shushes her and nods.*)

THE MAN. Howdy do little Dot?

DOROTHY. Alright. Howdy do Papa?

THE MAN. Alright.

DOROTHY. You're all wet.

THE MAN. I just come from the creek.

DOROTHY. You been gone a long time.

(THE MAN *does not respond.*)

I knew you'd come back.

THE MAN. What you doin' out here all alone Dot? The night is damp and full of mysteries not fit for little girls.

DOROTHY. Thinking. Feeling lonesome. Logan broke my guitar when I ain't hardly got a chance to play it yet.

(THE MAN *picks up the shattered fragments of her guitar.*)

THE MAN. This it?

DOROTHY. Mmm-hmm.

THE MAN. That's nothing but wood and strings Dot. The person who plays is the music… Tomorrow morning, you take a spade and dig a hole right at the base of the buckeye tree and see what you find.

DOROTHY. Alright Papa.

THE MAN. Your great-grandmamma used to play the mandolin. She'd fill fourteen hungry bellies every suppertime, then fill fourteen hungry souls with music when the stars came out. Reckon she'd want you to have what's in the hole at the base of the buckeye tree.

DOROTHY. Alright Papa.

(*A train whistle blows in the distance.*)

THE MAN. Gotta go now Dot.

DOROTHY. Where to Papa?

THE MAN. ……

DOROTHY. Take me with you.

THE MAN. Can't do that Dot. You mind your mama and go back inside now.

DOROTHY. When will you be back?

THE MAN. I'll see you again Dot. That's a promise.

DOROTHY. G'night Daddy.

THE MAN. G'night Dot.

(THE MAN *heads off in the direction of the train's whistle.* DOROTHY *waves to him until he's out of sight, then exits into the house.*)

FLORENCE REECE GOES TO CAMP
by Diana Grisanti

PART 1: CAMPFIRE.

Around the campfire. A group of kids sings "Which Side Are You On?" For a somber labor anthem, it sure sounds fun.

PART 2: NAN'S OFFICE.

NAN, *the boss, stands before* HALEY *and* JENNA. *She is <u>very disappointed</u>.* HALEY *and* JENNA *are used to this.*

NAN. I gotta say, y'all

I have to say

I am very disappointed.

HALEY. Sorry, Nan. My bad.

NAN. "My bad"? That's it?

HALEY. Full disclosure? I don't actually know what we're talking about.

NAN. Dammit, Haley! Get your head outta your butt.

HALEY. Is this about us smoking pot on the archery course?

NAN. What?! No.

Is that true?

HALEY. I mean, not the archery course exclusively.

NAN. Holy hell, y'all—

Okay we're gonna table that

The marijuana conversation

We're gonna table that for later

JENNA. We're supposed to be leading a nature hike in ten minutes.

NAN. The nature hike is cancelled. Everything is cancelled. Camp is cancelled.

JENNA. You're cancelling camp. Because you're disappointed in us.

NAN. *I'm* not cancelling anything. I'm not the bad guy here. But, I tell y'all what, it's only a matter of time before Steve Beshear swoops down from Frankfort and calls the whole damn thing off.

     (HALEY *giggles.*)

JENNA. Steve Beshear?

HALEY. Steve / Beshear!

JENNA. The governor of Kentucky. He's gonna shut us down?

     (HALEY *cracks up.*)

NAN. Are you high right now? / Is she high?

HALEY. (*Annoyed exhale.*) / Rude.

JENNA. Nan, why are we here?

NAN. You're here because of a certain song.

(NAN *recites the first four lines of "Which Side Are You On?"*)

What in the hell were y'all thinking?

HALEY. Um…it's a camp song.

NAN. I have worked here since I was sixteen years old. I know my way around a damn camp song. And this!—this is a song about *labor unions*.
We are funded by the *Commonwealth of Kentucky.*
You can't go around spouting your personal political beliefs at a state-run camp!

JENNA. Why not?

NAN. We're government employees. They got us under a microscope here. We're supposed to be neutral.

JENNA. Harlan County is *fifty miles* from here. We're talking major labor strikes. Haven't you read Howard Zinn?

HALEY. You guys. It's just a song.

JENNA. It's not just a song. Every student in this state should know those words by heart.

HALEY. Nan, on behalf of both of us, it won't happen again. Byyyye.

NAN. Don't— Stop— Quit moving. I'm your boss, and I'm telling you to stay put.

JENNA. You're only our boss because me and Haley didn't wanna be in charge.

NAN. Clearly! So here I am busting my hump, so y'all can smoke reefer and and and
give hand jobs to Karl Marx.

HALEY. What the fuck?

NAN. I'm sorry. I'm frantic. I'm I'm

(*Takes a breath.*)

Be here now, Nan. Be here now.
Someone has captured the incident on film.

HALEY. How?
How would they even
Nobody has their phone

JENNA. One kid does. One kid has her phone.

HALEY. Oh shit. The diabetic girl.

NAN. The diabetic girl.

JENNA. Carly Ann DeWitt.

HALEY. I'm sorry but when I was a camper there were like eight diabetic kids, and nobody needed an *app* to track their insulin.

NAN. Well Carly Ann does and now she's gonna destroy us.

HALEY. How is a video going to destroy us?

NAN. She'll put it on the Internet. It'll go viral.
And and Mitch McConnell—
And taxpayers—
I don't know!
I don't know how it's all gonna play out, but our days are numbered.

JENNA. That kid is such a bitch.

> (*This tickles* HALEY.)

NAN. Jenna!

HALEY. Dude. She's like thirteen. And she has juvenile diabetes.

JENNA. Then I guess that makes her a thirteen-year-old diabetic bitch.
And y'all should know I do not use that word lightly.
But her?
That girl's gonna grow up to be one of these Sheryl Sandberg, Lean-In, Man-Up, Fuck-You-poor-people bitches.

HALEY. That's pretty spot on.

JENNA. Do you know who her parents are?
They're bourbon magnates. They *own* Sweet Acres bourbon.
Why that child is going to a government-funded camp, I have no idea. But I do know that she's rich and awful, she terrorizes the other kids, and now she's terrorizing us.

> (*A knock at the door.*)

NAN. Ohmygodit'sher.

HALEY. Breathe, / Nan.

JENNA. Come in.

> (CARLY ANN *walks in. She's just sweet as can be.*)

CARLY ANN. Oh hi, Miss Jenna. I didn't know you and Miss Haley were gonna be here.

JENNA. Well, we are here.

CARLY ANN. Okay, well, I was wanting to talk to Miss Nan?

JENNA. So talk.

CARLY ANN. Oh um okay

NAN. (*Overly formal.*) Carly Ann, I viewed the film you sent me.

CARLY ANN. Oh good! That's what I wanted to talk with you about.

NAN. I am so sorry about this.

CARLY ANN. Sorry about what?

JENNA. You were saying about the video—

CARLY ANN. Right yeah well it's really great.
I don't know if y'all two have seen it, but it turned out great.
And I'm not saying this to brag, but my daddy says I'm a natural filmmaker?
I mean, I think he's just being cute, but still.
So anyway, I showed it to the lady who does marketing for my daddy's company.
My daddy's the CEO of Sweet Acres bourbon distillery?

JENNA. We know what your father does.

CARLY ANN. Yeah so the lady who does marketing really liked the video and the song,
And she thinks it'd be great for like an ad campaign, you know?
Which would be amazing for me, for like college applications and stuff
Like, can you imagine? Having a national spot under my belt before high school?
And yeah so she wanted to know if we could use the video for a commercial.
I mean, we'd have to re-shoot most of it. And stage some B-roll, you know, no big.
But yeah, she's gonna call y'all about dates and times and stuff,
But I wanted to touch base first, you know, since I'm the director.

HALEY. Is this for real? Sweet Acres wants to shoot a commercial here?

CARLY ANN. Yeah! Everyone was totally inspired by the "Which Side Are You On" theme?
We're gonna have Kentucky bourbon on one side and, like, random Tennessee whiskey on the other.

HALEY. Totally.

CARLY ANN. Right? And then: voiceover:

(*Imitating a pitchman.*)

"Which side are *you* on? Sweet Acres Bourbon."

HALEY. Nan, can we do it?

NAN. I don't
The protocol
Oh wow
Oh boy
This is unprecedented!

JENNA. Are you kidding me?

NAN. This is a great opportunity for the camp.

JENNA. We're talking about turning a protest song into a jingle.

HALEY. You said that every kid in the state should learn it.

JENNA. Okay:

Protest song. Jingle.

NAN. It's good for the camp, and it's good for the Commonwealth.

JENNA. Having *children* in a *whiskey commercial* is good for the Commonwealth?

CARLY ANN. Oh, it'll be real classy. It'll be like:

a gauzy shot of singing around a campfire…

crossfade to the Sweet Acres logo.

JENNA. Lemme ask you something, Carly Ann, do you know who Florence Reece is?

CARLY ANN. Is that the old lady who works in the mess hall? She's adorable.

JENNA. Florence Reece wrote the lyrics that you and your *marketing team* are so in love with. She was a coal miner's daughter and a coal miner's wife.

Do you know what that means?

CARLY ANN. Um. Not really.

JENNA. It means she spent her whole life fighting against people like your dad.

CARLY ANN. /Okay…

NAN. Jenna!

JENNA. So no. Sweet Acres cannot use this camp or the song. And by the way, the mess hall manager is Shirley Mills. Learn her name.

NAN. Carly Ann, sweetie, why don't you step out for a second?

CARLY ANN. Of course, Miss Nan. Absolutely.

(CARLY ANN *goes.*)

NAN. Jenna, what is wrong with you? This is the greatest thing to ever happen here, and and

JENNA. And what?

NAN. I just don't know what your deal is.

JENNA. My deal is that co-opting a song about workers' rights to sell alcohol—to sell *anything*—is completely fucked.

HALEY. But how cool will it be for the kids to see themselves on TV?

JENNA. This camp is for kids in the state who have nothing. Poor kids. We are the poor-kid camp. So I don't see how helping Sweet Acres Bourbon— helping Carly Ann's *dad*—

I mean, the guy literally has more money than this *entire county*.

NAN. Look, Jenna, I know you're in college and your mind is expanding, and that's great. But your job is to lead nature hikes and make sure nobody dies. We're not trying to start a revolution here.

JENNA. Why not?

HALEY. That'd be hilarious.

JENNA. Seriously, *why not?*

Which side are *you* on, Haley? Nan?

There's no such thing as neutrality. We're in charge of the future, so why don't we do something about it?

WHICH SIDE ARE Y'ALL ON?

(*But* NAN *and* HALEY *are already gone.*)

PUNKBITCH

by Jeff Augustin

The frame of a house, a porch. SHAW, a tall lanky thirteen-year-old boy, is listening to his headphones. He takes a sip of a cup of milk. He places it down gently. A beat. He begins to dance, it's a sort of square dance. Maybe he's singing as well. A beat. JAY and DEE enter. SHAW doesn't see them. He's lost in his own world. They creep up behind him and push him.

SHAW. (DEE *and* JAY *are laughing.*) What the f— (*He sees them.*) Oh. Hey Dee, Jay.

JAY. What you doing?

SHAW. Nothing

JAY. Looks like you were trying to square dance

SHAW. No, I'm just dancing

JAY. Like that?

SHAW. Yeah

(JAY *and* DEE *look at each other.*)

DEE. You ain't listening to no black music, dancing like that

SHAW. I am

DEE. What you listening to?

SHAW. Ummm…you know

JAY. She wouldn't have asked if she knew, now would she?

SHAW. I'm listening to something old school

DEE. Old school?

SHAW. Yeah

(*A beat.*)

DEE. Like old school rap?

(*A slight beat.*)

SHAW. Uh, sure

JAY. Lies.

SHAW. Truths.

JAY. Let me listen

SHAW. It's on shuffle

DEE. What song was it?

SHAW. Can't remember

JAY. You listening to some old ass country shit. You don't know no old school rap, that's for hardcore niggas

SHAW. I'm hardcore

JAY. Boy, you not even whole black

DEE. Yeah, you're like a quarter black and a bunch of other shit

JAY. Like Indian and Canadian and probably German

DEE. Yeah, you probably a Nazi

JAY. (*Doing the Nazi salute.*) Heil Hitler

DEE. Heil Hitler

(*They crack themselves up.*)

SHAW. I'm not a Nazi.

JAY. Yeah, they would lynch you cause you got those pretty black features.

DEE. But he ain't got no coordination and no rhythm like a nigga

SHAW. I got rhythm.

JAY. Like a homo

DEE. Yeah, like a homo and rap ain't homo music

SHAW. Why ain't it?

JAY. Cause homos ain't hardcore

SHAW. Then what do they listen to?

JAY. Why so curious?

DEE. Cause he's a homo

SHAW. I'm not

DEE. Prove it

SHAW. How?

DEE. Name three hardcore gangsta rappers

SHAW. Okay. Tupac, Biggie—

JAY. Naw, non-commercial

SHAW. They're all commercial. They got to make money

DEE. No, like you know people no one knows

SHAW. Alright.

(*A slight beat.*)

But what do I get?

DEE. What you want?

SHAW. To jam—

JAY. To jam?

SHAW. You know, rap and beat-box and stuff with y'all after school. I want to join for a whole year

DEE. Abso-fuckin-tutely not

JAY. You can continue square dancing on your porch by yourself.

SHAW. I'm not square dancing, I'm just dancing

JAY. You say hetero, I say homo

SHAW. And I'm not always alone. Jamie hangs with me sometimes

JAY. Where Jamie at now?

DEE. I heard Jamie called him a punk-bitch

JAY. Oh, shit!

SHAW. No he didn't

DEE. That's what he told me

JAY. And me

> (*A beat.*)

SHAW. Well, if I'm a punk-bitch I ain't going to know any hardcore rappers so why not give me a year?

JAY. He's right. Punk-bitches don't listen to rap

DEE. You right.

> (*To* SHAW.)

We got a deal.

> (*They do a complicated handshake agreement.*)

Go ahead.

SHAW. Alright.

> (SHAW *thinks. A beat.*)

JAY. Look at him, he don't have a fucking clue. What I tell you?

DEE. He thinking so hard, he going to hurt himself

JAY. Don't hurt yourself now punk-bitch

> (*They laugh.*)

Let's go this shit is pathetic

> (*They walk away but just as they're about to be gone,* SHAW *utters…*)

SHAW. Treacherous Three; Funky Four Plus One; and The Sugar Hill Gang

> (SHAW *drops the mic.*)

DEE. Fuck

> (*A beat.*)

Guess we'll have to see your punk-ass tomorrow

> (DEE *and* JAY *begin to exit.*)

JAY. I can't fucking believe it.

> (*They're gone.* SHAW *watches them go. Then he puts back on his headphones, hits play. Suddenly, the house, the porch becomes lit like we're at a concert. Very Grand Ole Opry. A band, consisting of a cellist, acoustic guitarist and two female singers appear. They or stagehands place a stool and a whiskey glass*

filled with milk next to SHAW, *who is now holding a mic. It sounds as if they just finished a number. We hear audience applause or maybe other actors in the audience or surrounding area applaud. The band continues playing.)*

SHAW. Thank you, thank you

(SHAW *grabs the glass of milk off the stool, takes a sip.*)

Whooo, Joe really knows how to pour it like I like 'em. I love to leave the night a little tipsy. Charlie knows what I'm saying. Ain't that right sweetie? Kathy here waits till after the show to get wasted.

(*He takes another sip. To the band.*)

Y'all still playing?

JAMIE. We trying to keep you from talking

SHAW. The talking is the best part

JAMIE. The folks are here to hear you sing, not talk shit

SHAW. You got to talk before you sing. Otherwise it would be like sex without the foreplay. You always got to give them foreplay. Keeps it exciting. You don't just go for it, do you Jamie?

(JAMIE *begins playing the first notes of "Man of Constant Sorrow" on his cello.*)

Don't be shy now

(JAMIE *starts playing more vigorously/louder.*)

I'm just messing with you baby.

(*He goes over to* JAMIE, *maybe strums the cello or does something playful to stop him from playing.*)

I know you love your foreplay.

(JAMIE *begins playing the song again.*)

You want me to sing

JAMIE. Yes

SHAW. That song?

JAMIE. Everyone loves it

SHAW. Alright baby

(*To audience.*)

You see I can mess with Jamie, cause he and I go way back to Pre-K

JAMIE. Daycare

SHAW. That's right. See he's got the memory. Been best friends our whole life.

JAMIE. This ain't the song

SHAW. I'm getting there.

(*A slight beat.*)

I remember when we first met

JAMIE. No you don't. We were toddlers.

SHAW. My first memory of us then. We were on the playground. Hanging out with Genie here

(*He points to one of the singers,* GENIE *waves.*)

She a real sweet, beautiful girl, ain't she

(*The audience cheers.*)

So we're on this playground. We playing X-Men. We all big X-Men fans. It's what we like to do when we're not playing for lovely folks like y'all. Tom there

(*Pointing to guitarist…*)

He's trying to get us into his Dungeons and Dragons. But he don't know that black people don't play that. Anyhow. We playing X-Men. See, I'm always Rogue. Cause I'm southern like her. And Jamie is always Cyclops and Genie is always Jean Grey. We running around killing the "bad guys" when Genie and I run right into each other face first. We drop to the ground, crying. Jamie trying to calm us down, but nothing is working. When all of a sudden he whips out his penis—now that's the first time I had seen a penis other than my own—and he just starts pretending to shoot laser beams out of it.

JAMIE. Shaw we got to stay on—

(*Putting his finger over* JAMIE's *lips.*)

SHAW. Shhhh…

It gets me laughing and feeling something I never had before then. But Genie here won't stop crying. So Jamie goes to her, holds her until she stops crying. Then I realize why he wanted to be Cyclops. I needed him to be Gambit, cause every Rogue needs her Gambit, a man to love her. But he had to be Cyclops cause Genie was Jean Grey. And everyone knows Jean and Cyclops are forever. Gambit and Rogue never last. And I realized that thing, that I had never felt before, that thing was sorrow. And I've been feeling it ever since.

(*He looks to* JAMIE. *A beat.* JAMIE *begins playing, the band slowly joins in.* SHAW *downs the rest of his milk. He begins to sing "Man of Constant Sorrow." After a verse or a verse and a hook/refrain, he begins to rap a la Gangstagrass. It should live in the world of Lauryn Hill, before she went crazy. As* SHAW *reaches the end of his rap/song, he's once again alone on his porch, dancing to music.*)

THE PEACE OF WILD THINGS*
by Cory Hinkle

A ramshackle shack in the midst of the Kentucky hills
The light of the moon through a roof full of holes
The place is decayed, falling apart
But in the midst of it
Stands KADEE, bundled in a parka and scarf and a hat cause it's cold as
shit outside.

KADEE. My sister disappeared into the hills of Kentucky.

(*She smiles at the thought.*)

Sounds strange
Strange like it's not real
Or like my sister's a character out of some old forgotten song.

Jane never left here like the rest of us
Me in Chicago
My older brother Eric in Nashville.
My asshole brother, Chip, he's out West
Adam's in New Hampshire
And Brant? Who the fuck knows where Brant is. He's fucking Brant.

But Jane
Of the faded Reebok tennis shoes and the silvercapped front tooth
Jane of the wild animals and trees
Of the cracked fiddle and the lonesome howl.
Jane stayed back. Here.
Until the house collapsed around her, the debris of our lives like snow through a hole in the roof and through that hole the sky beckoned, it reached out and said…

Come.

(*Beat.*)

That's what they say anyway. They say Jane flew up and out of here like the wind…

(*As KADEE looks up at the hole in the roof, the sound of the wind begins and then builds until it's the sound of blizzard-like conditions outside the house. KADEE sits down and wraps herself in a blanket.*
From a great distance, the sound of voices, in harmony, sing notes from Bill Monroe and the Bluegrass Boys' "In the Pines."
KADEE falls asleep.

---

* The title was inspired by Wendell Berry's poem, "The Peace of Wild Things."

The sound of the voices fades away.
A moment.
And then, a hand comes up from out of the floorboards
The hand knows what it's looking for
The hand, and then an arm, stretches out across the floor to KADEE's
knapsack, reaches inside, rummages around and finally, victorious, the hand
pulls out an apple.
The hand goes back under the floor. We hear the sound of ravenous eating.
The sound makes KADEE *start. Awake now, she listens. She crawls out from*
under her blanket, over towards the noise; she lifts up a floorboard, looks inside.
KADEE *jolts, takes a step back.)*

KADEE. What are you doing down there?

> (*A young* GIRL, *in tattered clothes, under-dressed for the cold, pokes her head*
> *up from the floor.*)

GIRL. Eatin' an apple.

KADEE. *My* apple.

GIRL. Thanks for it! It's good.

KADEE. I didn't give it to ya. And yeah it is. It's a Honeycrisp.

GIRL. Honeycrisp?

KADEE. They invented 'em in a lab in Minnesota, ya never heard?

GIRL. You can't invent an *apple*. God made apples.

KADEE. God!?! I hate to break it to you, but God (if there even is one) didn't make that apple. No, he made a much shittier apple and then *we* made that apple.

> (*The* GIRL *goes back to eating the apple.*)

Why are you in my house?

GIRL. Don't look like nobody's house.

KADEE. Has to belong to somebody, no matter how it looks.

GIRL. Needed a place to stay. Since this polar vortex started up.

KADEE. It didn't used to look like this. We lived here. My whole family. Jane, me, my brothers. All kinds of things used to happen here, before it fell apart.

GIRL. Can't imagine it.

KADEE. Jane and Dad used to sit right there and play their fiddles and we'd dance all night.

GIRL. Hey! Then maybe this is yours?

> (*The* GIRL *reaches down into the hole in the floor.*
> *She pulls out a fiddle.*
> *She holds it up to* KADEE.
> KADEE *takes it from her.*)

KADEE. It's Jane's … But she left it behind? It used to hang right there on the wall.

(KADEE *stares at the fiddle.*)

GIRL. Where'd you get that nice, warm parka?

KADEE. I don't know. A store?

(KADEE *is still transfixed by the fiddle.*
The girl shivers.)

GIRL. I don't like cold. I like heat. Sweaty, swampy heat like down south. The heat hits ya like you're inside an oven and the insects singing up in your ears like they're messing with your mind. I love that! Everyone sitting on their porches all day cause it's too hot to move! You know, if it's *not* hot, I'm like, what am I going to do today? But if it *is* hot, I know *exactly* what to do. Sit on my front porch. *On my ass.*

KADEE. Did you see my sister? When you got here? On your way up?

GIRL. What's she look like?

KADEE. About my height // and—

GIRL. Don't know her.

KADEE. I didn't finish my description.

GIRL. Don't know anyone your height.

(*A beat.*)

You got any more of them apples?

KADEE. Yeah.

GIRL. Can I *have* one?

KADEE. They're Honeycrisps. Man-made, or woman-made (human-made?) I want 'em for myself.

GIRL. Got anything else? A Red Delicious or something?

KADEE. Red Delicious? Are you joking!? A Red Delicious is what happens when *God* makes an apple. *He fails.*

(*Small beat.*)

I got a tangerine.

(KADEE *hands the* GIRL *a tangerine and she peels it in that cool way that some people do where they do it all in one piece and it makes a spiral.*
The girl drops the spiral gently on the floor.)

GIRL. Eating fruit in the middle of winter. Weird world.

(*She takes a bite of tangerine. Smiles. Chews.*)

You want to know why she disappeared?

KADEE. That's why I came back. To find out.

GIRL. It's cause she lived here. Who wouldn't want to get the hell out of *here*? And she was lonely—So lonely!—It hurt being left behind. It was an insult to everything she knew and loved, to be abandoned, as if these hills where y'all grew up was some kind of hovel fit only for animals. Why'd you leave her alone like that?

KADEE. No— That's— We kept in touch!

GIRL. Sure ya did.

KADEE. I did the best I could! She's not gone cause of me!

GIRL. If you say so.

> (*As* KADEE *yells*
> *It becomes less directed at the* GIRL
> *And more towards herself,*
> *Or her sister, or us*
> *And as she rails and rants, the* GIRL *recedes unnoticed by* KADEE.)

KADEE. She's gone cause nothing goes right!
How could I have caused that!?
That's God's fault! (Not mine!)
God takes people whenever he wants
The good ones, the beautiful souls, like my sister
And He lets foolish people destroy—like—the trees! The bees! The animals! The flowers! (There won't even be fruit soon!) *God* did that, he let 'em all build filth and shit in the place of everything beautiful. Why does he let the good die and the terrible live?
He doesn't answer!
WHY???
YOU DON'T ANSWER! WHY DON'T YOU ANSWER!?

> (*As* KADEE *finishes*
> *The sound of the wind picks up again, bigger, larger*
> *The* GIRL *has disappeared.*
> KADEE *looks around. She doesn't see the* GIRL.)

Hello? Where'd ya go?

> (*No answer.*
> *The sound of voices, from off.*)

CHIP. (*O.S.*) How the hell did you get the wheels stuck!?!

ADAM. (*O.S.*) I couldn't see!

BRANT. (*O.S.*) Are you sure this is the place!?!

ERIC. (*O.S.*) Come on! Hurry!

BRANT. (*O.S.*) Dude! My boots are full of snow!

> (ERIC, CHIP, *and* ADAM *enter.*
> *Followed by* BRANT *who has one boot off … he's hitting the boot … getting*

the snow out.

All the boys have big-ass coats on.)

ADAM. I knew it! I told you! She's here.

CHIP. Oh my God. Look at this place. How long have you been here!?

BRANT. It's incredible! It's, like, so decrepit! This is *really* where we used to live!?

CHIP. Yes! Why do you keep asking // the same—

ADAM. Will you stop being a dick to Brant?

CHIP. *I'm* a dick?

ADAM. You've been *on his ass* since Nashville.

CHIP. And you drove us *straight* into a snow bank!

ERIC. Guys!

Shut the fuck up!

We came here to get Kadee

To bring her *home*

And I have *got* to get back

Tonight.

Okay?

I left my wife alone

WITH OUR NEWBORN TWINS!

Do you know how fucking *tired* I am!?!

CHIP. We need like a piece of wood? Or something? To get the car out.

> (CHIP *walks up to a wall*
> *He grabs a plank of wood*
> *He pulls really hard.*
> *An entire piece of the house rips off in his hands, it's a big-ass plank of wood.*)

CHIP. Holy shit! It came right off!

ERIC. So can we go?

CHIP. Yeah, Kadee, let's go.

> (*They move to leave.* KADEE *doesn't move. She just glares at them.*)

ERIC. What's the deal?

CHIP. Are you coming with us or not?

> (*Small beat.*)

KADEE. You just *disrespected* our childhood home.

CHIP. It's not a home. It's a shack of rotten wood.

KADEE. I'm not going anywhere with any of *you.* I'm staying right here and I'm going to wait for Jane. If I have to sit here for years! If I get covered in snow and freeze—

ADAM. You can't stay here alone.

KADEE. I'm not alone. I have a friend! She likes fruit! We're going to stay here and eat Honeycrisps and *be human*.

CHIP. There's no one here.

BRANT. Did we *really* used to live here? Seriously! Or are you guys fucking with me!? Is this a joke!?! Cause this is *weird!* It's like I completely blocked this place out of my mind.

> (*Small beat.*)

Or, I don't know, maybe it just looks different.

CHIP. We have to get the car out or we're going to get snowed in.

> (*She won't move.*)

Why do you always do this? You're like this little stray animal that keeps running away and we have to keep catching you and bringing you back. Everyone always worried sick about Kadee! I'm done worrying about you.

> (CHIP *exits. Small beat.*)

ERIC. I have to get back to the twins.

> (ERIC *sighs, shakes his head.*)

Why twins!? We weren't ready for two. And our parents had six! What were *they* thinking? (*He has a sudden realization.*) Ohmygod. Now they only have five... I just realized that.

KADEE. Unless Jane comes back. She might come back. It's possible.

CHIP. (*O.S.*) Come on! I need some help!

ERIC. Coming!

> (ERIC *exits.*
> BRANT *is clueless about what to say, so he just vaguely gestures and mumbles...*)

BRANT. I'm gonna... Go and...

> (BRANT *does an awkward wave and exits. A moment.*)

ADAM. "Polar vortex"... Sure is cold, huh?

> (*Beat.*)

Do you know what the cold makes me think of?
Summer!
Or it makes me *miss* summer.
My porch.
I like to write poetry on my porch.

KADEE. Poetry? I never knew that.

ADAM. It's a new thing.
I like to put my desk out on my porch
So I can watch all the animals while I write...
I used to see all these deer
And loons

I saw like hundreds of chipmunks
And skunks
Birds. Blue jays, finches and whatnot
I saw a barn owl once?
And wild rodents
An albino possum with a litter of babies
And a moose.
But just one
Just one moose…
I named him Moose.
Anyway, I don't see many animals anymore.

>(*Beat.*)

KADEE. What was the point of all that?

ADAM. The animals are gone? I guess. I don't think they're ever going to come back.

>(*Beat.*)

She's not coming back.

KADEE. Lies.

ADAM. No, truth.

>(*Beat.*)

It's like one of those old songs.
No one knows who wrote 'em.
Anonymous, right?
You always liked those the best.
The weird, unexplained endings
Vanished people
Good folk that walk up into the hills never to be seen again
A vengeful God reaches down and plucks 'em off the earth for no good reason.

KADEE. I don't believe in God anymore.

ADAM. I didn't used to. Till I started watching those animals. Then I started to see God everywhere. In every thing.

>(*Beat.*)

KADEE. Where'd she go?

ADAM. She's up in the hills. Singing songs with all the other wild animals.

>(ADAM *howls like a coyote*
>KADEE *follows his lead and howls too*
>*At first, it's funny.*
>*They're having fun howling together like animals.*
>*But then, suddenly,* KADEE'*s howl transforms into tears.*

It's a cry of grief that comes spontaneously out of her.
ADAM hugs her. She cries into his arms, and then quiets.)

BRANT. (*O.S.*) Hey, guys!

CHIP. (*O.S.*) The piece of wood worked!

ERIC. (*O.S.*) Time to go!

(ADAM *looks at her.*)

ADAM. You ready?

(KADEE *nods.*
She gives the place one last look
And they walk out.
A moment of silence.
The GIRL reappears
She holds the last slice of tangerine in her hand
She pops it in her mouth
She chews
She swallows.
She sees the fiddle on the wall and takes it down.
She looks at it closely.
She hums the first vocal part of Bill Monroe's "In the Pines"
Then plucks the first verse on the fiddle
And as she does
Music, from somewhere distant, up in the hills, rises from the voms to accompany her.
The GIRL looks up through a hole in the roof...
And the lights snap out.)

MISS FAYE AND THE BANJO
by Charise Castro Smith

An ancient woman in a rocking chair and a teenage boy sit in the shade of a front porch.
A long pause.

MISS FAYE.
Listen closely now.
You listening to me?

SAM.
Yes ma'am.

MISS FAYE.
Are you sure?

SAM.
Yes ma'am.

MISS FAYE.
This is very important.

SAM.
I'm listening.

MISS FAYE.
You're gonna bust your eardrums right out of your damn head
If you keep listening to your music so loud.
You hear what I just said?

SAM.
Yes ma'am.

MISS FAYE.
Lies.

SAM.
Truths.
You said I was gonna bust my damn eardrums right out of my head
If I kept listening to my music so loud.
Then you asked me if I heard what you just said.
Which I did.
So truths.

MISS FAYE.
Well. Alright then.

SAM.
Well?

MISS FAYE.
Well what?

SAM.

What were you going to tell me?

MISS FAYE.

I'm a ghost.

SAM.

What's this now?

MISS FAYE.

I am half ghost, half human.

SAM.

Ma'am?

MISS FAYE.

When you're as old as I am, that's not actually the strange part.
The strange part is that the ghost that is wrestling for my everlasting soul is the ghost of a banjo.

SAM.

Huh.

MISS FAYE.

Yes.

SAM.

You're a banjo ghost?

MISS FAYE.

Half a banjo ghost.

SAM.

When did you first begin to believe ah…
How come you think this?

(MISS FAYE *opens her mouth and a thrilling banjo lick emerges. When she closes her mouth, it stops.*)

MISS FAYE.

That's how come I think it.

SAM.

I did not expect that.

MISS FAYE.

Sometimes I wake up in a haze in the middle of the night,
And I feel strange fingers stroking my skin.
They start out strumming real slow and soulful.
But that's just the foreplay—

SAM.

Oh my God Grandma—

MISS FAYE.

Then they pick up speed and start moving me in all sorts of wild ways that

I've never felt before. And the ghost part of me feels like it finally gets to
come fully to life.

And the woman part of me is scared but also excited.

(*A pause.*)

SAM.

Is this real?

MISS FAYE.

To the best of my knowledge, it is.

And every day I'm a little more banjo and a little less me.

SAM.

So what will you do?

MISS FAYE.

I suppose that one day soon I'll wake up transformed.

SAM.

Into a banjo?

MISS FAYE.

Yes.

And here is my one wish—you listening?

SAM.

Yes ma'am.

MISS FAYE.

When that day comes

That I don't show up for breakfast

And they turn down my covers

And find a fine stringed instrument where my body used to be,

You make sure I land in good hands.

SAM.

Yes ma'am.

MISS FAYE.

Alright then.

(*The creaks of* MISS FAYE's *rocking chair somehow transform into the sound of strings.*)

SPRING BREAK *DOS MIL QUINCE*
by Diana Grisanti

A packed karaoke bar in Acapulco.
On the dance floor: Scads of college kids from the U.S., plus a few locals.
Onstage: A trio of Kappa Kappa Gammas, plus ANTONIO, sing the final bars of "Blue Moon of Kentucky."

KARAOKE JOCKEY. Gracias, chavas. Un fuerte aplauso para las mujercitas de la Universidad de Kentucky. [*Thanks, gals. Let's give it up for the ladies of the University of Kentucky.*]

    (*The girls shout in bad Spanish.*)

KAPPA GIRL 3. Vamos gatos! Universidad de Kentucky por vida! [*Go Cats! UK for life!*]

KAPPA GIRL 2. Kappa represent!

KAPPA GIRL 1. Yo amo México! [*I love Mexico!*]

ANTONIO. I lobe Kentucky!

CARLITOS. Cousin, those girls are from your eschool! Do you know them?

ALEX. UK has thirty thousand students.

CARLITOS. Eh?

ALEX. (*Tentative.*) Muchos estudiantes.

    (ANTONIO *leads the girls offstage and calls to* CARLITOS.)

ANTONIO. Oye guey vamos a la esa lagunita por allí abajo. [*Yo, man, we're gonna go to the lagoon down there.*]

CARLITOS. Ahorita, guey, permíteme tantito. [*Gimme a sec, man.*] Do you want to go eswimming? In the lagoon?

KAPPA GIRL 3. Vamos a la playaaaa! [*Let's go to the beeeeach.*]

ANTONIO. ¡A la esa laguna, guey! [*To the lagoon, man!*]

ALEX. Y'all go ahead. I got a buzz goin'.

CARLITOS. A what?

ALEX. A buzz—

KAPPA GIRL 1. It means he's druuunk!

CARLITOS. ¡A huevo! ¿Qué te dije? [*Fuckin' a! What I tell you?*] You come out with me, you forget all your problems!

    (*They all start to go.* ANTONIO *pulls* CARLITOS *with him.*)

KAPPA GIRL 2. Vamos a nadar. [*Let's go swimming!*]

KAPPA GIRL 1. (*Parroting a ubiquitous phrase she doesn't understand.*) ¡No mames guey!

CARLITOS. I see you later, cousin. You take care!

KARAOKE JOCKEY. Atención, damas y caballeros, un aviso super importante: allí en el bar hay shots de gelatina, o sea Jell-O shots. Dos por uno. Two for one. [*Attention, ladies and gentleman, a super important announcement: there are Jell-O shots at the bar.*]

> (*Shouts of joy/drunkenness as the group stumbles out.*
> ALEX *sits there and drinks.*
> LANEY *approaches. She looks lost.*)

LANEY. (*Super stilted.*) Con permiso, señor? Has visto a un grupo de chicas de los Estados Unidos? [*Excuse me, sir? Have you seen a group of girls from the United States?*]

ALEX. Those Kappa girls?

LANEY. ¿Mande? [*Pardon?*]

ALEX. I said, "Those girls from Kappa Kappa Gamma?" From UK?

LANEY. Ohmygod that was English sorry.

ALEX. Yup.

LANEY. Sorry. I've been trying to use my Spanish. Which obviously sucks.

ALEX. Mine too.

LANEY. You said you saw those girls?

ALEX. They walked out like two seconds ago. You can prolly catch 'em.

LANEY. Ugh. It's fine. There's no point.

ALEX. Literally, it was two seconds ago.

LANEY. It's really okay. They're all terrible.

ALEX. Cool.

LANEY. Right?

ALEX. I liked that song they sang.

LANEY. It was so random. This place only has like three songs in English.

ALEX. I'm from there. Kentucky.

LANEY. Ohmygod are you in Sigma Chi?

ALEX. No, I'm a free agent.

LANEY. Okay well you really look like this one guy in Sigma Chi. I seriously think I've met you.

> (*A semi-nude* FRAT GUY *runs through.*)

FRAT GUY. Last night in paradise, people. Make it count. Spring Break!

LANEY. I hate Spring Break. There's all this pressure to have an amazing, memorable time and it's really just shitty and boring, and all your friends are shitty and boring, and drunk and like having sex with the most random dudes. And it's like, I'm not a prude. I wanna have sex with random dudes. Or, you know, hook up at least. But I always get stuck cleaning up vomit and making sure people use condoms, and like buying actual food. It's because I'm the oldest child. It's compulsive.

ALEX. I'm the oldest too.

LANEY. It's a mind fuck, right? So much anxiety.

ALEX. Yes.

LANEY. So what's your deal? Do you go to UK or…? Oh shit, are you with that group from Ohio State? Those girls are so trashy, no offense.

ALEX. I live here.

LANEY. Whoa. That is so intense that you like *live* here. Like all the time? Wait I thought you said you were from Kentucky.

ALEX. Well I got deported so.

LANEY. What? Fuck. What? Like recently?

ALEX. Couple weeks ago.

LANEY. Oh my *God*.

ALEX. Yeah / well.

LANEY. I thought Obama was supposed to—
like he gave that big speech or whatever—
like about the Dreamers and people with kids?
—sorry I don't really know what I'm talking about.
My aunt who's more like my cousin because she's only a few years older than me? anyway my aunt is super up-to-date on all this stuff—
This is so fucked up.

ALEX. Me and my roommate sold Adderall.

LANEY. Shit.
That's how I know you.
I had a statistics midterm.
I bought Adderall from you.

ALEX. For real?

LANEY. You can get *deported* for that?

ALEX. I mean, *you* can't.

LANEY. I am so sorry.

ALEX. For what?

LANEY. For *this*. You *live* here now. And I didn't even *need* Adderall! That test was so easy. It was like, "Hey, what's five plus five."

ALEX. Say *five* again.

LANEY. (*Not sure where this is going.*) …Five.
        (*The I [ahhh] is perfectly Kentucky.*)

ALEX. I like the way you say that.

LANEY. I just said it like I say five.

ALEX. Where'd you learn how to say five like that?

LANEY. It's called Somerset. It's really small.

ALEX. I know Somerset. I grew up in Richmond.

LANEY. Oh yeah, I always go through Richmond on my way to school.

ALEX. Straight shot up 75. I could do that drive with my eyes closed.

LANEY. Totally.

KARAOKE JOCKEY. Damas y caballeros, en este momento les toca a unos gueros mamones para variar. [*Ladies and gentlemen, next up, a group of bourgie white boys. Surprise, surprise.*]

> (*The* GUEROS MAMONES *get up and sing a surprisingly lovely rendition of* "Man of Constant Sorrow"—"Hombre de Gran Tristeza"—*in Spanish.*)

GUEROS MAMONES.
Vive en pena desde que él nació

Yo soy un hombre de gran tristeza
He visto líos desde niño
Yo me despido de mi Kentucky
Es el lugar donde crecí yo

Es el lugar donde él creció

Por seis años largos he tenido líos
Ningún placer se halla aquí
Porque en este mundo soy vagabundo
Ni una mano me han echado a mí

Ni una mano echada ahí

Yo te digo adiós, mi fiel amante
Que no me veas con desdén
Porque es mi destino ir por el norte
Quizá me muera en este tren

Quizá se muera en este tren

Tú puedes enterrarme en valle hondo
Y el monte se derrumbará
Cuando regreses a amar a otro hombre
Dormiré en mi tumba ya

Dormirá en su tumba ya

Tal vez me piensen forastero
Fuimos uno, y ahora dos

Pero te prometo que nos vemos pronto
En la costa de oro de Dios

En la costa de oro de Dios

ALEX. Let's dance.

> (*They're dancing closer.*
> *They're doing the touchy-flirty-dancy thing. They're about to make out.* LANEY
> *pulls away.*)

LANEY. Do you miss it?

ALEX. What, Kentucky?

LANEY. Sorry, that was a stupid question,
obviously, of course you miss it,
it's home,
of course you do

ALEX. I don't know if *miss* is the right word, cause it's like, my *life.*
Like, there, I was me.
And here, I'm the awkward cousin who doesn't talk. You know?

LANEY. Yeah.

ALEX. This sounds kinda dumb, but: I think maybe I miss myself.

> (*She kisses him. They kiss.*)

LANEY. (*Breathless.*) My hotel room's empty.

ALEX. Awesome.

> (*He kisses her some more.*)

LANEY. Hang on a / second.

ALEX. Are you / okay?

LANEY. I'm amazing, I'm doing math.

ALEX. I love math.

LANEY. Our flight's at 7:30. I should get there by six, and I still need to pack,
so we have till about five.

ALEX. (*Prompting her.*) We have till five?

LANEY. That's right. Fiiive.

> (*They clasp hands and run out of the bar. End of scene.*)

IT SOUNDS LIKE THIS

by Cory Hinkle

> *Dance Party*
> SHAW *comes onstage.*
> *He acts as DJ for the end of the show.*
> *He hits a key on his computer and we hear cellos, then vocal harmonies.*
> SHAW *scratches a record over the cellos.*
> *It's its own unique thing. DJ'ing meets bluegrass. As the scene progresses,* SHAW
> *layers on more music via computer and vinyl.*
> *Note: The music is loud. People have to yell to be heard.*
> URE *enters and starts dancing.*

URE. Nice music!

SHAW. Thanks!

> (JOSH *enters.*)

JOSH. Whatcha doing!?

URE. Dancing!

JOSH. Well, all right!

> (JOSH *dances too. In comes* MAX.)

MAX. Hey, guys!

URE and JOSH. Hey!

> (MALLORY, LEXI, *and* ALI *enter. They ad lib greetings and start dancing.*
> ERIKA *and* AARON *enter.*)

MAX. (*Re: the music.*) How good is this shit?

> (*Ad lib responses.*)

ERIKA. Usually I only like country, but I love this!

AARON. Me too!

LEXI. I love the music under the music! The folk or whatever—!

SHAW. It's bluegrass!

LEXI. Right! How'd I forget that? Bluegrass! My grandma—she used to play mandolin to me before she died and she told me once that she dug up her mandolin from under a tree.

ALI. That's awesome!

LEXI. I know! But now it sounds crazy like maybe I made the whole thing up.

KAYLA. It's like what my grandma used to say. How if you don't pass down history it becomes myth. Your grandma's mandolin is a myth.

BRIAN. *My* grandma turned into a banjo.

KAYLA. WHAAAAT?

BRIAN. I'm just fucking with ya!

(JOSÉ *is dancing near* MALLORY *and staring at her.*)

MALLORY. Have we met?

(*She looks at him, doesn't know him.*)

JOSÉ. You remind me of a girl. We had one great night. Spring Break in Acapulco! That wasn't you, was it? I swear you look like just her!

MALLORY. Sorry! …But I don't remember you!

(MALLORY *dances away from* JOSÉ.
The dance floor fills up.)

COLLIN. We used to dance on the hardwood floor of the old house where I grew up, but my sister says we didn't have hardwood floors.

MADDY. But you're always high!

COLLIN. Fuck yeah I am! And dancing makes me feel *higher!* I love that!

MADDY. You know what I love? People! And music! And just like *everything!* What about you? What do you love?

CAMERON. Oh… Um… Bourbon?

(SHAW *calls out to someone.*)

SHAW. What about you?

JOHN. The sound of banjos!

SHAW. And you?

BRIAN.
Guitars

(*People spontaneously call out the things they love.*)

TAYLOR.
Fiddles

BRIAN.
Mandolins

COLLIN.
Old school rap

MAX.
The ghosts in the hills

URE.
A blue moon

LEXI.
My heart's a blue moon

KAYLA.
It won't let me be

> **SHAW.**
> What do you love?

JOE.
Time

MAX.
Passing

JOSÉ.
Getting older

AARON.
Wiser

> **SHAW.**
> What's that sound like?

MADDY.
Like something I can't name

LORENZO.
It's stuck in the back of my throat

> **ERIKA and MALLORY.**
> It's a mandolin buried under a tree
>
> **LEXI, MAX, and LORENZO.**
> A shattered guitar
>
> **CASEY, ALI, COLLIN, and BRIAN.**
> A fiddle under the floorboards
>
> **AARON, JOSH, URE, JOHN, and MALLORY.**
> It's a kid on his front porch dancing to Funky Four
> Plus One

> > **TAYLOR, MADDIE, and
> > KAYLA.**
> > It's forgetting
> >
> > **JOE, CAMERON, and LEXI.**
> > Where you come from

MALLORY and JOSÉ.
And who you once were

> **KAYLA, MAX, COLLIN, ALI, BRIAN, TAYLOR,
> CASEY, URE, JOHN, and ERIKA.**
> It's lonesome as hell
>
> **SHAW.**
> What's *that* sound like?

> > **EVERYONE.**
> > It sounds like…

SHAW.
What's it SOUND LIKE?
EVERYONE.
It sounds like…
                    SHAW.
                    IT SOUNDS…LIKE…
                    THIS.

(SHAW *cuts out the music.*
And together, the entire company makes a HIGH LONESOME SOUND.
Maybe it's a few notes from a sad, lonesome bluegrass tune.
Silence.
And the lights snap out.)

End of Play